Peter the Great's Revenge: The Russian Siege of Narva in 1704

Boris Megorsky

Translated by Stuart Britton

'This is the Century of the Soldier', Falvio Testir, Poet, 1641

Helion & Company

Helion & Company Limited
Unit 8 Amherst Business Centre
Budbrooke Road
Warwick
CV34 5WE
England
Tel. 01926 499 619
Fax 0121 711 4075
Email: info@helion.co.uk
Website: www.helion.co.uk
Twitter: @helionbooks
Visit our blog http://blog.helion.co.uk/

Published by Helion & Company 2018
Designed and typeset by Mach 3 Solutions Ltd (www.mach3solutions.co.uk)
Cover designed by Paul Hewitt, Battlefield Design (www.battlefield-design.co.uk)
Printed by Henry Ling Ltd, Dorchester, Dorset.

ISBN 978-1-911628-02-6

British Library Cataloguing-in-Publication Data.
A catalogue record for this book is available from the British Library.

For details of other military history titles published by Helion & Company Limited
contact the above address or visit our website: http://www.helion.co.uk.

We always welcome receiving book proposals from prospective authors.

Contents

List of Illustrations & Maps

Illustrations

Maps

List of Colour Plates

Dedicated to my family and friends

Introduction

The City by the Sea

It is rare to see such a sight – two castles of the Middle Ages facing each other across a wide, rapidly flowing river. Initially the citadels were opponents, but later became allies and today they are neighbours. Narva and Ivangorod are connected by a rich, common past; they have seen much over the centuries, but one of the storylines of the past became particularly dramatic and entered the towns' names into the chronicles of world history. This was the Great Northern War of 1700 to 1721 and the two battles for Narva. The first is widely known for the Russian army as the "Narva confusion" and as the greatest victory of the young Swedish king Charles XII in November 1700. The second battle, this time successful for the Russian Army, was the Russian siege of Narva in 1704, which usually remains in the shadows. Since the Great Northern War became largely a war of sieges and assaults (field battles were relatively rare), only when taking Narva did the Russian troops employ all possible tactics and methods – from a blockade and bombardments to a formal attack and a successful grand assault; there was never before such a battle in the history of Peter the Great. It is to this, the second Narva campaign of the Russian Army, that this book is dedicated.

Narva was founded in 1223 by the Danes, but in 1326 came under the power of the Livonian Order; the Russians called the town Rugodev. Ivangorod was built under Ivan III in 1492 as a counterweight to Narva and as "a window looking out on Europe" for the Grand Duchy of Moscow. Troops of Ivan IV (Ivan the Terrible) conquered Narva in 1558, and for the next 23 years both towns presented a solid "doorway to Europe" for Russian trade by sea. However, with the passing of the Livonian Order from the stage of European politics, the growing Kingdom of Sweden arrived to replace it. In 1581 Narva was taken by Pontus De La Gardie (the most renowned Swedish military commander of the 16th Century), while Ivangorod fell to the Swedes in 1611 and together with the other ancient Russian fortresses of Koporie [Swedish Koporje], Yam [Jamburg] and Oreshek [Nöteborg] went to Sweden under the Treaty of Stolbovo in 1617 that ended

the Ingrian War between Russia and Sweden. Thus, both banks of the Narova River became Swedish, and Ivangorod ultimately became Narva's bridgehead fortification after the latter grew and flourished on its own bank of the river. In 1658 Russian troops reached Narva, but conducted no full-blown siege of the town, and the Treaty of Cardis in 1661 between the Tsardom of Russia and the Swedish Kingdom again consolidated the latter's control over the fortress. In the 17th century Narva became the largest Swedish port in the region according to the volume of trade, exceeding those of the neighbouring cities of Vyborg, Reval and Nyen. Through the centuries, the town primarily became populated by Germans, Russians, Estonians, Finns, as well as by Swedes, Chudes, Vodes and a small number of Latvian families. The most prominent citizens and businessmen were primarily Germans.

Narva's fortifications included the tower of the Hermann Castle and the fortress walls around the town that had typical medieval towers and gates. In the 1620s the Swedes strengthened the fortress with bastions according to the latest Italian system of fortifications. A conflagration in 1610 destroyed the town's wooden structures, while rich stone development in the Barocco style began after the next conflagration in 1659. In present-day Narva, the preserved Town Hall with its spire and high front staircase, which was built in the period between 1663 and 1671, recalls this period of time.

In the autumn of 1681, Erik Dahlberg, the Swedish General Quartermaster, chief of fortifications and a leading engineer, who took part in the updating of a multitude of fortresses in the Swedish Kingdom, arrived in Narva to inspect it. He noted the disrepair of the stone walls, the

The city plan and the condition of Narva fortifications in October 1698. Narva's bastions were completed over two years before the start of the war; however, only one ravelin was finished, which covered the King's Gateway between the Honor and Gloria Bastions. (Sweden, 1698 Krigsarkivets kartsamlingar)

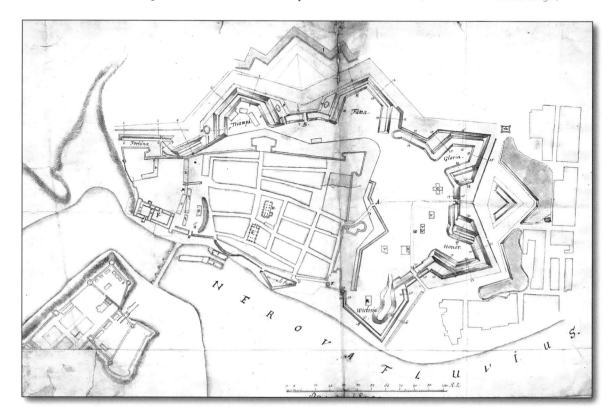

inadequacy of the bastions, and the extended, undefended suburbs. In 1684, work began according to Dahlberg's design on five new bastions: Honour, Gloria, Victoria, Fama and Triumph. The Old Town remained within the boundaries of the medieval walls, while the New Town rose between them and the new outer fortifications. By 1700–1704 the greater part of the work had been completed; only three of the five ravelins projected by Dahlberg remained incomplete. Despite the unfinished work, Narva became the most impregnable Swedish fortress in the region thanks to its successful design and obviously the fact that Dahlberg himself, who occupied the post of the General-Governorship of Livonia from 1696 could personally oversee the construction work. The renovated Narva fortress impressed the Danish emissary Just Juel, who in 1709 wrote:

> Narva has been fortified so well that it can be considered one of the strongest fortresses in Europe. A river flows next to the town and separates it from Ivangorod. The moats around the fortress are dry; however, those that were cut into the rock, upon which it was built, are so deep that it is impossible to scale the walls without assault ladders and are so precipitous that plainly it is impossible to descend them without falling to one's death or getting killed when leaping from them. The fortress's parapet has been constructed from large stones. The fortress has been furnished with several splendid bastions: the names of them have been written in Latin lettering on posts, expressly for those erected by the Swedes.[1]

The siege of Londonderry in 1698; a fragment.
The etching contains a clear view of the configuration of the fortifications of a bastion fortress: the gentle slope of the glacis (5) rises from the field up to the palisade, or the stockade, behind which runs a "covered way" – protected space for deploying and shifting the defenders. This structure on the field side of the moat was collectively called a "counterscarp." In the moat stands a separate structure, a "ravelin" (4) which protects the gate from direct artillery fire. The moat, dry or filled with water, was the final obstacle on the path to the rampart of the fortress, which consisted of pentagonal bastions with walls (curtains) (1) between them. Round and quadrangular Medieval towers often remained in the cities, but no longer met the demands of the modern fortifications. (Amsterdam, Collection Riiksmuseum)

---

1   Juel, J., *Zapiski datskogo poslannika v Rossii pri Petre Velikom* [*Notes of a Danish emissary to Russia under Peter the Great*], pp. 69–70.

Note on Sources

A large number of accessible sources allow us to write in detail about the events around Narva. The main narrative sources are the two official histories of the war published back in the 18th century – *Kniga Marsova* [*Book of Mars*][1] and the *Zhurnal ili Podennaia zapiska Petra Velikogo* [*Journal or Daily notes of Peter the Great*], as well as the fuller version of the latter *Podennyoi zapiski – History of the Swedish War*.[2] Certain supplementary information is contained in the so-called *Journal of Baron Henrich Freiherr von Huyssen*, the tutor of Tsarevich Alexis, who starting in 1703 wrote reports about the events in Russia for the European press, and later compiled a history of the war with Sweden by order of Peter the Great.[3] These official descriptions of the war overall and of the Narva operation in particular were written and edited under Peter the Great on the basis of a multitude of primary sources. Such sources include the documents and daily entries that make up the *Campaign Journal of 1704*, which contains a more detailed description of the siege.[4] Certain information about the actions, numerical strength and losses of separate formations can be found in the war campaign diary of B.P. Sheremetev and in P.M. Apraxin's journal of the Swedish services.[5]

---

1   *Kniga Marsova* is a book about the military exploits of the troops of the Russians' Tsarist Kingdom when taking very famous fortifications, or of those explits pulled off by the brave battalions in various places over the troops of the Royal Swedish Majesty. From the second printing of the first Saint Petersburg 1713 edition (SPb, 1766). Henceforth, the *Book of Mars*.
2   *Gistoriia Sveiskoi voiny (Podennaia zapiska Petra Velikogo)* [*History of the Swedish War (Chronology of Peter the Great)*] in two volumes (Moscow, 2004). Henceforth, *Gistoriia Sveiskoi voiny*; *Zhurnal ili Podennaia zapiska, blazhennyia i vechnodostoinyia pamiati gosudaria imperatora Petra Velikogo* [*Journal or Chronology, the blessed and eternally worthy record of His Majesty Emperor Peter the Great*] (Saint Petersburg, 1770). Henceforth, *Zhurnal ili Podennaia zapiska*.
3   Von Huyssen, "Zhurnal Gosudaria Petra I c.1695 po 1709", *sochinennyi baronom Gizenom. Polovina pervaia: Sobranie raznykh zapisok i sochinennii, sluzhashchikh k dostavleniiu polnago svedeniia o zhizni I deianiiakh Gosudaria Imperator Petra Velikogo. Izdannoe trudami i izhdiveniem Feodora Tumanskago. Tom 3* [*Journal of His Majesty Peter I between 1695 and 1709, compiled by Baron von Huyssen. First half: Collection of His Majesty Emperor Peter the Great. Published by the labours and means of Feodor Tumansky. Volume 3* (Saint Petersburg, 1787).
4   *Pokhodnyi zhurnal 1704 goda* [*Campaign Journal of 1704*] (Saint Petersburg, 1854).
5   B.P. Sheremetev, "Voenno-pokhodnyi zhurnal (s 3 iunia 1701 goda po 12 seniabria 1705 goda) general-fel'dmarshala Borisa Petrovicha Sheremeteva: Materialy voenno-uchenogo arkhiva glavnogo shtaba" [War campaign diary (from 3 June 1701 to 12 September 1705) of General

Sketch of the fortress of Narva that was luckily taken by assault by His Tsarist Majesty's troops under the command of his Excellency General Field Marshal Baron von Ogilvie on 9 August 1704.

This separate page with captions in the Russian and German languages was the official report regarding the victory. The drawing was etched in the Armory in 1704 and served as the source for later etchings; the plan of the fortress and fieldworks and even the reference letters of the legend were copied from it without changes. The map is oriented to the east, and it shows the two ravelins on either side of the Gloria Bastion that had been built by the moment of the city's fall. The "Sketch" was published by Jakob Keiser in Amsterdam in the 1710s with the addition of a genre scene in a cartouche. The same picture, oriented to the west, became part of the Book of Mars in 1712-1713. (Workshop of the Armory Chamber, Moscow; Russia, 1704 Bibliothèque nationale de France)

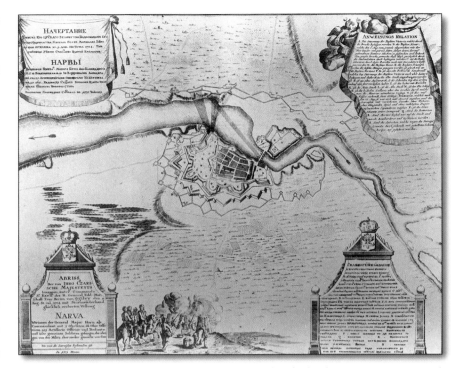

Swedish official historiography of the deeds of Charles XII is represented by the works of Gustav Adlerfeld and Pastor Jöran Andersson Nordberg; both histories were written by contemporaries of the events on the basis of documents accessible to the authors.[6] Because Narva in 1704 was a distant and secondary theatre for the King, and the authors were not eyewitnesses to the events, their descriptions of the siege are sparse. One can also assign the *History of Livonia* to the narrative sources from the Swedish perspective;[7] its author Pastor Christian Kelch was a contemporary of the events and a resident of Estonia. His work is of undoubted interest, but one must keep in mind that he was not an eyewitness of the siege of Narva and used information from newspapers,[8] and obviously tales contained in the reports of other eyewitnesses.

Field Marshal Boris Petrovich Sheremetev: Materials of the military studies archive of the main headquarters] (Saint Petersburg, 1871), Volume 1; Volynsky, N.P., *Postepennoe razvitie russkoi reguliarnoi konnitsy v epokhu Velikogo Petra s samym podrobnym opisaniem ee uchastiia v Velikoi Severnoi voine*. Kn. 3 [*Gradual development of the Russian regular cavalry in the epoch of Peter the Great with a most detailed description of its participation in the Great Northern War. Book 3*] (Saint Petersburg, 1912), pp. 33–36.

6   Adlerfeld, G., *The military history of Charles XII, King of Sweden, written by the express order of his Majesty by M. Gustavus Adlerfeld*, Vol. 1–3. (London, 1740). Henceforth: Adlerfeld; Nordberg, J.A., *Histoire de Charles XII, Roi de Suede, Vol. 1– 3* (Naue, 1748).

7   Kelch, C., *Lieflandische Historia oder Kriegs-und Friedens-Geschichte. Continuation (1690–1706)* (Dorpat, 1875).

8   Many of the details cited by Kelch were published in the news digests: *Mercurius: Welcher in sich enthält und vorstellig machet den gegenwärtigen Zustland von Europa, alles was in denen Europäischen Höfen sich ereignet, und vorfällt, das Interest der Printzen und Staaten, ihre Staats-Streiche, und überhaupt alles dasjenige, was da merkwürdig und curieux*. (Nürnberg,

The preserved diary entries of the residents and garrison are most valuable. Adlerfeld cited a most important military source from the Swedish side – "Journal of what happened during the siege of Narva from 1 April to 24 August 1704", which was written by an officer who was possibly the commander of the Ivangorod garrison.[9] In its time the recollections of an anonymous resident of Narva was published, which also contained information from several other personal diaries.[10] Certain citizens, who moved to the Swedish Reval (present-day Tallinn) after the fall of the city, later wrote letters from there about the events that took place; these letters rather quickly entered broad circulation throughout Europe, as one can judge from the articles in the newspapers. One such letter is published in translation and with commentary in the appendix.[11]

Since the majority of histories were written after the fact, the correspondence of participants in the events immediately in the course of the siege, about the siege, are particularly valuable. They include information about the orders that were issued, the accounts of how the orders were carried out, the testimony of prisoners, etc. To such correspondence one can assign the letters of Tsar Peter himself, Alexander Menshikov, Boris Sheremetev, Georg Benedikt von Ogilvy, Peter Apraxin and others. These sources were published in the third volume of "Pisma i bumagi Petra Velikogo" ["Letters and papers of Peter the Great"] and other collections of material.[12] The personal experience and emotional turmoil of direct participants in the events are preserved in memoirs, which are extremely rare for the Petrine army. For the first siege of Narva, these are the notes of a Saxon general in the Russian army, Ludwig Nikolai Hallart, and the anonymous "Letopisets 1700 goda" ("Chronicler of 1700"); for the second siege, the notes of Prince Boris Ivanovich Kurakin and Count Grigorii Petrovich Chernyshev.[13] Other

---

9   1704). October, pp. 1183–1185; *Der neubestellte Agent von Haus aus, mit allerhand curieusen Missiven, Brieffen, Memorialen, Staffeten, Correspondencen und Commissionen, nach Erforderung der heutigen Staats- und gelehrten Welt* (Freyberg, 1705), Vol. 6, pp. 492–496.

9   Adlerfeld, Vol. 2, pp. 1–28.

10   *Narva's Belagerung und Einahme von den Russen, nach Aufzeichnungen dasiger Einwohner in Jahre 1704: Archiv für die Geschichte Liv -, Esth -, und Curlands*. Band VI. Heft (Reval, 1851), pp. 225–287.

11   Letter from Reval dated 5 September 1704, preserved among the papers of General Lewenhaupt in the collection of manuscripts in the Linköping library (LiSB H 79:4, no. 159).

12   *Pis'ma i bumagi Petra Velikogo [Papers and letters of Peter the Great]*, T. 3 (1704–1705). (Saint Petersburg, 1893). Henceforth *Letters and Papers*; Ustrialov, N.G., *Istoriia tsarstvovaniia Petra Velikogo*, T. 4, Ch. 2 *[History of the reign of Peter the Great, Vol. 4, Part 2]* (Saint Petersburg, 1863); *Severnaia voina 1700–1721: K 300-letiiu Poltavskoi pobedy. Sbornik dokumentov [Northern War 1700–1721: For the 300th Anniversary of the Poltava victory. Collection of documents]*.

13   Hallart, L.N., *Das Tagebuch des Generals von Hallart uber die Belagerung und Schlacht von Narva, 1700* (Reval, 1894). Henceforth, Hallart; "Letopisets 1700 goda": Letopis' zaniatii Arkheograficheskii Komissii, 1865–1866 [Chronicler of 1700: Chronicle of works of the Archaeographic Commission, 1865–1866], Vol. 4 (Saint Petersburg, 1868), pp. 131–157. Henceforth: Chronicler of 1700; Kurakin, B.I., *Russko–Shvedskaia voina. Zapiski. 1700–1710: Arkhiv kn. F.A. Kurakin, Kn. 1 [Russian–Swedish War. Notes. 1700–1710: Book archive of F.A. Kurakin, Book 1]* (Saint Petersburg, 1890); Kurakin, B.I., *Voennaia khitrost' tsaria Petra Alekseevicha pod Narvoiu 8-go iiunia 1704: Rasskaz ochevidtsa kniazia B.I. Kurakina: Arkhiv kn. F.A. Kurakin, Kn. 3 [Military ruse of Tsar Peter Alekseevich at Narva on 8 June 1704:*

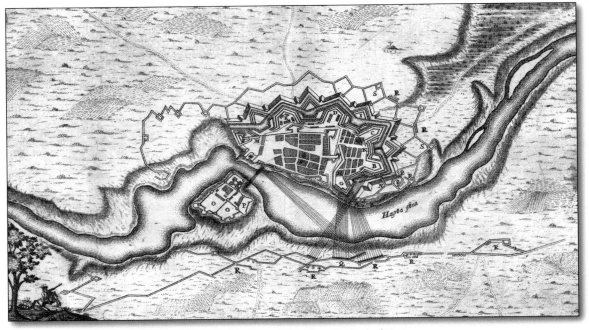

The map of the siege of Narva from the Book of Mars.
The lettering shown on the outline: A. Approach to the Viktoria Bastion, into which they climbed through a breach. B. The Honor Bastion faces of which crumbled from the foundation up on the day of 6 August from both attacked directions, together with the battery cannons that had been standing on them, thus making a breach so large that the attackers conveniently mounted the breach using ladders. C. The Gloria Bastion, into which they also climbed across its own ravelin with ladders. D. The Fama Bastion. E. The Triumph Bastion, toward which a feigned attack was conducted, as well as toward the Fortune Bastion (F). G. There is an old bulwark called the Sandwall, which they also climbed with ladders during the assault of the Viktoria Bastion, and then entered the Old Town. H. The old exterior fortress, which the Swedes immediately abandoned during the first attack. I. The King's Ravelin, toward which they assaulted. K. The New Town. L. The Old Town. M. The Old Castle. N. The covered passage above the moat, across which they wanted to "attach a miner". O. The strong Ivangorod Castle, which on 17 August was surrendered by agreement, and the garrison with inverted muskets, without banners or a drum beat, and with unbared swords was compelled to leave. P. The new entrenchment outside of Ivangorod. Q. Batteries. R. Mortar pits, from which the town and fortress was bombarded, and pounded by cannons. S. Approaches or trenches, which due to the rocky soil were all built with filled gabions. (Workshop of the Saint-Petersburg Printshop; Russia, 1712-1713. Russian State Library)

primary personal sources are service autobiographies written by officers of the Russian Army in 1720; these sometimes contain valuable information about these authors' participation in combat operations.[14]

New details regarding the wartime daily life and supply of the Russian Army, which reports rarely mentioned, can be extracted from the unpublished orders to the army that were issued at Narva. For example the selection of documents from 9 July to 28 August, which are preserved in the Russian State Military History Archive in the files of the headquarters of the Life

Story of the eyewitness Prince B.I. Kurakin, Book 3] (Saint Petersburg: 1892); Chernyshev, G.P., "Zapiski G.P. Chernysheva" ["Notes of G.P. Chernyshev"], RS (Vol. 5, no. 6), pp. 791–802.

14   For example, the stories of officers of the dragoon regiments published in N.P. Volynsky's book *Postepennoe razvitiie russkoi reguliarnoi konnitsy v epokhu Velikogo Petra s samym podrobnym opisaniem ee uchastiia v Velikoi Severnoi voine*, Book 4 (Saint Petersburg, 1912).

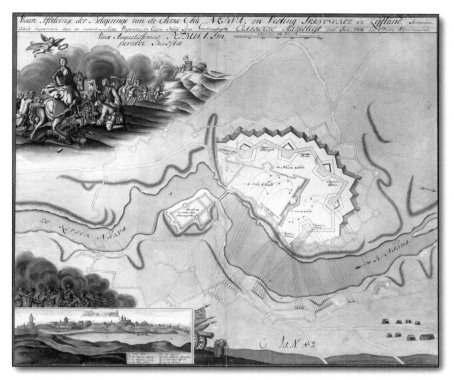

Depiction of the siege of the strong city of Narva and the Ivangorod fortress. This beautiful hand-drawn picture with captions in the Dutch language, unfortunately lacks value as a source. The plan of the fortress and the trenchworks, most likely, were copied from the Book of Mars, and the cross section – from Bodenehr's etching. (Artist unknown, 1728 Krigsarkivet, Sveriges Krig)

Guard Semenovsky Regiment in the form of a typewritten copy from early in the 20th century.[15] A number of orders related to the siege period and the life in the town after its fall are found in the files of A.D. Menshikov's campaign Chancellery in the Saint Petersburg archive of the Russian Academy of Science's Institute of History [SPbII RAN].[16] In addition, documents of the Artillery Administration (*Prikaz artillerii*) from the archive of the Saint Petersburg Military History Museum of Artillery [VIMAIViVS] contain information about the preparation, delivery and expenditure of ordnance and supplies to the besieging army.[17]

Since the author has set himself the task of illustrating the described events to the maximum possible degree, he has selected quite a few rare engravings and maps from the beginning of the 18th century, including the previously unpublished plans of the first and second sieges of Narva, discovered in Peter I's collection in the Library of the Russian Academy of Sciences. The text is accompanied by a large series of original illustrations, created especially for this publication by leading artists – specialists in illustrating military history.

The siege of 1704 has been repeatedly described in Russian historiography in more or less detail. These include such works as scholar Nikolai Gerasimovich

---

15 RGVIA, F. 2584, Op. 1, D. 6; The author wants to express his deepest gratitude to Kirill Vasilievich Tatarnikov for his help in making me familiar with this document.

16 Arkhiv SPb II RAN [Archive of the Saint Petersburg Russian Academy of Science's Institute of History], F. 83, Op. 2.

17 Arkhiv VIMAIViVS, F. 2, Op. 1, D. 3, ll. 307-311; F.2, Op. 1, D. 4, ll. 133–139.

Ustrialov's *Istoriia tsarstvovaniia Petra Velikogo* [*History of the reign of Peter the Great*] (1863), military engineer Fedor Fedorovich Laskovsky's *Materialy dlya istorii inzhenernogo iskusstva v Rossii* [*Materials for the history of the engineering art in Russia*] (1861), historian of Narva Aleksandr Vasil'evich Petrov's *Gorod Narva, ego proshloe i dostoprimechatel'nost'* [*The city of Narva, its past and sights*] (1901), as well as specialist on the history of Estonia in the 17th and 18th centuries Heldur Palli's *Mezhdu dvumia boiami za Narvu: Estonia v pervye gody Severnoi voiny 1701–1704* [*Between two battles for Narva: Estonia in the first years of the Northern War 1701–1704* (1966). In Swedish literature, a detailed description of the military operations of 1704, based on archival sources, can be found in the work of Carl von Rosen, *Essays on the events that immediately preceded the fall of the great power of Sweden* (1936). The books of the aforementioned authors rather fully cover the chronology of the events of 1704 but are little known to the modern reader.

Today, relying on a wide circle of sources from both sides, we can recreate a chronicle of the second Narva operation of Peter the Great's army on a day by day basis – in the form of diaries or "chronologies" that were common in

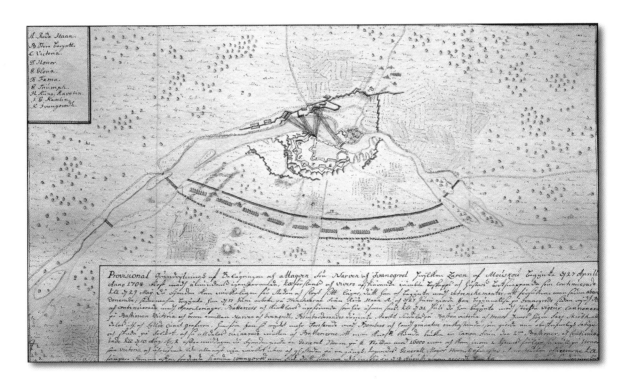

A provisional plan for the siege and attack of Narva and Ivangorod in 1704.
The previously unknown plan of the second siege of Narva from the collection of Peter the Great's hand-drawn maps contains details not found on other plans. The siege camp on the Narva bank, the countervallation line and *chevaux de frise* in place of the circumvallation line, and the bridges across the Narova River are depicted. It shows the opening of the trenches on the Rotenhan farmstead; the zig-zag pattern of the approaches seems to have credence; and the rising ascents along the steep bank of the river toward the Viktoria and Honor Bastions look logical. Possibly, the condition of the trenches is shown not on the day of the city's capture, but earlier, when the besiegers hadn't yet managed to link all of the approaches to the continuous system of trenches, which have been shown on the other plans above. The captions have been written in Swedish and the dates have been given in the Swedish style. (Artist unknown, Library of the Russian Academy of Sciences, Department of Manuscripts)

that epoch. The Narva events are viewed in a broad context, and the book also describes why the year of 1704 was so noteworthy in European military history; the parallel events of that year are mentioned as they appeared in the Russian newspapers. In passing, the specifics and traditions of siege warfare are disclosed, and there are discussions about certain more or less famous participants in the events – people of that time. The appendix contains reference information on the composition of the Russian and Swedish forces, gathered on the basis of published and archival sources.

All of the dates in the book are given according to the old style, which is to say according to the Julian calendar that was in effect at that time in Russia and Great Britain; that same calendar in Sweden was ahead of the Russian calendar by one day. The Gregorian calendar, which is to say the new style, was in effect in the majority of Europe's countries back then and was different by 11 days. Thus, the storming of Narva took place on 9 August 1704 according to the Russian calendar, 10 August according to the Swedish calendar, and 20 August according to the new style.

A view of the siege of Narva from the second edition of the Book of Mars.
We know of two versions of the etching with the side view of the siege of Narva. Here, the first is presented – with a high skyline and the inscription "NARBA" in the ribbon. The second repeats the image in almost identical fashion, but is done in a panoramic format (printed on a narrow horizontal band), without a ribbon, with the caption "Narva" in the lower left corner. (Workshop of the Saint-Petersburg Printshop; Russia, 1715. [Library of the Russian Academy of Sciences, Department of Cartography])

The Chronology of the 1700–1704 Period of the Great Northern War

1700

February	Saxon attack against the outskirts of Swedish Riga and the capture of Kobron-Schantz.
March	The Saxons capture the fortress of Dünamünde near Riga.
April	The Danes attack the fortress of Töningen in Schleswig-Holstein.
July	Swedish landing in Zeeland; Denmark exits the war.
August	Russia declares war on Sweden and initiates a campaign against Narva.
November	Victory of Charles XII over the Russians at Narva, which lifted the first siege of the city.

1701

January	Swedish General Kronhjort attacks a Russian border post on the Lava River in the direction of Ladoga and Novgorod.
February	Swedish General Spens attacks the Pechory Monastery in the direction of Pskov.
June	A Swedish fleet in the mouth of the Northern Dvina River attacks the Novodvinsk fortress that is under construction near Arkhangelsk.
July	Charles XII defeats the Saxons in the Battle of Duna [Western Dvina or Daugava] River near Riga.
December	The Saxon and Russian garrison of the Dünamünde fortress surrenders after six months of a Swedish siege. General Sheremetev defeats the Swedes at the Battle of Erastfer in Swedish Livonia.

1702

July — Charles XII defeats the Saxons in the Battle of Kliszów in Poland. Sheremetev gains another victory over Swedish General W.A. von Schlippenbach at Hummelshof in Livonia.

August — Tsar Peter's march with his court and Guards from the White Sea across woodland towards Lake Onega. Sheremetev's forces capture the fortress of Marienburg in Livonia.

October — The Russians besiege and capture the fortress of Nöteborg at the outflow of the Neva River from Lake Ladoga.

1703

March — Victory of a Swedish–Lithuanian detachment over a mixed force of Russians and Lithuanians at Salaty in Lithuania.

May — The Russians besiege and capture the fortresses of Nyenschantz, Koporie and Jam in Swedish Ingria. Foundation of Saint Petersburg.

October — The Saxon garrison holding the fortress of Thorn (Torun) in Poland surrenders to the Swedes after a five-month siege.

1704

July — The Russians capture Dorpat [modern-day Tartu]. A Swedish–Lithuanian detachment defeats a mixed force of Russians and Lithuanians in the Battle of Jakobstadt in Livonia.

August — The Russians capture Narva and Ivangorod. The Swedes in turn capture Lwow in Poland.

October — Victory of the Swedes over the Saxons in the Battle of Poniec on the border of Silesia.

November — Victory of a Russian–Lithuanian detachment over a mixed force of Swedes and Lithuanians in the Battle of Skuodas [Schoden] in Lithuania.

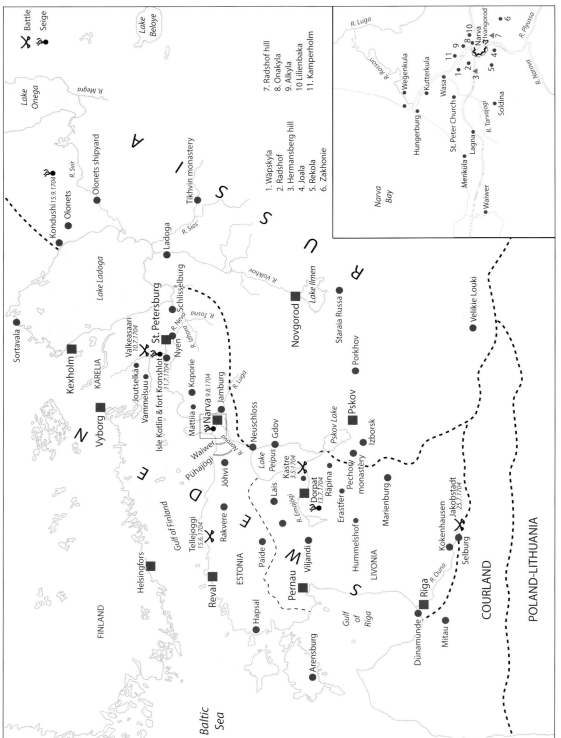

Map 1 The Narva Campaign of 1704.

Inset legend:

7. Radshof hill
8. Onakyla
9. Alkyla
10. Lilienbaka
11. Kamperholm

1. Wäpskyla
2. Radshof
3. Hermansberg hill
4. Joala
5. Rekola
6. Zakhonie

Battle
Seige

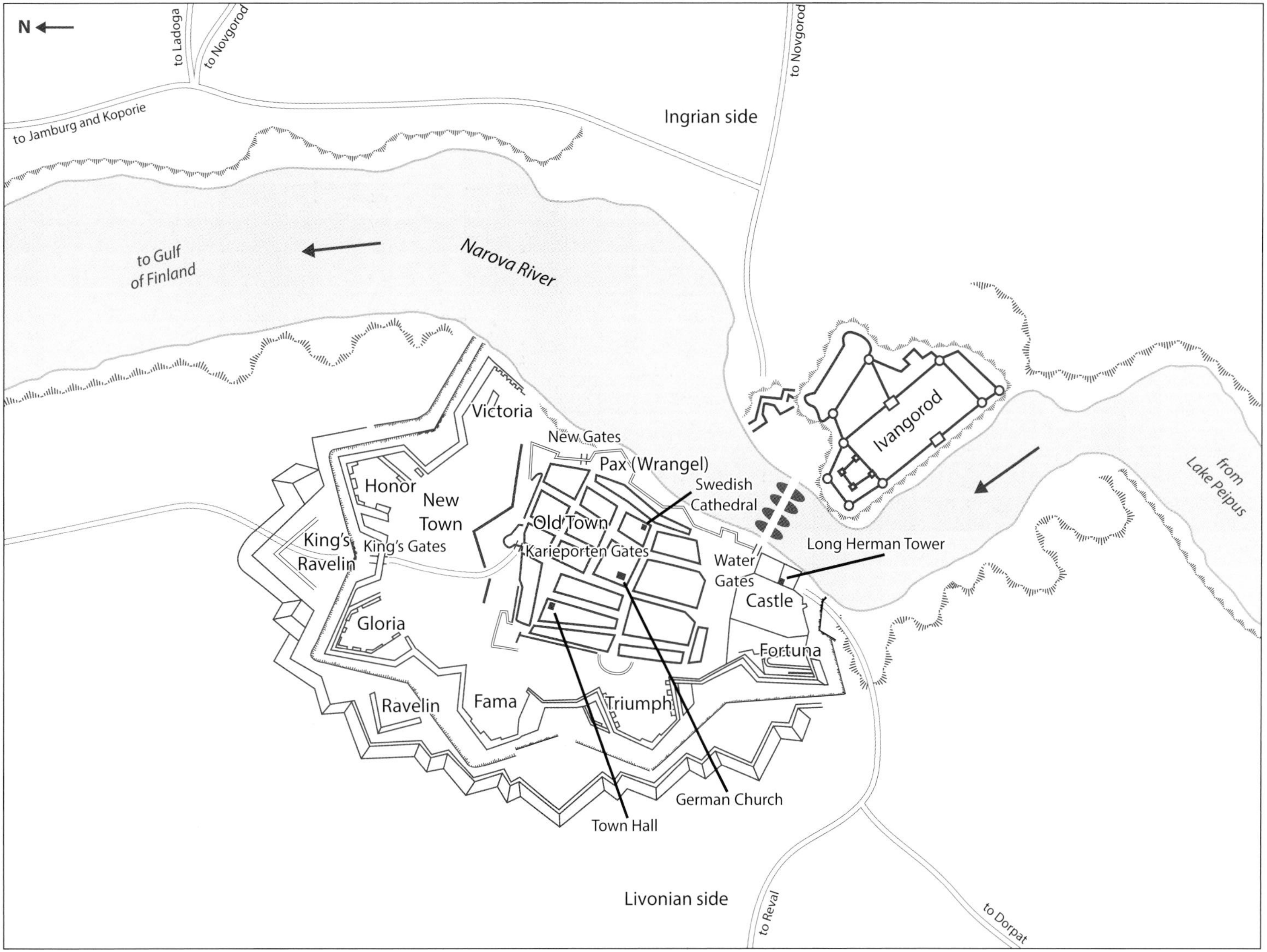

Map 2 Narva and Ivangorod with their fortifications and suburbs in 1704.

Ivangorod

from Lake Peipus

Long Herman Tower

Swedish Cathedral

Water Gates

Castle

Fortuna

Pax (Wrangel)

New Gates

Old Town

Karieporten Gates

Triumph

German Church

Town Hall

Victoria

Fama

Honor

New Town

King's Gates

Gloria

King's Ravelin

Ravelin

Narova River

to Gulf of Finland

Ingrian side

to Novgorod

to Novgorod

to Ladoga

to Jamburg and Koporie

to Novgorod

to Dorpat

to Reval

Livonian side

N

xxiii

1

The Start of the 1704 Campaign

2 January

On the evening of the second day of the new year of 1704, just before the closing of the city gates, the peasant Andrei Nikulaev slipped out of the city of Narva together with the Swede Hanno Mitkalev. Together they crossed the ice of the Narova River and headed to the east, towards the Russians. Having encountered Tsarist dragoons in the village of Kotly, Andrei told them that he had intentionally left to find the Petrine troops. He was sent to Petersburg, but not before answering questions and writing down his testimony. A year earlier, Nikulaev had lived with his wife and son in the village of Matveeva near the Retel farmstead of the Koporie district, 40 km north-east of Narva. In the Russian documents they were called Letts (*Latyshy*) – as were all the tribes back then that had settled the southern coastline of the Gulf of Finland together with the Russians.[1] In the village there were three households, and the households were owned by the retired Swedish Captain Frans von Knorring.[2] In the spring of 1703, when the Russians captured Nyenshantz, Jam and Koporie, but during the planting season the owner arrived in the village and "took all of the residents together with bread and livestock to Rugodev." In the city all three families with their women and children lived together in Knorring's household. Many of the displaced residents could not tolerate life in such cramped conditions, hunger and cold; among others, Nikulaev's wife and son died, and there was nothing left to keep him in Narva.

---

1   The Vodes and Ingrians were the native Finno-Ugric tribes of Ingermanland [Ingria], where they were living in the 18th century along with Russians and with Finns who had resettled to the area while under Swedish dominion. Judging from a map of the ethnic settlements in the region, the villages belonged to the Vodes, which means Nikulaev was a Vodian.

2   Frans Henrik von Knorring (around 1650–1726), a participant in the war with Brandenburg in 1678; in retirement from 1680. He owned the Rättilä estate. He was brought to responsibility for insulting the Crown, for the fact that for more than six months he had not buried his wife, and repeatedly for violating public order. He presumably passed away in Vyborg in 1726. The author expresses his gratitude to the genealogical resource www.vonknorring.com for making the information available, and to its administrator Harald von Knorring.

PETER THE GREAT'S REVENGE

Fireworks in Moscow on 1 January 1704 in honor of the taking of Nyenschantz and the conquest of Ingria in 1703.
(Adriaan Schoonebeeck 1661-1705 Russia, 1704)

A snowy winter.
(Christoff Weigel 1654-1725 Nuremburg, 1700, Collection Rijksmuseum, Amsterdam)

Building 12 on Ritter (Rüütli) Street
in the Old Town of Narva.
(Otto Kletzl 1897-1945 and Richard
Hamann-MacLean 1908-2000,
Estonia, 1940-1941, Bildarchiv Foto
Marburg)

It became known to the Russians from this "fugitive" that the Narva garrison had 3,000 Swedish infantrymen, 400 cavalrymen, 150 grenadiers and 50 cannoneers; in Ivangorod were soldiers of the Nöteborg, Nyenshantz, Jamburg and Koporie garrisons that had been released upon surrendering the fortresses. In the city there was apprehension over the Russians' approach; in the summer new earthworks studded with cannons had been built around Narva and Ivangorod, and in the winter the ice of the river channel at the bridge across the Narva River was chopped up in order to restrict a crossing to the bridge itself.[3]

6 January

In Reval, the Governor-General of Estonia Count De La Gardie reported to the Defence Commission in Stockholm that it seemed to him impossible to send wagons loaded with provisions to Narva. Such was his reply to a decree from King Charles XII dated 27 October 1703 to send as much foodstuffs to Narva as soon as possible. With the onset of autumn, navigation was already coming to an end, and now De La Gardie did not want to send cargo by land, since some of the route presumably ran through territory now occupied by the Russians.

The Narva commandant Horn, starting in the summer of 1703, had repeatedly requested that provisions be supplied to the garrison. In the fall of

---

3   Archive of the SPbII RAN, F. 83, Op. 1, D. 83, l. 1 ob. – 3; Op. 2, D. 1; Book of copies 1, l. 273 ob. – 277. Published: Volynsky, Book 3, pp. 250–251.

1703, several ships arrived in Reval with food for Narva; there were intentions to send the provisions by horse-drawn wagons, then this was postponed until winter so that sleds could be used to transport the provisions. However, that winter they decided that it was simpler to wait until springtime and send the foodstuffs by sea. As a result of the lack of food, mortality in the city was sharply increased.[4]

7 January

The Russian dragoons who had met the peasant Nikulaev belonged to the regiments under the command of Morel de Carriere and Souvas; they were spending the winter in Kotly (the Kotly estate) between Jamburg and Narva. Their horses were so gaunt due to the lack of fodder that they had to send the men out on assignments on foot. Prince Mikhail Meshchersky's company from Balabanov's infantry regiment, at an order from Major General Chambers, had set out from Jamburg to capture prisoners willing to talk; two versts[5] outside of Narva they captured "eight Lett residents of Narva", who had ridden out of the city looking for firewood. The unlucky woodcutters reported information that was going around in the town that the Swedish King was in Poland and had no intention to come to Narva (there was "a letter from him to the general presently he was not going to help against the Russian men outside of Rugodev"), that General Otto Welling was being sent in order to replace the current commandant Horn, and that an earthen rampart had been built around Ivangorod with four bastions containing one cannon each, and that mines had been dug underneath.[6] In Swedish sources, this rampart with bastions protecting the Ivangorod castle was called a hornwork.

The hit-and-run raid became the first in the surroundings of Narva in 1704 but was far from the first in the years of the war. After the defeat and withdrawal from Narva in November 1700, the Tsarist warriors returned more than once – either with the aim of gathering intelligence from prisoners or in the tactical framework of devastating hostile territory. One of the largest attacks took place on 1 January 1703, when Field Marshal Sheremetev sent a detachment under Prince Vasilii Alekseevich Vadbol'sky consisting of three regiments of dragoons and 1,000 Cossacks, Kalmyks and Tatars to attack the Swedish troops, who were in their winter quarters on the estates and in the villages around Narva. The Swedish infantry and cavalry on the outskirts of Ivangorod were scattered, and losing flags and drums, they fled into Narva. During the pursuit of the fleeing enemy, Vadbol'sky himself had been killed, but his cavalry, having dealt with the enemy, burned four ships docked at a wharf beneath the city walls, before riding around the surrounding hamlets and villages, burning buildings and killing local residents or taking them prisoner.[7]

---

4   Rosen, p. 179; Palli, p. 246.
5   A 'verst' was an old Russian unit of measurement roughly equal to 1.1 kilometres.
6   Aleksei Balabanov's letter to A.D. Menshikov. Archive of the SPbII RAN, F. 83, Op. 2, D. 1, l. 1704 g. Book of copies 1, ll. 240 ob.–242 ob. Chambers reported to Menshikov about the same event, but in less detail. See Volynsky, Book 3, pp. 335–336.
7   Volynsky, Book 1, pp. 147–148; Adlerfeld, Vol. 1, p. 196.

13 January

A Russian detachment marched from Ingria across the ice of the frozen Gulf of Finland and attacked a Swedish post on the coastline in the Vyborg area. Several days later, in return, the commander in Finland General Maidel dispatched a party, which attacked sentries on watch on the Russian shore.[8]

16 January

Peasants Savelii Mikhailov and Mikhail Pankratiev from the Jamburg District caught a secret agent in the village of Orlova and brought him to the authorities. Major General Ivan Ivanovich Chambers ordered to torture the spy in his presence, who confessed that his real name was Sen'ka, and he had been sent by the Narva commandant to gather information about the number of Russian infantry and cavalry that were quartered in the villages.[9]

11 February

Once again, Horn demanded from De La Gardie to deliver food to Narva.[10]

18 February

The Ladoga military governor Petr Matveevich Apraxin sent reports to the Tsar, in which in particular he asked about directives for the start of the campaign. Peter I wrote brief instructions: After the rivers were freed from ice to cross the Luga River, Apraxin was to position the regiments at the coastline at the point where the Rosson' River flows into the estuary of the Narova River, and prevent enemy ships from reaching Narva. Later, when the Russian troops on a different axis entered Livonia, he could cross the Narova, but in the meantime this plan should be kept secret.[11] The order about blockading Narva from the sea was repeated on 7 March.[12]

Meanwhile: the Rákóczi Uprising

News was reporting: "From Vienna they're writing … that the two great fortresses on Hungarian soil of Munkács [Munkatsch; today Mukachevo in Ukraine] and Mórocz surrendered to the rebels"[13] and "Rákóczi has taken the Munkács fortress."[14] The Austrian garrison after a three-month siege on 16 February had surrendered the castle in the Transcarpathian town of Munkács; previously in January, Tokaj had been seized. The anti-Hapsburg uprising that had started in 1703 with the support of France enveloped Hungary and Transylvania. Peasant militia units – of Hungarians, Ruthenians and Slovaks – which taken together were known as the Kuruc were headed by son of

---

8   Adlerfeld, Vol. 1, pp. 303–304.
9   Archive SPbII RAN, F. 83, Op. 2, D. 1, 1704. Book of copies, pp. 271 ob.–272.
10   Rosen, p. 179.
11   PiB, Vol. 3, p. 32.
12   Palli, p. 244.
13   *Vedomosti – Moskva (Pechatnyi dvor)* [News – Moscow (Print yard), 22 April 1704, p. 4.
14   *Ibid.*, 3 April 1704, p. 2.

View of the Munkacs Castle. In 1686-1688, the Hungarians under the leadership of Ilona Zrinyi, the mother of Ferenc Rákóczi II, held a defense here for two years against Austrian forces. The castle was rebuilt and strengthened in the 1690s and in 1705. Today the castle carries the name of Palanok. The word "palanok" or "palanka" in Turkey and southeastern Europe means earthen and timber fortified structures with a palisade; they were encircled by a moat at the foot of the castle hill. (Nicholas de Fer 1646-1720; Paris, 1692 Collection Rijksmuseum, Amsterdam)

an old noble family Ferenc II Rákóczi. In the spring and summer of 1704, battles took place at Biskupice, Koroncó and Smolenice. The capital of the "Kaiser" – the Emperor of the Holy Roman Empire of the German Nation – after the legendary Turkish siege of 1683 was again in danger. French and Bavarian troops were threatening Vienna from the west, and the majority of the Austrian Army had been sent to face them; meanwhile, Kurucs rebel units were approaching the city from the east. An extended embankment was hastily being built in order to protect the immediate environs of the capital. England and the Netherlands were seeking to draw Saxony to help the Emperor, but the alliance between August and Peter and their war against King Charles XII prevented it. In the same year, Rákóczi was selected as Prince of Transylvania. In 1711 the rebellion was put down, the Hungarian War of Liberation ended, and the Prince's palace, the Munkács castle, was again occupied by Austrian troops.[15]

23 February

Tsarist cavalry officer Colonel Karl Ewald von Rönne conducted a raid against the Bjorke Islands in the Gulf of Finland and the ironworks two miles outside of Vyborg. The route across the ice ran through Kotlin Island and was complicated by deep snow. The unit consisted of dragoons and a select

15 Delegan, M. and Filippov, A., *Istoriia Mukachevskogo zamoka (v dokumentakh)* [*History of the Monkasc castle (in documents)*] (Uzhgorod, 2010).

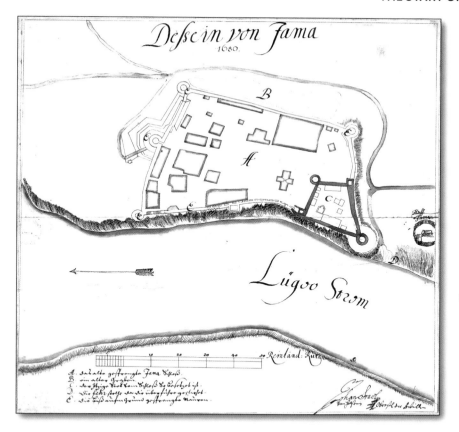

Plan of the fortress of Jama. The walls of the old Russian fortress were so decayed that as a result of Dahlberg's inspection, the Swedes demolished them in 1682, leaving only the stone citadel in the southwestern corner on the precipitous bank of the Luga River. After the town was taken by Russian troops in May 1703, it became known as Jamburg, while the medieval fortifications were strengthened by new earth and timber bastions – their ramparts have been preserved up to the present day. (Author unknown; Sweden, 1680 Krigsarkivets kartsamlingar)

company of Novgorod nobles, Ukrainian Cossacks, and infantry. They found neither iron nor combat troops in the works. Colonel Treiden together with soldiers remained to occupy the works, while von Rönne took the cavalry and 200 infantrymen on skis headed towards the village of Kalolakhti, where according to the testimony of a prisoner, a Swedish guard detail was located. A participant of this march, Petr Andronovich Kalinin, a private in Ivan Ridder's infantry regiment, later recalled that an enemy company of pickets had been captured at the time.[16]

26 February
The Tsar announced his plans for the 1704 campaign in conversation with Colonel Joost Friedrich Arnstedt, the General-Adjutant of the Polish King and the Saxon prince-elector: Field Marshal Sheremetev had been ordered to march to Dorpat, take it, and then push further into Courland. Peter himself with the rest of his army would set out in the spring towards Kexholm;[17] after

---

16 Volynsky, Book 3, p. 252; Tatarnikov, K.V. (ed.), *Ofitserskie skazki pervoi chetverti XVIII veka: Polevaia armiia (v dokumentakh)* [*Officers' tales from the first quarter of the 18th century: Field army (in documents)*] (Moscow, 2015), Vol. 2, p. 1417.

17 A place located on the north-western shore of Lake Ladoga on the Karelian Isthmus, Kexholm, under Swedish rule since 1611, used to be an old Russian town Korela, today known as

taking this fortress he would make an attempt on Vyborg in order to ensure the security of Saint Petersburg, which had been founded the year before. Afterward, he had in mind the possibility of linking up with Sheremetev at the Western Dvina River and blockading Riga from the sea.[18]

14 March
As Chambers reported to Menshikov, the regiments from Apraxin's command were quartered in the Koporie District: Shakhovsky's regiment on the Soikino peninsula and Krakolne, Bils' regiment – in the village of Pilova.[19]

25 March
Peter Apraxin arrived from Ladoga in Jamburg – the westernmost town that had just been captured by the Russians. At the same time a drummer arrived from Narva, who was delivering correspondence to the Swedish prisoners in Moscow before carrying back letters to the Russian prisoners in Narva. Apraxin sent a letter in the Swedish language from Narva commandant Horn to Menshikov, because a translator could not be found in Jamburg.[20]

General Anikita Ivanovich Repnin's infantry regiments were encamped in villages along the coastline of the sea around Koporie; judging from the letter to Menshikov, Repnin's soldiers were in acute need of clothing and footwear. At the same time, they remained in readiness to repulse a possible Swedish attack out of Narva or from out of Vyborg across the ice of the Gulf of Finland. About the enemy's condition, it was known in particular from a prisoner's interrogation that "very many were dying in Rugodev from illness and hunger."[21]

29 March
Apraxin dispatched a cavalry unit and directed it towards Narva and further on to the west "for finding out", which is to say with the aim of gathering information and along the way inflicting damage to the enemy. Three hundred dragoons from Colonel Morel de Carriere's regiment under the command of Lieutenant Colonel Ivan Matveevich Novikov, at a point along the road to Reval 20 versts from Narva, "laid waste to many hostile residences and in those residences thrashed around 200 men of all types and captured 30 prisoners." From the captured Swedish cavalry, foot soldiers, servants and peasants, among other things he learned that Major General Henning Rudolph Horn remained the commandant in Narva, that the Nöteborg commandant Gustav Wilhelm Schlippenbach was sitting in the fortress under arrest, because he had prematurely surrendered the town, and that Johann Apoloff [Ivan Grigorievich Opalev], the former Swedish commandant of Nyenschantz of Russian descent was also located in Narva, but at liberty. The prisoners provided details about conditions in Narva: There were four regiments in

Priozersk.
18   PiB, Vol. 3, p. 40.
19   NIA SPbII RAN, F.83, Op. 1, D. 137, l. 1.
20   *Ibid.*, D. 150, l. 1–1 ob.
21   Volynsky, Book 3, p. 302.

Military troops on a square.
(Joseph Parrocel 1656–1703,
France, late 17th century,
Collection Rijksmuseum,
Amsterdam)

the fortress, but over the winter more than half of the men had died, and six men were continuing to pass away each day; there remained fewer than 2,000 infantry and cavalry in the garrison; only around 600 soldiers remained healthy, and the entire burden of sentry duties fell on their shoulders – after two days 300 men would be relieved at their posts; and finally, that there no fewer than 300 cavalrymen in the garrison, but many of their horses had died due to lack of fodder. In the city they experienced the lack of food and were in dread of a siege, in which they might not hold out for long. Notices had been posted along the roads, so that by springtime each estate would prepare wagons for transporting Swedish troops to Narva.[22]

30 March

A supply train carrying grain that had been sent from Reval reached Waiwer [today Vaivara], a village about 25 km west of Narva, where it ran into a Russian unit that was crossing at Wasa. Some of the peasants accompanying the train were killed, but later a covering party was sent out from Narva which escorted the wagons into the city. The first entry in the journal of a Swedish officer in the Ivangorod garrison was dedicated to the raid conducted by Novikov's dragoons: the Russians had left Jamburg and had crossed the ice of the Narova River to the Livonian side at Kutterkuhl,[23] killing and capturing peasants.[24] Obviously, this was the last possibility of crossing the river before the ice melted; for example, the Neva River at Schlisselburg by 3 April was already open and ice was beginning to flow downstream from Lake Ladoga.[25]

22   Volynsky, Book 1, p. 238; Ustrialov, Vol. 4, Part 2, p. 303.
23   In the sources of the 17th and 18th Centuries, this village is alternatively spelled Katterkyhla, Kutterkull, and Gutterkull. Today it is Kudruküla, which lies on the western bank of the Narova River three kilometres from the sea.
24   Rosen, p. 179; Adlerfeld, Vol. 2, p. 2.
25   NIA SPbII RAN, F. 83, Op. 1, D. 167, l. 1.

Soldiers plundering a village. An etching from a series about the sufferings and tribulations of war. France, 1633.
Rural lands in those times were a source of provisions and fodder, while troops were quartered in populated places. Therefore, the warring armies sought to deprive the enemy of these resources by laying waste to the lands adjacent to the border. Both sides began to resort to the tactic of devastation already in December 1700, and over time the Russian side achieved much greater "successes" in this practice. Field Marshal Sheremetev reported to the Tsar about the actions of his troops in Livonia in the summer of 1702: "I sent men in every direction to imprison and burn; as a result, nothing remained intact; everything has been left desolate and burned, and your Majesty's warriors have taken prisoner several thousand men, women and children, as well as working horses, and rounded up 20,000 or more head of cattle; in addition, all of the regiments have been fed, and whatever couldn't be gathered has been slaughtered or massacred; meanwhile I expect that there will be twice more." As a result, the Swedish forces in the region couldn't conduct any sort of major operations. (Jacques Callot 1592-1635)

4 April

Apraxin's force that had arrived in Jamburg was not ready for a further march towards Narva. In the first place, cannons were absent in the regiments, and the commander asked the Tsar to issue orders so that the artillery administration would distribute the necessary guns. The infantry regiments were short of men, especially Inglis' regiment, into which since autumn all of the "most emaciated, doddering and blind" soldiers from General Repnin's troops had been collected. Apraxin complained about the lack of weapons and regimental supplies and requested the hasty dispatch of everything necessary.[26]

8 April

Rumours regarding the impending siege of Narva began to pass around in the Swedish command staff even before active operations got underway against the city, and even before the Tsar himself decided to initiate a full-scale siege. News was already spreading in Riga that the Russians had already constructed fieldworks at the mouth of the Narova River and were blockading the fortress from the sea and land; soon the Tsar himself would arrive with his grand army, but in the meantime the Muscovites were supposedly eradicating each

---

26   PiB, Vol. 3, pp. 609–610.

View toward the castle and Old Town from the southeast.
In addition to the centerpiece buildings that exist today – Hermann Tower and the Town Hall – two more bell towers had been rising above the city back in 1704. (Otto Kletzl 1897-1945 and Richard Hamann-MacLean 1908-2000; Estonia, 1940-1941 Bildarchiv Foto Marburg)

village together with its inhabitants. On this day, 2,000 men set out from Reval in order to reinforce the Narva garrison, as did ships loaded with provisions.[27]

9 April

Sheremetev reported from Pskov that according to the testimony of a Swedish soldier who had deserted from Dorpat, the Swedes were building a large, new ship, and after the Emajõgi River was freed of ice, they would set out along the river channel with all their ships armed with a total of 150 cannons to where the river entered Lake Peipus; from there they would cross the lake to the Russian side in order to pillage and devastate the countryside.[28]

11 April

At dawn, Russian dragoons rode up to Ivangorod – one company under Lieutenant Terentii Unkovsky and Ensign Prince Vasilii Kropotkin from Morel de Carriere's regiment. Unnoticed, they managed to reach a point beneath the walls themselves, where sentry huts were standing in the moat. Having driven in the doors, the dragoons broke into the huts and in the course of a fleeting combat took three Swedes prisoner, but "stabbed and shot the other cavalrymen and peasants, because they would not give up alive"

---

27   Volynsky, Book 3, p. 77.
28   NIA SPbII RAN, F. 270, Op. 1, D. 41, l. 26.

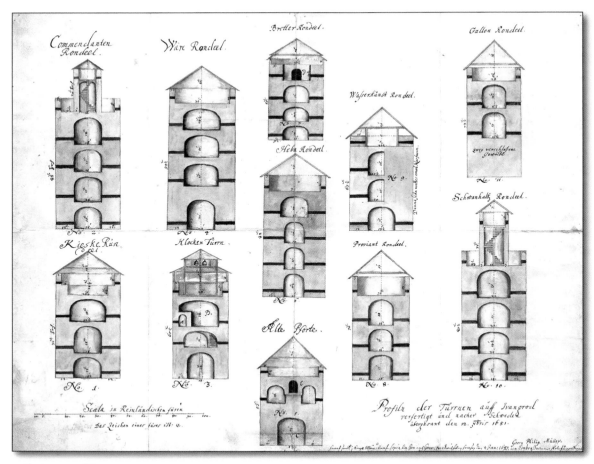

The Ivangorod Towers in profile.
Dahlberg back in 1681 highly rated the power of Ivangorod's fortifications, but recommended that roofs be added to the towers, lest they fall into decay and develop cracks. The recommended bastions on the Ingrian side were in fact never constructed. (Georg Philip Müller; Sweden, 1681 Krigsarkivets kartsamlingar)

(six men were killed and four wounded according to the Swedish source). Several rounds were fired from the hornworks' cannons, but the attackers had already disappeared behind a hill. On this same day the prisoners were brought to Jamburg, and they revealed that because of the die-off of horses, many Narva cavalry and dragoons were heading out to the picket posts on foot; that all of the city dwellers were fearing a Muscovite siege; that they were expecting the arrival of 2,000 troops from Reval; and that mines had been dug around Ivangorod. The soldiers of the Narva garrison were living in root cellars and they rarely had heating because of the lack of firewood in the city, but they did not travel outside of the town, fearing the Russians.[29]

12 April

Responding to Apraxin's request, Tsar Peter promised to send 20 regimental cannons from Saint Petersburg and advised the commander to take three large cannons from the Jamburg fortress; together with the 4,000–5,000 soldiers and dragoons, which were to come under Apraxin's command,

---

29   *Ibid.*, F. 36, Op. 1, D. 693, l. 31 ob.; Volynsky, Book 3, pp. 10 and 28; Adlerfeld, Vol. 2, p. 2; Laskovsky, Vol. 2, p. 394; Archiv., p. 241.

this should be enough to blockade the mouth of the Narova River. The Tsar implored Apraxin not to waste time and assured him that with such a force he had nothing to fear. The Swedish military ships could not enter the river – the depth of 2.5 metres was adequate only for cargo ships (Peter had personally measured the depth in the estuary back in the autumn of 1700).[30]

Sheremetev received an order to occupy the mouth of the Emajõgi River at Lake *Peipus*, and once the grass emerged to set out with the cavalry and to operate with it against the Swedes "to frighten them"; then he was to follow the given "articles" which instructed him to go to Lithuania and to drive the Swedes out of Courland.[31]

21 April

The Swedish convoy of 10 supply ships arrived off the Narva Roads from Reval. It was being guarded by Captain Schnack's squadron consisting of the 20-cannon frigate *Snaren Sven* and the 14-cannon brigantines *Jungfrun* and *Väduren*.[32]

---

30   PiB, Vol. 3, p. 50.
31   *Ibid.*, pp. 46–49.
32   Archiv., p. 242; Rosen, pp. 165–166, 181.

23 April

Apraxin sent a detachment from Jamburg on reconnaissance towards the Narova estuary. Two companies of dragoons (Captain Leontii Shishkov's company from Souvas' regiment and Timofei Choglokov's company from Morel de Carriere's regiment), as well as a platoon of soldiers from Balabanov's regiment examined a meadow where the Narova and Rosson' Rivers flowed together and selected a place for a military encampment. Captured civilians – four peasants who had been fishing on the Rosson' River – reported that on the day before, two Swedish military ships and four ships carrying rye had approached the estuary, while six more ships were standing out to sea.[33]

Information about the navigability of the Rosson' and Luga Rivers for ships had been gathered in August 1703 by Colonels Bauer and Kropotov at Sheremetev's order. Through a personal examination and the interrogation of local residents they found out that only small boats could travel from Luga to Narva along the Rosson' River, which links the Narova and Luga Rivers just before they enter the Gulf of Finland; the channel was impassable for large ships because the Luga estuary had a depth of just two metres, and in addition had "large rocks".[34]

25 April

Ships loaded with oats and malt entered the Narova River and moored at the bridge. Apraxin sent word to the Tsar about the arrival of the ships from Reval and reported he would set out on the next day from Jamburg towards the estuary and take position on the coast between the Narova and Rosson' Rivers in order to intercept the Swedish flotilla. In order not to delay in setting out, it was decided not to wait for the reinforcements and to march out with the available forces – a total of 2,456 men (380 in Shakhovsky's regiment, 780 in Titov's regiment, 496 in Bils' regiment, 300 from Balabanov's regiment, which was serving as Jamburg's garrison, and 500 men from Souvas' dragoon regiment); and three 6-pound cannons and six 3-pound cast iron cannons from the Jamburg fortress. Frenchman Robert Ducrot and the Brandenburger Johan Schmidt served as the artillery sergeants with Apraxin's cannons.[35] Since a supply train would slow down the march, for speed the soldiers carried provisions in their backpacks. There were only 400 cannonballs for the regimental 3-pound cannons; the others that had been delivered were of incorrect calibre – 4-pound and 5-pound cannonballs. Such a number was insufficient for a lengthy defence of the coastline. Apraxin requested the Tsar to send cannonballs, cables for laying down a pontoon bridge, and other supplies.[36]

---

33 Volynsky, Book 3, p. 29.

34 Sharymov, A.M., *Predistoriia Sankt-Peterburga, 1703: Kniga issledovanii* [*Pre-history of Saint Petersburg, 1703: Book of studies*] (Saint Petersburg, 2004), pp. 664.

35 Archive VIMAIBiBS, F. 2, Op. 1, D. 37, ll. 77–79; Brandenberg, N.A., *Materialy dlia istorii artilleriskogo upravleniia v Rossii: Prikaz artillerii 1701–1720* [*Materials for the history of the artillery command in Russia: Artillery Administration 1701–1720*] (Saint Petersburg, 1876), p. 465.

36 Archiv., p. 242; Ustrialov, Vol. 4, Part 2, p. 304; PiB., Vol. 3, pp. 610–611; Volynsky, Book 3, p. 10.

Who was Petr Matveevich Apraxin?

Major General Petr Matveevich Apraxin, born on 1659, was a high-ranked *okol'nichii* (palace courtier in pre-reform Russia), the older brother of Fedor Matveevich Apraxin, a member of the Admiralty and the governor of Azov, as well as the brother of Marfa Matveevna Apraxin, who was the widow of Tsar Fedor Alekseevich, which meant he was a relative of Peter the Great. Apraxin participated in the Chigirin campaign of 1677 against the Turks. Until 1699 he served as the military governor of Novgorod. In 1700 he was with the Tsar at Narva as a "volunteer", which means he did not have an official post. From April 1701 he became the military governor of Ladoga and received troops under his own command, with which he protected Ladoga from General Kronhjort's Swedish troops that were standing on the border. In 1702 he advanced to the west and drove Kronhjort away from Nöteborg, after which he took part in capturing this fortress. In 1703 he took part in the capture of Nyenschantz, and then arrived in Jamburg with his troops, where they moved into winter quarters, while the commander himself went to Moscow for the winter.[37]

Frederick IV, King of Denmark and Norway (see page 40). (Christoff Weigel 1654-1725, Germany, 1710 Anne S.K. Brown Military Collection)

26 April

While Apraxin was in route with his troops, the Swedish convoy sailed up the Narova River to the city and unloaded the cargo of oats and malt. On this occasion rye was not delivered.[38]

27 April

Apraxin's force arrived and set up camp at the village of Wegenkulle[39] on the Narova River next to the mouth of the Rosson' River. It became known that the day before this, enemy ships had arrived at the estuary, three of which were standing opposite the mouth of the Rosson', two of which were standing inshore; in addition, four ships and four scows were visible out to sea. In Narva they noticed the appearance of Russian cavalry close to the mouth of the river.[40]

---

37   Volynsky, Book 3, pp. 33–36.
38   Archiv., p. 242; Rosen, p. 181.
39   In the sources, this village also figures as Wagenkyla and Wegenkull. This village on the southern bank of the Rosson' River at a point 1.5 kilometres from where it merges with the Narova River is today known as Venekiula.
40   Ustrialov, Vol. 4, Part 2, p. 304; Adlerfeld, Vol. 2, p. 2.

Meantime: the Danish King Travels to Norway

The news was reporting: "From Copenhagen … they are writing that the Danish King intends to travel to Norway, and on April 27th will go to Bergen or Trondheim."[41] Norway was part of the Danish kingdom under the terms of a united commonwealth, and in 1704 King Friedrich IV, who had ruled Denmark since 1699, visited his overseas territory for the first time. By now, Denmark had succeeded in being one of the first to enter the Northern War in the springtime of 1700 and was the first to exit it in August of the same year. On its southern borders, the Duchy of Holstein-Gottorp, which was traditionally supported by Sweden, was a subject of long-time Danish claims. However, after the Danes joined the war, the Swedish Army with the support of a powerful British and Dutch fleet made a landing in the Copenhagen area and compelled Denmark to sign the Peace of Travendal with Holstein, which virtually obligated Denmark to leave the anti-Swedish alliance. However, the diplomatic efforts of Peter and Augustus to return Denmark to the Northern Union never ended. In subsequent years, Danish regiments were available on hire to the Allies and took part in the War of Spanish Succession; in the ranks of the Imperial troops they fought against the French in Italy and Flanders, as well as against the rebels in Hungary.

28 April

Under a gentle breeze, two brigantines entered the Narova River at 2:00 p.m., sailed up the channel as far as Apraxin's positions and opened fire, in order to knock out the battery that had been set up on the riverbank opposite the village of Kutterkuhl; other ships were firing with their cannons from long range. In response the Russian artillery spoke up, and a furious cannonade began from both sides. Several men in the battery were wounded, and one cast-iron 3-pound gun blew up when firing. Nevertheless, the battery was able to develop rapid fire, and one of the brigantines in the course of the battle received several hits in the side; both ships were forced to retire – they were towed away by oared boats beyond the range of the Russian cannons. So the attempt by the enemy fleet to reach the city was repulsed. Of the entire squadron of Swedish ships, three were left not far from the estuary, while six others headed out to sea. On this same day, Commandant Horn had ridden out of the fortress in order to observe the enemy's actions from the opposite bank of the river, but he came under fire from the battery. Apraxin, reporting to the Tsar about the results of the action, advised to head out to sea and to attack the Swedish fleet, but also requested doctors for his unit.[42]

29 April

The Russians continued to labour and expanded their fortifications on the riverbank; now a ship on the roads could not reach the port, while those

41 *Vedomosti – Moskva*, 29 May 1704.
42 NIA SPbII RAN, F. 83, Op. 1, D. 213, l. 1–2; Adlerfeld, Vol. 2, p. 2; Ustrialov, Vol. 4, Part 2, pp. 304–305; PiB, Vol. 3, pp. 615–616; Volynsky, Book 3, pp. 10–11, 30, 35; Laskovsky, Vol. 2, p. 394; Archiv., p. 242.

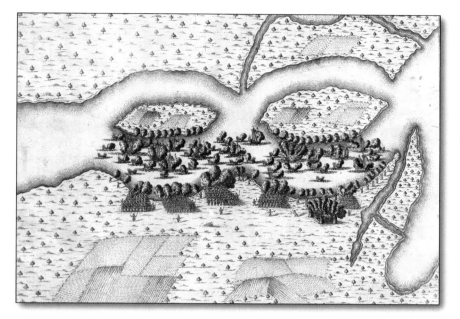

Von Werden's infantry battles the Swedish squadron on the Emajõgi River; fragment of an etching from the Book of Mars.
Judging from the testimonies of the surviving Swedes, the Russian infantry was firing from the banks; there was apparently no boarding from boats. At the moment of encounter, the Kastre Castle stood upstream from the battle location, but artists depicted it at the place of battle as a landmark. (Workshop of the Saint-Petersburg Printshop; Russia, 1710s Russian State library)

standing at the city under the protection of the fortress cannons could not exit into the sea. The Swedes lost any and all hopes for the delivery of provisions to Narva.[43]

30 April

Sheremetev was preparing, according to the previously received instructions, to head out to the Polish borders and simultaneously sent nine infantry regiments to the mouth of the Emajõgi River; among them was Andrei Scharf's infantry regiment from the lower Volga, the men of which were accustomed to being on water, as well as two Pskov *streltsy* regiments, which had experience with water campaigns.[44] On this same day the Tsar cancelled Sheremetev's campaign into Lithuania and Courland and ordered him to set out with his infantry and initiate a siege of Dorpat; in order to "reassure" the Lithuanians and Poles, Sheremetev was to send one dragoon regiment to Major General Korsak.[45]

1 May

A portion of Apraxin's force boarded boats and crossed the Narova River. On the Livonian bank, they occupied the villages of Hungerburg[46] and Kutterkuhl, dug retrenchments there, and dispatched mounted patrols towards Waiwer; from this day on, they daily harassed the Swedes and attempted to drive off the cattle and horses that were grazing around Narva. Swedish attempts

---

43   Adlerfeld, Vol. 2, pp. 2–3; Laskovsky, Vol. 2, p. 394; Archiv., p. 242.
44   NIA SPbII RAN, F. 270, Op. 1, D. 41, l. 30.
45   PiB, Vol. 3, p. 53.
46   A village on the west bank of the Narova where it enters the Gulf of Finland, today known as Narva-Jõesuu.

to get provisions to Narva aboard small boats at night continued but were thwarted by the Russians who had appeared on the river in boats and were attacking the enemy scows.[47]

In the early days of May, Tsarist instructions went out to the combat groupings from Saint Petersburg with the final plans for the starting campaign. Field Marshal Boris Petrovich Sheremetev was ordered to march from Pskov and to besiege Dorpat, and to prepare to march further into Courland; the Kiev military governor Dmitrii Mikhailovich Golitsyn was ordered to lead his infantry and Cossacks from Kiev to link up with King Augustus in Poland, where they would come under the command of the secret adviser Lieutenant General Johann Reinhold von Patkul; Hetman Ivan Stepanovich Mazepa together with his Little Russia[48] troops were ordered to head to the Polish border and there, at the directions of Augustus, devastate with fire and sword the domain of the King's enemies; Major General Bogdan Semenovich Korsak was to march from Smolensk to Lithuania in order to link up with Lithuanian troops at Biržai.[49]

The bas-relief medallion in honor of the victory of "the Russian ships on Lake Piepus" that is on the Emajõgi River. (Carlo Bartolomeo Rastrelli 1654-1744, Andrei Konstantinovich Nartov 1693-1756, Russia, 1720s)

Meanwhile: the Battle on the Emajõgi River

Having learned that a flotilla of military ships had been prepared in Dorpat for sailing into Lake Peipus and Lake Pskov, the Tsar ordered Sheremetev to occupy the mouth of the Emajõgi River. The assignment was given to Major General Nikolai von Verdin with a force of six soldier and three *streltsy* regiments with a combined strength of 7,066 men and 18 regimental cannons. The Russians only had a matter of hours to be on time to intercept Swedish ships before they broke through to the open lake. On 2 May the Swedish Commodore Karl Gustav Löshern von Herzfeld left Dorpat with 13 pennants and under sail travelled down the river to Lake *Peipus*. Von Verdin's unit aboard boats headed up the channel from the mouth of the river to meet him. The Swedes failed to organise reconnaissance of the banks as they travelled down the river; they were informed about the enemy by fishermen, but the route column of ships became extended. Major General von Verdin had sent boats carrying soldiers and *streltsy* to the ruined castle of Kaströ that was nine kilometres from the lake. There, having noticed the approach of the Swedes early on the morning of 3 May, they descended the river back to

---

47   Laskovsky, Vol. 2, p. 394; Archiv., p. 243; Adlerfeld, Vol. 2, p. 3; Rosen, p. 182.

48   Little Russia (*Malorossiia*) was the name used in Russia for its part that is now territory of Ukraine. It was semi-autonomously governed by Hetmans, hence was also called the Hetmanate (*Getmanschina*).

49   *Pokhodnyi zhurnal 1704 goda*, pp. 19–21.

the mouth and warned the six regiments of soldiers, that were positioned along both riverbanks. The Swedish commodore was forewarned and had time to make dispositions before the battle; the officers' wives and civilians who had remained on board after the banquet in honour of the squadron's departure from Dorpat were disembarked from the ships. The lead ships one after the other came under fire from both banks and entered battle; they had no possibility of manoeuvring or falling back along the narrow and rapid river. In turn the ships became grounded on riparian shoals and after fleeting battle were abandoned by their crews. The heavy musket and artillery fire from both sides of the river continued for not less than an hour. Von Verdin's troops lost 58 killed and 162 wounded; approximately 190 Swedes were killed, 142 were captured, and more than 240 men were able to escape back to Dorpat. The flagship, the brigantine *Carolus*, was third to arrive at the scene of battle and soon blew up. The remaining 12 ships, equipped with 86 cannons, other weapons and supplies, were captured and triumphantly brought back to Pskov. That is how the struggle, which since 1701 the Dorpat squadron and the "floating warrior hosts" from Pskov had conducted with alternating success, came to an end. With the destruction of the Swedish flotilla, the path to Dorpat and Narva from the direction of Lake *Peipus* was now open for the Russians.[50]

4 May

Apraxin was ordered to build a bridge across the mouth of the Narova River and a fieldwork on the opposite bank, so that cavalry could cross to the Livonian bank and hamper the unloading of ships on the seashore. Peter I was concerned that ships, unable to reach Narva via the river, would unload their cargo on the seaside and deliver it to the city over the land. Therefore, on 6 May Sergeant Shchepotev arrived from the Preobrazhensky Regiment with two sailors in order to construct the bridge. To embolden the commander, the Tsar wrote that he had nothing to fear, because there were no enemy troops in Livonia, and Sheremetev had been sent to besiege Dorpat.

Meanwhile Commandant Horn asked Schlippenbach to gather forces and to come to Narva, in order to clear the Russians from the estuary and to escort ships loaded with provisions to the city. In the meantime, however, the commandant had doubts that it was worth taking in reinforcements into Narva, because there were not enough available provisions.[51]

50 Sheremetev's Campaign Journal, pp. 142–149; Kelch, pp. 373–374; Laidre, pp. 108–109; Sidorov, D.A., *Shvedskaia Derptskaia flotiliia 1701–1704: bor'ba za Chudskoe ozero // Menshikovskie chteniia – 2014: nauchnyi al'manakh* [*The Swedish Dorpat flotilla, 1701– 1704: struggle for Lake Peipus// Menshikov's Readings – 2014: scientific almanac*] (Saint Petersburg, 2014), pp. 168–224; Lukoshkov, A.V., *Issledovaniia po lokalizatsii mesta srazheniia na reke Emaigi 3 Maia 1704// Menshikovskie chteniia – 2105: nauchnyi al'manakh* [*Research to identify the places of fighting on the Emajõgi River 3 May 1704// Menshikov's Readings – 2015: scientific almanac*] (Saint Petersburg, 2015), pp. 171–183.
51 PiB, Vol. 3, p. 57; Rosen, p. 182.

Who Was Mikhail Ivanovich Shchepotev?

His origins are unknown. In 1693 he accompanied Tsar Peter on his trip to Arkhangelsk, where together with the military governor Fedor Apraxin he was left for the winter in order to build ships and prepare for the Tsar's naval campaigns along the White Sea in the summer of 1694. He was a sergeant of the military unit that was closest to the throne – the bombardier company of the Preobrazhensky Regiment and in this role carried out Peter I's special assignments. He was one of the organisers of the laying down of the path of more than 170 kilometres through the taiga from the White Sea to Lake Onega in August 1702; this feat is still known in local folk memory as the *Osudareva doroga* (the Monarch's Road). After the conclusion of the 1702 campaign, he escorted the Swedish prisoners from Ladoga to Moscow, where he took part in a triumphal parade. In February 1703 Shchepotev led raids against the surroundings of Nyenschantz. With the start of the siege of this fortress, he commanded a scouting party to the mouth of the Neva River in order to keep watch for the enemy fleet and reported on the arrival of the Swedish ships. Thanks to the received information, Peter I and Menshikov at the head of a boatload of units of Guardsmen on 7 May 1703 attacked and seized two enemy warships, the *Gädda* and the *Astrild*. This famous battle entered history as the *"Nebyvaemoe byvaet"* ("The impossible happens"), but whether or not Shchepotev took part in the boarding of the ships is unknown. That summer a boeier was under construction at the Olonets shipbuilding yard, and Shchepotev was serving as the captain when she was launched into the water. In the winter of 1704 he was engaged in receiving new recruits for the regiments in Novgorod. As one of the Tsar's trusted individuals, Mikhail Petrovich was not only in charge of constructing the bridge across the Narova River, but also looked after Apraxin and reported on how the things were going to Peter I.

8 May

Every day the Apraxin's cavalry crossed to the Livonian side, before setting out and riding in different directions along the coastline, the road to Reval, and towards the very fortress of Narva. The garrison's distant patrols were pushed back into the city and were showing no activity. Petr Matveevich himself on this day rode around the city to the very island, where Sheremetev had been standing in 1700 (in general, both Apraxin and Shchepotev, when describing the terrain, referred to the events in 1700, for example, where Peter I's battery or A.M. Golovin's encampment were located). A lot of people were visible on the walls of the fortress, and twice cannons fired, but nobody rode out of the city. A Swedish mounted patrol was standing in the suburban area beside the walls, and in the field the Russians captured two prisoners. Narva dragoons Denis Iuriev and Osip Piartulev related that in 1703 an earthen rampart standing head high and a moat that was two metres deep had been built around the Ivangorod castle at a distance of 8–10 metres from the stone walls. Thirteen mines had been dug into it, and on the Narva bank, three mines had been made at the ship wharf. The prisoners testified on the numerical strength and commanders of the garrison and announced that in May the soldiers had been given rotten rusk and did not receive their pay.[52]

9 May

The Swedish fleet was standing as before on the Narva Roads but demonstrating no activity. P.M. Apraxin could count eight warships and eight scows, of which one or two ships approached the estuary each day for observation. Apraxin complained of a shortage of cavalry – as before he had only the single dragoon regiment under Souvas, and only 400 of the dragoons had mounts, but the rest were dismounted, because back in the autumn many of the horses had perished. The infantry did not have enough swords and bayonets, and in place of the absent flags, the empty flag covers were on display on the flagpoles in the camp. Petr Matveevich was awaiting the arrival of Morel de Carriere's dragoon regiment and requested the dispatch of Astafiev's and Gorbov's dragoon regiments, which were billeted in the villages around Jamburg. On this day, the soldier Semen Spitsyn from the Preobrazhensky Regiment's bombardier company arrived from the sea via the Luga River and Rosson' River, bringing the cables that were needed for the pontoon bridges.[53] Although Apraxin was confidently reporting to the Tsar that he "would not allow them to unload anything or let them reach the shore", the Swedes nevertheless conducted a landing over a beach, 30 kilometres west of the Narova River estuary. On the night of 9–10 May, 700 infantrymen of Colonel Rebinder's regiment were ferried ashore from the ships in boats and quickly disappeared into some woods. The Russian horse patrols either did not notice them, or else could not interfere with the landing and failed to inform higher command.[54] Meanwhile the preparations for the Tsar's campaign towards Kexholm was underway: eight navigation pilots, who knew the route from Schlisselburg to Kexholm, were dispatched from Olonets.[55]

10 May

Apraxin's troops continued to set up their position: around the "baggage train" they erected a "town with four bulwarks", which is to say, a fortified camp with a bastion at each corner; the battery overlooking the river was increased to 13 cannons. On the opposite bank, they still had not put the finishing touches to the fieldwork – they were waiting for the bridge to be put in place. Shchepotev squarely reported to the Tsar that the preparation of pontoons would be completed on this day, and that the cables would be stretched across the river. In the sea, five kilometres from the mouth of the river, 16 Swedish ships were visible, including smacks [or smaks], snows [or snauws], and fluyts. In order to repulse a possible second ship attack, local boats were gathered and men were sent to Jamburg to bring more boats;

52   NIA SPbII RAN, F. 83, Op. 1, D. 232, ll. 1–2.
53   NIA SPbII RAN, F. 83, Op. 1, D. 233, ll. 1-2; Ustrialov, Vol. 4, Part 2, p. 305; PiB, Vol. 3, pp. 616–617; Volynsky, Book 3, pp. 11 and 413.
54   Volynsky, Book 3, pp. 12–13, 414–415.
55   RGA VMF, F. 223, Op. 1, D. 9, l. 46.

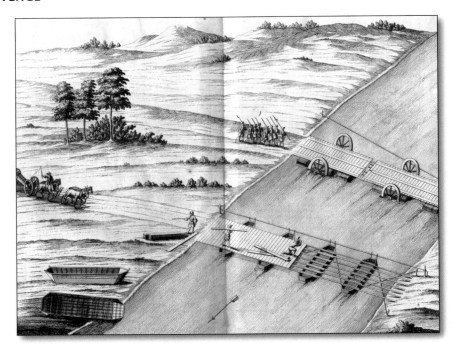

Types of pontoon bridges from the military encyclopedia *Der Vollkommene Teutsche Soldat*. (*The Contemporary German Soldier* by Hans Friedrich von Fleming; Artist unknown Leipzig, 1726)

perhaps, the sergeant was getting ready to repeat the exploit of the preceding year – the "Impossible", when the Tsar and his grenadiers in boats had seized two Swedish warships in the Neva estuary.[56]

Meanwhile, Rebinder's regiment was moving towards Narva from its landing site along the Reval–Narva road. In order to meet it and escort it back to Narva, 300 infantrymen from Colonel Lode's regiment and 250 cavalrymen from Morath's regiment marched out of the city. Russian sources say nothing about this episode, though the Swedes have drawn a fully dramatic picture. The Swedish units linked up in the area of the estuary just at the same time when the Russians were purportedly beginning to construct the pontoon bridge; they completed in "great haste" and immediately crossed troops to the Narva bank in order to attack the enemy. The Swedish colonels consulted with each other and decided that to accept battle with fewer troops and without artillery would be too risky; moreover, Rebinder's men were poorly supplied with muskets, and there was not a single tool in the entire regiment which might be used to dig an entrenchment in the case of extreme necessity. So, the Swedes turned around and withdrew towards Narva with Rebinder's regiment at the head of the column, followed by Lode's men, while the cavalry and 30 grenadiers served as the rearguard. They managed to escape the pursuit, only having destroyed the bridge across the Tarvajegi stream behind themselves.[57] By nightfall the unit entered Narva in formation, and the soldiers on sentry duty counted seven flags (which meant seven companies) in Rebinder's newly-arrived regiment. This regiment, as one of

---

56   Volynsky, Book 3, p. 413.

57   Today known as the Tõrva jõgi, this stream crosses the Tallinn road and enters the Narova River at a point six kilometres from the sea.

the Swedish soldiers captured later reported, assembled in 1701 out of territorials, which meant it was a militia unit. Commandant Horn was very dissatisfied with the conduct of his colonels and called for a military counsel on this matter. The reinforcements brought with them neither baggage nor provisions.[58]

11 May

Apraxin travelled to Ivangorod and sent Shchepotev out together with several dragoons on reconnaissance towards the Narva side of the river. The patrol captured prisoners, and in the diary of the resident of the city, it is noted that the Russians had desolated the territory between Narva and Waiwer.[59]

12 May

Swedish Vice-Admiral De Prou's squadron arrived at the Narva Roads; from shore, the Russians could see

A column of infantry. (Artist unknown; in Hans Friedrich von Fleming, *Der Vollkommene Teutsche Soldat* Leipzig, 1726)

that the Swedish fleet had increased to 35 ships, including seven 28-cannon and 30-cannon warships with a flagship under the command of the Vice-Admiral. In Narva, they could easily hear the powerful cannonade in the estuary.[60] Meanwhile, elsewhere on this day, Peter I confirmed the order to Sheremetev to besiege Dorpat.[61]

Who Was Jacob De Prou?

"A vice-admiral with the name of De Prou, a Frenchman by birth, whose left hand is made of silver, now stands at the head of the naval fleet; his left hand had been blown off many years ago by a grenade."[62] Vice-Admiral Jacob De Prou was born in 1651. As a Huguenot, he left France because of religious persecution and resettled in Sweden, where he became a colonel quartermaster of an infantry regiment in 1681; captain of a fleet in 1688; and vice-admiral in 1700. As an army officer he lost his right hand, which hindered

58   Adlerfeld, Vol. 2, pp. 3-4; Laskovsky, Vol. 2, pp. 394–395; Archiv., p. 243; Rosen, p. 182.
59   Volynsky, Book 3, p. 12; Laskovsky, Vol. 2, p. 395; Archiv., p. 243.
60   Ustrialov, Vol. 4, Part 2, p. 305; Volynsky, Book 3, pp. 12, 30; Adlerfeld, Vol. 2, p. 4; Laskovsky, Vol. 2, p. 395; Archiv., p. 243.
61   PiB, Vol. 3, p. 68
62   Volynsky, Book 3, p. 16.

Warships.
(Peter Schenk 1660-1711, The Netherlands, 1700 Collection Rijksmuseum, Amsterdam)

his field service, so he began to make a career in the navy, having replaced his hand with a steel mechanical prosthesis (apparently, the rumours that had reached the Russians contained twisted information – his right hand became his left hand, and the steel prosthesis was now silver). During the war against France in 1691–1692, he had served in the Anglo-Dutch fleet at his own expense, and then up until 1695 he continued service in it at the expense of a Swedish prince. He accepted his first independent command in 1704, having assumed command of a squadron of 15 ships. He received orders to defend the coastline of the Gulf of Finland against Russian invasion. Having set sail, he was supposed to leave Karlskrona and secure the supply of Narva with troops and provisions from Reval, and then to prevent the Russians from digging in around the Neva estuary and on Kotlin Island.[63]

13 May

On the Ivangorod side of the river, the Swedes saw a strong party of Russian troops – perhaps this was yet another mounted patrol conducted by Apraxin or perhaps the approach of the regiments that had been left behind which had been assigned to Apraxin's unit, Inglis' infantry else Strekalov's or Baishev's

---

streltsy; Apraxin himself is silent about a battle with ships and the arrival of reinforcements on this day.[64]

14 May

De Prou made another attempt to attack Apraxin. After noontime, a 28-cannon warship reached the squadron, and together with the other ships they attempted to bombard the Russian camp until nightfall from 24-pound cannons and three-pood (327 mm) mortars. However, the bombardment did not do any damage to Apraxin's troops: the deep-drafted warships could not approach closely and their cannon fire could not reach the encampment and batteries. Apraxin reported to the Tsar that the bridge had been completed, and once again complained of the lack of troops, especially in cavalry, in the event that the Swedish corps under General Wolmar Anton von Schlippenbach arrived from Reval.[65]

The testimony of the Swedes that had been captured on 11 May passed up the chain of command to Menshikov: towards the end of April, the Swedes had managed to get 30 wagons full of rye into the city, but had been unable to deliver anything more from the ships; grain reserves were assessed as "not scant", enough for five months, and were being stored in the castle; provisions were being issued to the garrison regularly, but the soldiers were not getting their pay; there were 12 companies in Horn's regiment, five companies each in the other two regiments, and in total, prior to the arrival of reserves, there was up to 2,000 infantry and 200 cavalry; in the fortress mines had been dug to the wharves below the Butchers' Gates;[66] and that Schlippenbach had 4,000 cavalrymen at Reval.

Schlippenbach at this time was continuing to hold at Neuhof in the Pernau [modern-day Pärnu] area and conducting an exhaustive correspondence with De La Gardie and Horn, explaining the impossibility of moving out towards Narva due to the lack of supplies, wagons and so forth.[67]

15 May

Shchepotev and his detachment of dragoons rode along the sea on the Narva side. They did not encounter any Swedish troops, but captured 40 Letts, peasants of both genders.[68]

16 May

The Tsar received Apraxin's intelligence and informed Sheremetev that in Narva they were despairing of getting the ships through and were awaiting

---

64 Laskovsky, Vol. 2, p. 395; Archiv., p. 243.
65 Apraxin's original letters about the events of 12 and 14 May have been dated "14 May". Ustrialov mistakenly dates this letter to 12 May, Volynsky to 13 May. NIA SPbII RAN, F. 83, Op. 1, D. 243; Ustrialov, Vol. 4, Part 2, p. 305; Volynsky, Book 3, pp. 12, 30.
66 The gates of the Old Town, which emerge on the river between the Wrangel (Pax) and Victoria bastions. These gates were also known as the Dark, Little Waterside and Butchers', the latter in connection with the fact that the stalls of Russian butchers were located at the gates.
67 NIA SPbII RAN, F. 83, Op. 1, D. 238, ll. 1–2 and D. 243, 1–2; Volynsky, Book 3, pp. 12–13; Rosen, p. 183.
68 Volynsky, Book 3, pp. 414–415.

Estonian peasants from Oberpahlen (present-day Põltsamaa). (Johann Christoph Brotze 1742-1823, Russia, 1777)v

Schlippenbach and his 4,000 dragoons to come to the rescue. The Field Marshal was ordered to cut Schlippenbach's path with his cavalry. Sheremetev meanwhile learned from captured prisoners that the Swedish general was holding between Reval and Pernau.[69]

In execution of his intentions that were announced back in February, the Tsar initiated the campaign towards Kexholm: Lieutenant General Adam Schönbeck was ordered to head out of Schlisselburg to the north with his regiments, and before reaching the Swedish fortress, to wait for the rest of the troops from Petersburg; one battalion of the Preobrazhensky Regiment set out on the campaign by land, while the others were preparing to board ships.[70]

Meanwhile: the Siege of Susa in Italy

News sources were reporting "The French have besieged the fortress of Susa in Savoia."[71] The events of the War of Spanish Succession were unfolding in particular in northern Italy. The town of Susa on the border of the Duchy of Savoy with France lies in the foothills of the Alps, 50 kilometres west of Turin. The French General Louis d'Aubisson duc de la Feuillade began the siege on 18 May with 20 battalions of infantry and four regiments of dragoons, and in just two weeks the 1,500-man garrison surrendered according to terms of an agreement, without waiting for the walls to be breached. The citadel

69   PiB, Vol. 3, pp. 69–70, 613.
70   *Pokhodnyi zhurnal 1704 goda*, p. 25.
71   *Vedomosti – Moskva (Pechatnyi dvor)*, 4 June 1704.

was subsequently destroyed by the victors.[72] After the Duke of Savoy Victor Amadeus II went over to the side of the anti-French coalition in 1703, the French campaign in Italy in 1704 was successful for France; Louis XIV's military commanders captured seven towns: Vercelli, Ivrea, Verrua Savoia, Revere, Robbio, Rosasco and Susa. In other theatres of the war, success was on the side of the Allies. On the whole, over the years of the War of Spanish Succession (1702–1714), there were no less than 115 sieges in various areas of Western and Central Europe, which depending on the strength of the fortifications and the forces engaged on both sides lasted from several days to many months.[73]

17 May

A peasant captured near the fortress, Mikhail Martynov, passed along information he heard from his master, Captain Renter of Horn's regiment: 80 casks of gunpowder had been placed in mines around Ivangorod, and in the event of an attack by "Muscovite troops" against the castle, the gunpowder would be ignited.[74]

18 May

Shchepotev sent a report off to the Tsar and Menshikov about the fulfilment of his mission: the bridge was in place across the Narova River and fieldworks had been built on the opposite bank, in which 200 soldiers had been posted; he had nothing more to do for Apraxin. Since he was knowledgeable about naval affairs, the sergeant wrote in detail about the composition of the Swedish fleet that was visible offshore, which had been reinforced to up to

The fall of Suza. After its capture by the French in 1704, this town, encircled by mountains and with a castle on a hill, was won back by Imperialist troops in 1707. (Paul Decker 1685-1742, Augsburg, 1712-1715, Collection Rijksmuseum, Amsterdam)

---

72 *Campagne de Monsieur le maréchal de Tallard er Allemagne L'An MDCCIV*, Vol. 1 (Amsterdam, 1763), p. 300; Description of all the seats of the present wars of Europe (London, 1704), p. 63; *Neu-eröffneter Historischer Bilder-Saal*, Vol. 6 (Nürnberg, 1725), p. 767; Salmon, T., *Modern History Or the Present State of All Nations*, Vol. 2 (London, 1745), p. 282.

73 Ostwald, J. "Vauban's siege legacy in the War of Spanish Succession, 1702–1712". Dissertation (Ohio, 2002), pp. 319–325.

74 NIA SPbII RAN, F. 83, Op. 2, D. 1. Book of copies 1, p. 43.

40 units. In addition to the infantry on board, the ships were holding a large amount of grain, malt, butter, herring and meat. Shchepotev also reported on the weakness of the troops under the Ladoga military governor: men were few, reinforcements for the regiments had not arrived from Moscow, many of the soldiers lacked cold steel, and the dragoons lacked horses. Moreover, the men had not been paid for three months. Titov's regiment was in particularly bad shape – it had just six officers, no flags, and there were neither swords nor bayonets.

Apraxin passed along the information that he had received from his captives that the Swedish fleet with 1,500 soldiers aboard the ships was expecting on 20 May the arrival of Schlippenbach, whose corps had been strengthened to up to 7,000 men and had already left Reval; this information was being confirmed by one peasant (apparently, Mikhail Martynov from the Letts that had been taken by Shchepotev), at whose place a lieutenant that had been sent by Schlippenbach to Narva with information of the corps' pending arrival had spent the night. A supply train of 240 wagons was moving with Schlippenbach. On the basis of such alarming news, Apraxin once again requested reinforcements and in a letter to Menshikov gave the following comparative assessment between the Russians and Swedes: "… it is known to you, my lord, that twice as many of our good-hearted troops are needed against them."[75]

Prince Repnin with his generalship was also assigned to the Kexholm campaign. He was ordered to wait for further instructions in Schlisselburg.[76]

Who Was Petr Vasilievich Griaznoi?

Originating from the Bezhetsky Verkh in Tver region, Petr Griaznoi was a servant to squire Gavril Ivanovich Batiushkov. In 1702 he voluntarily ("of his own will") signed up as an enlisted man in Moscow at the Military Chancellery; in 1703 he was appointed as a sergeant to Titov's infantry regiment, with which he took part in Apraxin's campaign to the Narova River estuary.[77]

19 May

The Tsar, together with his entourage and Guards, set out aboard ships from Petersburg towards Kexholm, but after sailing five kilometres a special courier from Apraxin caught up with him with the message about the Swedish fleet's build-up and word that Schlippenbach was closing on Narva with 7,000 troops. After receiving such news, Peter "held a military council and after sound reasoning he thought it better at present to set aside his intentions for Kexholm for a while." The blockade of Narva was already yielding its fruits – the city was short of provisions and would be unable

75   Ustrialov, Vol. 4, Part 2, pp. 305–306; Volynsky, Book 3, pp. 13–15, 414–415; NIA SPbII RAN, F. 83, Op. 1, D. 250, l. 2.
76   *Pokhodnyi zhurnal 1704 goda*, p. 25.
77   Adamovich, pp. 96–97.

to withstand a lengthy siege; however, if Apraxin was not supported, then the Swedish fortress would receive a strong reinforcement and supplies and taking it would become much more difficult. Such an opportunity should not be missed, and therefore all the Russian troops that were in movement towards Kexholm (some of the regiments and all of the artillery were already in Schlisselburg) were ordered to return, disembark from the ships, and march towards Jamburg and Narva.[78]

20 May

That morning Russians boldly approached the fortress of Narva itself, rounded up officers', burghers' and artillery draft horses that were grazing in the fields, captured several prisoners, and made off with their booty under fire from the fortress cannons.[79]

The transfer of troops to Narva began: two dragoon regiments under the command of von Rönne and Pflug, together with the Novgorod noble cavalry crossed the Neva River and hastily headed out to Jamburg. Peter I informed Sheremetev of his decision to abandon the siege of Kexholm and reaffirmed the order to move towards Dorpat quickly.[80]

A cavalry mount.
(Bernard Picart 1673-1733, The Netherlands, 1708-1717 Collection Rijksmuseum, Amsterdam)

21 May

Yet another mounted Russian patrol – Lieutenant Ivan Illarionovich Laptev's dragoons from Morel de Carriere's regiment – moved out from Narva to the west along the road to Reval and along the coastline and managed to capture more valuable prisoners than simple peasants – 13 soldiers, cavalry troopers and cannoneers, as well as one particularly important prisoner: Captain Staël von Holstein, who was carrying a bundle of Schlippenbach's coded messages to Narva, which were addressed to Commandant Horn. For such a valuable catch, each dragoon was awarded a rouble – Corporal Iurenev of this unit recalled this 16 years later.[81]

On this day Major General Chambers with the Guards and General Repnin with his generalship set out via an overland route towards Jamburg

---

78   *Pokhodnyi zhurnal 1704 goda*, pp. 25–26; PiB, Vol. 3, pp. 628–629.
79   Adlerfeld, Vol. 2, Part 4; Archiv., p. 243.
80   *Pokhhodnyi zhurnal 1704 goda*, p. 27; PiB, Vol. 3, p. 71.
81   Volynsky, Book 4, pp. 337, 345; Tatarinov (ed.), *Ofitserskie skazki pervoi chetverti XVIII veka*, Vol. 1, p. 359.

from Petersburg. Lieutenant General Schönbeck and five regiments were ordered to march out of Schlisselburg directly towards Jamburg and Narva. In addition, 24 new brigantines and scampavia [both galley-type vessels] arrived in Petersburg from the Olonets shipyards and berthed at the citadel [now known as the Peter and Paul Fortress].[82]

Who Was Georg Staël von Holstein?

Captain Georg Bogislaus Staël von Holstein (born in 1685). As a volunteer he served in the 1700 campaign with the Royal Life Guards and participated in the Battle of Narva. In 1703, he received the rank of captain in Adam De La Gardie's infantry regiment that had been recruited in Reval. The Staël von Holstein family owned estates in the Reval and Jamburg counties. Georg was the son of the Westphalian German colonel in charge of Narva's artillery; his mother and younger brother were living in a stone building in Narva; his older brother was serving in Charles XII's Guards; his cousin was a Guards colonel, and his uncle was a major general of the Duke of Holstein.[83]

22 May

The Tsar set out from Petersburg to Jamburg and Narva together with his closest circle: Governor-General Menshikov, Chamberlain Gavrila Ivanovich Golovkin and member of the Admiralty Fedor Matveevich Apraxin. A detachment of two companies of the Preobrazhensky Guards Regiment and a regiment of soldiers with tents, canvas and other items, including artillery and supplies, were sailing across the Gulf of Finland towards Narva in small watercraft. Lieutenant Colonel Hamilton's regiment that accompanied the ships returned to Petersburg after successfully delivering cargo.[84]

Sheremetev, whom Tsar Peter was lashing with orders to begin at last the siege of Dorpat, wrote the Tsar a letter, in which he assured him that the orders had been received, understood, and would be carried out by the Field Marshal with "all his inner and physical strength", and that his regiments were already moving out. In essence, Boris Petrovich was reporting that he had sent four dragoon regiments (under Meshchersky, Grigorov, Inflant and Astafiev) to reinforce P.M. Apraxin, and that the information about the pending arrival of Schlippenbach's 7,000-man corps did not seem credible to him.[85]

In the meantime, Apraxin sent the Tsar information he had gleaned from his prominent prisoner. The 19-year-old Captain Staël von Holstein not only talked about his family connections, but also related in great detail the composition, numerical strength and commanders of the Swedish units. Schlippenbach's cavalry in the surroundings of Reval consisted of the General's own regiment of 600 dragoons; Colonel Wachtmeister's Reval

---

82   *Pokhodnyi zhurnal 1704 goda*, p. 27.
83   Volynsky, Book 3, pp. 15–18.
84   *Pokhodnyi zhurnal 1704 goda*, p. 27; Tatarnikov (ed.), *Ofitserskie skazki*, Vol. 2, p. 1987.
85   PiB, Vol. 3, pp. 625–626.

regiment of 1,000 cavalry; Colonel H.J. von Burghausen's Vyborg regiment of 1,000 cavalry; Lieutenant Colonel Schlippenbach's regiment of 400 dragoons; Lieutenant Colonel Kaulbars' regiment of 400 cavalry. The infantry in Reval consisted of De La Gardie's regiment – 16 companies, each with 64 enlisted men and Colonel Liewen's regiment of 1,000 men (500 men of each of these two regiments had been assigned to General Schlippenbach's corps); Colonel Mellen's regiment of 800 men; Colonel Pahlen's regiment of 1,200 men aboard ships at the Narova estuary; and Colonel Rebinder's regiment of 600 men which had disembarked and passed to Narva. The captain gave similarly detailed information about the Swedish regiments in Pernau, Ahrensburg and Riga. Regarding the fleet, Georg knew not only that the admiral had a "silver hand"; according to him, De Prou had five warships (58-, 40-, 30- and 28-cannon), ten 12-cannon brigantines and two bombardment ships with mortars in addition to the cargo ships. The King, according to the latest news, was in Gdansk. In order to free Narva from the blockade, as Staël von Holstein was hearing, Schlippenbach was planning to move out 10–12 days after 16 May. Staël von Holstein knew details about the strength of the Narva garrison from letters from the garrison's officers, including from one of his relatives, Colonel Morath: Horn's regiment – 1,100 soldiers; Stefken's regiment – 300 soldiers; Lode's regiment – 300 soldiers; Rebinder's regiment – 600 soldiers; Colonel Morath's cavalry – 300 cavalry and dragoons; the town militia – 300 men; and Russians of the Ivangorod townsmen – 200 men.

Together with Staël von Holstein, another interesting, but less informative person was captured: "a Frenchman by birth, from the city of Lyon, called Nicolas Devgerin Lagarnad, who back in France served in the 1st Company [of Royal Musketeers]; arrived on Swedish territory, where they offered him the rank of ensign, but he did not accept this rank and served as a volunteer." The former Royal Musketeer did not provide any new information.[86]

24 May

In the wake of the Tsar, the boyar Fedor Alekseevich Golovin set out from Petersburg to Narva by land together with the Field Foreign Chancellery.[87]

25 May

While en route between Koporie and Jamburg, Peter I wrote his next directive to Sheremetev: since the Tsarist troops were already approaching Narva, while Schlippenbach, on the contrary, still had not made an appearance, his order for the Field Marshal to intercept Schlippenbach with his cavalry was being replaced: instead of this, he should be allowed passage to Narva, and then get behind him. Sheremetev was authorised to send three dragoon regiments, apart from Astafiev's, back to Dorpat.[88]

---

86 Ustrialov, Vol. 4, Part 2, pp. 307–309; Volynsky, Book 3, pp. 15–18.
87 *Pokhodnyi zhurnal 1704 goda*, p. 28.
88 PiB, Vol. 3, p. 73.

Troops approaching a town. (Simon Fokke 1712-1784, The Netherlands, 18th century Collection Rijksmuseum, Amsterdam)

26 May

At 2:00 a.m., the Russians drove away nine Swedish horses outside of Ivangorod. That evening the Tsar arrived at the Narova River estuary, followed in the next few days by the mounted and foot regiments and set up camp about half a kilometre from Apraxin's earthworks.[89] A resident of Jamburg, Butynsky, showed a road through a swamp and a ford across the Luga River.[90]

Meanwhile: the Swedes in Poland

News was reporting: "Burgomasters and senators of the city of Gdansk at the request of the Swedish king have signed an agreement, announcing that in Great Poland to remove the crown from the Polish king, King Augustus II, and to join the confederates … and promised to the Swedish king not to render any assistance to his adversaries."[91] King Charles XII spent the winter of 1704 in the Polish town of Heilsberg (today known as Lidzbark-Warmiński). The Swedes had remained in Poland in the preceding year of 1703, where after a lengthy five-month siege captured the fortress of Thorn [Toruń]; the strong Saxon garrison went into captivity, which noticeably weakened King Augustus II's army. Over all the years of the Northern War, this was the sole, successful formal siege of a major fortress for the Swedish army. In 1704 King Charles XII wanted to end the war in Poland, having replaced the Polish king with his proxy. Meanwhile King August II himself repeatedly offered proposals for a separate peace with Sweden, which went unanswered. The pro-Swedish Sejm in Warsaw announced the overthrow of King Augustus II, while the Swedish troops in Poland were busy gathering contributions and forcing towns and the nobility to join the Warsaw Confederation. In particular, the magistrate of the Polish city of Gdansk [Danzig] was forced to separate from King Augustus II and was burdened with cash payments. With the onset of the summer campaign, King Charles II and Field Marshal Rehnskiöld moved out with the Swedish army into the central regions of the Rzeczpospolita [the Polish name for the Polish–Lithuanian Commonwealth].[92] However, for

89   *Pokhodnyi zhurnal 1704 goda*, p. 28; Archiv., p. 244.
90   Petrov, p. 282.
91   *Vedomosti – Moskva (Pechatnyi dvor)*, 20 July 1704, p. 4.
92   Adlerfeld, Vol. 1, pp. 280–300.

The Tsar during the siege of Narva.
A fragment of a cartouche; illuminated map "Delineation … of the capture of the Narva fortress". (Jacob Keyser; The Netherlands, 1710s, Library of the Russian Academy of Sciences, Department of Cartography)

A view of the city of Danzig.
(Nicolas de Fer 1646-1720, Paris, 1692, Collection Rijksmuseum, Amsterdam)

The driving of cattle away from the fortress – a typical episode of the siege. (Aleksei Vladimirovich Temnikov, Vladimir, 2016)

Tsar Peter, the location of Charles XII in Poland gave him no confidence that the Swedish king could not suddenly shift troops to Livonia, as he had done back in 1700, in order to repulse a Russian offensive; therefore, all of the Swedish prisoners were unfailingly asked where their king was located.

27 May

The Tsar and Menshikov in the accompaniment of four dragoon regiments rode across the Narova River in order to examine the fortress of Narva. Cavalrymen – 20 dragoons of the previously mentioned Laptev, and 20 troopers of a select noble company – made their way up to the very ramparts of Narva, where they took seven captives and drove away cattle and horses. A Novgorod nobleman, Karaulov, was killed by shots from the city; he fell while chasing Swedes that were fleeing into the fortress with a broadsword, even after his horse was killed from under him.[93]

28 May

In the morning the Russians arrived in Joala, a village to the south of Narva near the waterfalls, and under fire from fortress cannons, captured several horses. At 4:30 p.m. a large troop of horsemen attacked an orchard on the outskirts outside the King's Gates; after resisting, the Swedish patrol of 15 cavalrymen fell back behind a counterscarp, while their commander, Captain Hochmuth [Wisocki-Hochmuth], was wounded and lost his horse. The pursuing Russians were driven back by fire from the bastions, losing several horses and a well-dressed Russian officer who was taken prisoner; "according to their habit, they carried away their own dead." The Russians advanced their outposts as far as Rothenhan,[94] and the infantry made camp closer to the city.[95]

A Finn by the name of Mohns, the son of carriage driver Johann and a hired worker employed by a Narva burgher, exited the fortress. In Narva he had been "taken by force", and for the next 12 weeks he had been detained under guard in order to enlist soldiers (impressment among the poor was

---

93   Tatarnikov, *Ofitserskie skazki*, Vol. 1, p. 359; *Pokhodnyi zhurnal 1704 goda*, pp. 29, 34.
94   Adlerfeld mentions this place without reference to its location. In the diary of the Narva citizen, such was the name of Colonel Stelen's farmstead on the northern outskirts of Narva beside the Narova River. In 1700, a Russian mortar battery had been positioned there.
95   Adlerfeld, Vol. 2, Part 4, pp. 4–5; Archiv., p. 245.

a normal practice in the Swedish forces together with voluntary enlistment).[96] On this day he had been freed in order to administer the oath, and Mohns used this as an opportunity to run away. His testimony on the whole repeated what was already known to the Russian command; in the city, even people of humble parentage had pretty good knowledge about matters regarding the town's defence. The colonel overseeing the garrison's artillery was called Kinnert (the Russian clerk from the Finnish speech heard and wrote down "Kilar"). Hunger was starting in Narva, and the soldier's bread ration had already been reduced. In the city they knew about the capture of Captain Staël and were sorry about him.

Ein Musquetirer.

Ein Grenadier.

Ein Piekenier Recroet.

Peasant-recruits: Head-piece to an illustrated manual of arms. Among the European armies, which were staffed with recruited hirelings and often foreign mercenaries, the Swedish army stood out by its means of recruiting. The system of *Indelta* – laying responsibility on peasants to supply soldiers from the community – supplied the kingdom with national units from Swedish and Finnish lands. Incidentally, a significant portion were hired, which is to say mercenary regiments – primarily comprised of Germans and residents of the Baltic provinces. The soldiers of Peter the Great's "newly-recruited" regiments by 1704 were drawn from "conscripts" (from landlords' and monastery domestic servants, but not from agricultural peasants) and from conscripted city paupers and coachmen. However, more than half of the personnel in the first years of the war fell to "all sorts of free men" – recruited volunteers and "tramps", most often from among runaway serfs. (Ernst Willem van Bilderbeek; first half of the 18th century, The Netherlands, 1730 Collection Legermuseum, Soesterberg)

Nevertheless, the contact with Schlippenbach had not ceased – messengers from him were riding along the Reval road as far as Waiwer, and then they were making their way through the woods along a circuitous route "through the empty villages of Räpennik and Sillomäe" to Narva.[97]

29 May

The Swedes observed the arrival in the Russian camp of a large mass of troops; they removed their outposts that were most distant from the fortress and fired importune salvoes in that direction without any particular hope of getting a hit.

Peter I ordered Kirill Alekseevich Naryshkin, commander in Pskov, to prepare ships for the delivery of cargo and supply wagons for the soldiers, so they would not be exhausted on the road, and to send to the Narva rapids 12 cannons with 300 cannonballs for each.[98]

30 May

General Repnin's infantry regiments, which had arrived from Petersburg and Schlisselburg, marched across a bridge over the Narova River in formation and began to set up camp next to the river about three kilometres from the town itself. Six dragoon regiments (under von Rönne, Pflug, Astafiev, Morel

---

96   See Palli, pp. 53–62 and pp. 103–109.
97   Volynsky, Vol. 3, pp. 18–19.
98   PiB, Vol. 3, p. 75.

The Town Hall Square in Narva. From the tower of the town hall, a view opens up not only over the buildings of the Old Town, but also toward the eastern bank of the Narova River. Such an observation post allowed the besieged to observe the enemy's movements. (Otto Kletzl, 1897-1945 and Richard Hamann-MacLean 1908-2000, Estonia, 1940-1941, Bildarchiv Foto Marburg)

de Carriere, Souvas and Gorbov), under the overall command of Colonel von Rönne, were sent out around Narva in order to block all the roads leading into the town. Apraxin with his infantry remained in their former position at the mouth of the Narova River, to where F.A. Golovin also arrived together with the Field Foreign Chancellery.[99]

On the Ivangorod side of the river, the Russians attempted to drive away the cattle, but they were repulsed by fire from the walls and withdrew behind the Radshof [Rathshoff] hill,[100] where they pitched tents and sent scouts up to the top of the hill. According to Swedish sources, this foray had been made by a regiment of green dragoons, supposedly under Major General Chambers, from the mouth of the river (in reality, of the six dragoon regiments, only Souvas' regiment remained on this side of the river). In addition, they occupied Copell-Berge hill [on the Ivangorod side of the river, as mentioned in the diary of the city resident], upon which a Swedish surveillance patrol had previously been positioned.[101]

31 May
Early in the morning, Menshikov and his dragoons rode up to the fortress and along the roads around Narva in order to examine the sentry posts; in the woods they captured a resident of Narva named Lange and a merchant, who had made their way into the town from the Swedish fleet. The prisoners shared the information that the squadron now consisted of 57 ships and that there were enough provisions in the city to last for two months. The Swedes attacked the strong detachment of Russian cavalry that was riding around the fortress several times.[102] On this day Adam Adamovich Veide, who had been wounded in the battle of Narva in 1700 and had been languishing together with other Russian generals in imprisonment in Stockholm, wrote

---

99   *Pokhodnyi zhurnal 1704 goda*, pp. 28–30, 34.
100   Judging from the Swedish 1678 and 1699 maps, this point was south-east of Ivangord.
101   Adlerfeld, Vol. 2, p. 5; Archiv., p. 245.
102   Von Huyssen, pp. 392–393; Adlerfeld, Vol. 2, p. 5.

a letter to Menshikov, in which among other things he reported that Swedes in Stockholm were dwelling in fear "and given up hope about Narva", which meant that they had resigned themselves to the pending fall of the fortress even before news about the onset of a full siege of the city could have reached Scandinavia.

Commandant Horn dispatched a letter to the King, in which he forewarned that communications would now be cut off. He also wrote in detail about the dispositions of the Russian forces: There was a chain of posts stretching from Wäpskyla to Joala, with units of up to 600 horsemen each in Goldenhof (where Trubetskoy's camp was located in 1700) and at Wäpskyla. Several squadrons had appeared on the Ivangorod side at Radshof. Below the village of Vasa, the Russians had laid down a bridge, across which fresh forces and supply trains were moving each day. The commandant estimated the enemy's total strength at up to 3,000 men, or 25 standards (squadrons) of cavalry, having clarified that it was difficult to determine the enemy's strength due to his constant marches and countermarches. Up to this point, he had seen no infantry.[103]

1 June

At dawn, a unit of 150 cavalry under the command of Lieutenant Colonel Friedrich Marquard was escorting prisoners to Ivangorod; on the way back, it was attacked by Russian cavalry, Souvas' dragoons. In the ensuing combat, the attack of the "Muscovites" was driven back. The Swedes pursued them over a hill towards some woods, where the Russians received reinforcements, reformed and in their turn forced the Swedes to retreat (in the words of the Swedish source, this retreat was done "in a gallant manner, with faces and pistols turned towards the enemy"). At the Ivangorod castle Major Funk's infantry compelled the Russians to abandon the pursuit, and now with the united forces of two service arms, it was possible to go over to a general attack. However, Funk rejected Marquard's proposal to attack with combined forces and to sack the nearest Russian camp – he did not have instructions for this from the commandant.

Later that day Horn caught sight of the Russian troops that were moving in the direction of Livonia and decided to undertake a strong raid against the Russian camp on the bank of the Narova River. He decided to sortie with 1,200 soldiers under Colonels Otto Rebinder [Rehbinder], Herman von Fersen, and Majors Adam Reinhold Nieroth and Berend Rebinder, as well as with Marquard's 200 cavalrymen. Combat ensued, but the commandant, having observed the reinforcement of the Russians from the roof of a building (Gorbov's regiment and infantry from the camp had hastened to assist Morel de Carriere's dragoons), gave a signal from mortars for the infantry to withdraw, while the on-duty adjutant Lieutenant Colonel Bloman withdrew the cavalry from the battle. In the action outside Ivangorod, Swedish Lieutenant Apoloff (a descendant of Russian nobility with the surname of Opalev, who had remained on the land occupied by the Swedes

---

103   Rosen, p. 183.

The portrait of Rudolf Henning Horn. (Georg Engelhard Schröder,1684-1750, Krigsarkivets porträttsamlingar)

after the Time of Troubles), Lieutenant Sparkuk and eight troopers were killed. The Russian losses were comparable: Lieutenant Stepan Iurievich Neelov and two dragoons of his company were killed, and nine dragoons were wounded, two of whom had received severe wounds from blades, while the rest received light gunshot wounds. One Russian dragoon was captured and gave the Swedes information that was plainly outdated, purporting that the Russians had no more than 6,000 men at Narva, while the arrival of the Tsar and 40,000 men was only anticipated.

Menshikov with 12 dragoon companies (two from each regiment) set out from a point near Narva in the direction of Rakvere (Rakovor – the old Russian name, also known as Wesenberg in Swedish and German sources) in order to gain information about Schlippenbach's forces; having travelled 30 km and without having encountered enemy troops, on the same day he returned by nightfall, bringing back several captives and Swedish deserter. Before turning back, he detached Colonel von Rönne and 400 dragoons to move on towards Rakvere in order to search for the Swedish general.[104]

Who Was Henning Rudolf Horn?

Henning Rudolf Horn af Rantzien was born in 1651 in Pomerania. He began service in 1664 as a volunteer in the artillery, then served in the cavalry and as a pikeman in the infantry. In 1671 he was promoted to lieutenant. He took part in the Sweden's wars against Brandenburg and Denmark. In 1680 he was a lieutenant colonel in the Ingermanland garrison regiment in Narva. Horn became commandant in Kexholm in 1681, and in 1695, a colonel and the commandant of Narva. For the defence of Narva in 1700 he was promoted to major general and simultaneously carried out the duty as commander of all the Ingermanland fortresses and of Kexholm County.[105]

2 June

A servant of one of the citizens arrived in Narva and related the information that he had heard somewhere, purporting that the Tsar was still not with the army, but they were expecting him soon.[106]

---

104 *Pokhodnyi zhurnal 1704 goda*, p. 32 and 35; Adlerfeld, Vol. 2, pp. 6–7; Archiv., pp. 245–246; Kelch, p. 376; Volynsky, Book 3, pp. 31–32.

105 Grauers, S., "Henning Rudolf Horn" in Svensk biografiskt lexicon <http://sok.riksarkivet.se/sbl/artikel/13821> (accessed 6 August 2018).

106 Archiv., s. 247.

3 June

After midday the Tsar together with Preobrazhensky soldiers went to the beach by the estuary, where two schutes of the Swedish flotilla had grounded on a shoal near Hungerburg – the day before during a gale force storm they had broken loose from their anchors. Tsar Peter started off across the shallow water on horseback, while the Guardsmen plunged into the water to wade or swim in their uniforms; both ships were captured, on which 25 sailors, Lieutenant Maidel and 75 soldiers

of Rebinder's regiment were taken prisoner. The loot included 100 muskets and a large cargo of grain. De Prou sent out a dinghy on reconnaissance, but when landing on shore the Swedes were attacked by patrolling dragoons and retreated, leaving behind one captured constable. Several Swedish ships closed within range of artillery fire, so two cast iron cannons were dragged to the shore from Apraxin's camp. However, both cannons were "old and badly-cast", and they blew apart with the first shot, killing one cannoneer and wounding another.

Pflug's dragoons at the outposts around Narva were continuing to detain people that were walking in and out of the town, and took 13 men; three were taken on the Ivangorod side and one man defected. Colonel von Rönne returned to Narva from around Rakvere, bringing back more than 100 villagers of both genders and driving back 800 oxen, 500 sheep and 40 horses. Apparently, this livestock had been prepared for Schlippenbach's corps; it was said that he was waiting in Rakvere with 3,000 cavalry and expecting three regiments of infantry to join him. From Narva, Russian infantry and cavalry were observed on the Livonian side, and that evening heavy gunfire was audible from the direction of the road.[107]

Schlippenbach, who was located at Rakvere, finally wrote directly to Governor-General De La Gardie that he could no longer go to the relief of Narva: Russians were marching towards Dorpat and Lais [Estonian Laiuse] and were threatening him from the rear. He wrote, "Therefore Narva has in fact been already encircled, so no hope remains for the plan to save it; … so now nothing remains but to attempt to defend that part of the country that has not been cut off." In his response, De La Gardie admonished the general, writing that the information about Narva's encirclement was unfounded rumours and asserting that Schlippenbach could gather 6,400 men, which was enough to save Narva.[108]

The Tsar seizes Swedish boats that have run aground. An illustrated German almanac, dedicated to European history, when describing the events of the Russian-Swedish War of 1704, probably relied on the information of Baron von Huyssen. From the entire siege of Narva, it was just this episode regarding the capture of transports by Peter I that had run aground that was worthy of illustrating. In the process the artist in Nuremberg preferred to depict the "Muscovites" in characteristic boyar hats, although the Tsar himself, as well as his Guardsmen, at this time looked fully European. (Artist unknown; Germany, 1710 Neu-eröffneter Historischer Bilder-Saal, Vol. 6 1700-1704, Nuremberg, 1710)

107 *Zhurnal ili pobednnaia zapiska*, p. 79; "Pokhodnyi zhurnal 1704 goda", pp. 33–35; Von Huyssen, pp. 392–394; Adlerfeld, Vol. 2, p. 7; Kelch, p. 375.
108 Rosen, p. 184.

Burned down homes and confiscated property – the fate of the poor peasants in the war.
(Artist unknown; Germany, 1750 Anne S.K. Brown Military Collection)

4 June

The ships carrying the groups of the Guards' and army's soldiers arrived from Petersburg at the camp near Narva; they brought with them belongings of the court and courtiers. In order to avoid the Swedish ships on the Narva roads, they entered the mouth of the Luga River and headed up river to where the Rosson' River enters it. A deserter, a servant of Major Rebinder, left Narva and reported information on the garrison's condition – it had 2,000 soldiers, 500 cavalrymen and 200 horses. Rye was no longer being distributed to the enlisted men; instead, each man was being allocated one fourth of a barrel of oats (approximately 33 kilograms, as one Tallinn barrel contained 133 kilograms) per month.[109] Officers were being paid only a cash allowance, so many of them were requesting the delivery of provisions from Horn; soldiers were openly saying among themselves that they would not tolerate starvation and would go over to the side of the Tsar's forces.[110]

Meanwhile a Russian drummer brought letters to Narva from Captain Staël, who had been taken prisoner on 21 May, and from the citizen Simon Lange, who had been captured on the 31st of May. The letters reported that on 3 June the Russians had seized two transport ships that had sick soldiers aboard. The drummer was immediately sent back, and he was told to return for a response on the following day.[111]

On this same day Field Marshal-Lieutenant Georg Benedikt Ogilvy set out towards the army from Moscow; he left with only light baggage, leaving behind his baggage train. However, before this he had "lingered" in the

---

109 Palli, p. 287.
110 *Pokhodnyi zhurnal 1704 goda*, pp. 35–36.
111 Adlerfeld, Vol. 2, p. 7; Archiv., p. 247.

capital, preparing for the campaign – procuring clothes, tents, wagons and so forth, and buying horses.[112]

5 June

The Russian drummer returned at noon for the letter of response. The Swedes observed some stirring in the besiegers' camp.[113]

What Was the Role of a Drummer in a Parley?

The warring sides frequently exchanged messages: the besieging army would make surrender proposals to the governor, and the besieged side would respond to these proposals depending on the situation; it was even possible to dispatch correspondence to civilians in the fortress or to a prisoner in the opposing camp. A musical signal to the adversary would indicate the desire to begin negotiations; this was called a *chamade* or parley. Thus, in European military tradition, the task to participate in negotiations rested on musicians, and they would be sent to the enemy camp with messages and letters. "He ought to be of a singular good carriage and descreet, to observe and take notice of all passages; that may give any intelligence to his officers of the state of the enemie." On their part, the besieged side sought not to reveal anything excessive to the enemy musician; when entering the place, they would be blindfolded and so forth.[114] During the siege of Dorpat, the governor ordered his drummer to get the Russian drummer drunk and to extract whatever information he could regarding the Russian plans. For this purpose, he also summoned a Russian-speaking citizen, but they were unable to accomplish anything – the Russian held his tongue and to all the questions only responded with bows and courtesies.[115]

A drummer.
(Artist unknown; in Hans Friedrich von Fleming, *Der Vollkommene Teutsche Soldat*, Leipzig, 1726)

Drummers and trumpeters in a parley enjoyed the status of inviolability. Such were the unwritten norms of international law of those years, and the sides never missed a chance to reproach each other over violations of "world-wide conventions". For example, even before the onset of the siege Horn demanded of the Russian command to return a Swedish drummer, who had been sent from Narva

112   NIA SPbII RAN, F. 270, Op. 1, D. 41, l. 38.
113   Adlerfeld, Vol. 2, p. 7.
114   Ward, R.I., *Animadversions of Warre*, 1639 – as cited by Pfeil, M., *Drumming in the English Civil Wars: Myths, Facts and Informed Guesses*, 2nd ed. (Bristol: Stuart Press, 1997), pp. 25–26; "*Voinskii Ustav, sostavlennyi i posviaschennyi Petru Pervomu Generalom Veide v 1698* ["Military Regulations, compiled and dedicated to Peter the First by General Weide in 1698"] (Saint Petersburg, 1841), p. 35; Tatishchev, V.N., *Izbrannye proizvedeniia* [*Selected Works*] (Leningrad, 1979), p. 178; *Voennyi Ustav s Artikulom Voennym* [*Military Regulations and the Military Code*] (Saint Petersburg, 1748), p. 203.
115   Laidre, p. 140.

An officer, writing a letter, and a trumpeter.
This painting by a well-known artist obviously illustrates the role of a musician, in the given case, a trumpeter, as a courier for delivering the letter. (Gerard ter Borch 1617-168, The Netherlands, 1659, Philadelphia Museum of Art)

with a letter back in December 1703. A series of demands to various levels of authority – from the commandant of Jamburg Balabanov up to Ingrian governor Menshikov – led to the fact that the Tsar himself became involved in the affair about the Swedish drummer. Tsar Peter ordered Sheremetev to find the musician and threatened that the guilty officers "would pay with their necks"; the Field Marshal in response pointed out that the truce envoy had been taken by a colonel of the dragoons, Mikhail Zybin, and had been sent to Moscow. In answer to Horn in the name of Menshikov as the governor of Ingermanland it was acknowledged that the drummer had in fact been detained, but in response it was pointed out that the Swedes themselves were holding two paroled officers, and it was suggested that "they look into a mirror" to find the guilty party. Nevertheless, 15 Swedish drummers who had been captured in 1702–1703 were found in Moscow and two with similar names – Yrjö Johansson and Yrjö Johann Anderson – were found in Moscow, and escorted by a minor official and three soldiers were sent to the Tsar when he was on campaign.[116]

During a siege, the dispatch of a drummer to the enemy implied a ceasefire: the two sides silenced their guns and stopped (or at least were supposed to stop) the construction of siegeworks and defensive works. Later, Horn decided to take advantage of this rule; in the hope of extending a truce that had started, he forcibly detained a Russian drummer.[117]

During the siege of Nyenschantz, on 30 April 1703 a Tsarist trumpeter had blown a *chamade*, and from the fortress they had responded with the beat of a drum. Afterward, officers had emerged and "ours in the trenches had pleasant exchanges of conversation with those from the place." A trumpeter by the name of Gottfried had been sent as an envoy; in the previous campaign he carried out the same mission in Nöteborg.[118] Apparently, he was a hired foreign professional musician who could easily converse with the Swedes. In other cases, including at Narva, drummers who were sent were ordinary company musicians who carried out the role of signallers in the infantry. The Narva governor, in order to pass messages to the Russian camp, sent a trumpeter by the name of Tobias.[119]

116 NIA SPbII RAN, F. 83, Op. 1, D. 297; PiB, Vol. 3, pp. 47, 72–73, 93, 608, 629–630 and 639.
117 Adlerfeld, Vol. 2, p. 20.
118 Von Huyssen, p. 334; "Pokhodnyi zhurnal 1703 goda" (Saint Petersburg, 1853), p. 16.
119 Archiv., p. 250.

6 June

In the daytime, between 1:00 and 3:00 p.m., the thundering of guns was heard in the fortress, and a plume of smoke rising high into the sky could be seen. This was due to several ships of the Swedish fleet which had approached the sandbar in order to burn the two abandoned schutes. They set one of them ablaze, but under the fire of sentry soldiers in the woods on shore, they returned to sea. The Russians made several attempts to seize cattle around the fortress, but cannon fire prevented them from doing so.[120]

7 June

Two soldiers from Narva deserted to the Russian camp. A dragoon arrived from Schlippenbach, who related that the general was standing at Rakvere with 3,000 troops, primarily mounted.[121]

What Was a Slogan Signal?

A participant of the events, Prince Boris Ivanovich Kurakin, explained the purpose of the exchange of signals as a system of recognising friendly forces and transmitting information at a distance: "through which they are made aware of each other, that one is on the approach nearby and the other is still holding is waiting to make contact."[122] The Tsarist Army's signal, or "slogan", consisted of three cannon shots, while the Swedes' signal consisted of two cannon shots. For example, at the very start of the war in March 1700, the garrisons of Riga and Dünamünde, besieged by the Saxons, exchanged double cannon shots, letting each other know that the defence was continuing.[123] Apparently, the Swedish signal was well known to the Russians. From maritime practice it was known that Swedish fortresses saluted military ships four times and cargo ships twice, while at the same time as in other countries they fired an odd number of times.[124] With a double cannon shot King Charles let Narva know about his approach from the Lagena Hills over a 10 km distance from the town on 18 November 1700.[125] Swedish ships gave the same signal when

120 Adlerfeld, Vol. 2, p. 7; *Pokhodnyi zhurnal 1704 goda*, pp. 36–37.

121 *Pokhodnyi zhurnal 1704 goda*, p. 37.

122 Kurakin, B.I., *Voennaia khitrost' tsaria Petra Alekseevicha pod Narvoiu 8-go iiunia 1704 g. Rasskaz ochevidtsa kniazia B.I. Kurakin* [*Tsaar Peter Aleseevich's military subterfuge at Narva on 8 June 1704. Story of eyewitness Prince B.I. Kurakin*]//Book archive of F.A. Kurakin, Book 3 (Saint Petersburg, 1892), p. 152.

123 Adlerfeld, Vol. 1, p. 24.

124 Gostev, I.M., "Teksty pervykh instruktsii komendantam beregovykh (primorskikh) krepostei 1702–1714 // Pamiatniki fortifikatsii: istoriia, restavratsiia, ispol'zovanie. Sbornik statei i materialov Pervoi mezdunarodnoi nauchno-prakticheskoi konferentsii, 18–19 sentiabria 2009 (Arkhangel'sk, 2012) Vypusk 1 ["Texts of the initial instructions to commandants of coastal (littoral) fortresses 1702–1714 // Monuments of fortifications: history, restoration, usage. Collection of articles and materials of the First International Academic–Practical Conference, 18–19 September 2009 (Arkhangel'sk, 2012), 1st ed., p. 40.

125 Petrov, A., "Narvskaia operatsiia" ["Narva operation"] *Voennyi sbornik*, No. 7 (1862), p. 21; Nordberg, J.A., *Histoire de Charles XII roi de suede*, Vol. 1 (Haye, 1748), p. 130.

Troops breaking down a camp. (Georg Philipp Rugendas 1666-1742, Augsburg, 1740s, Anne S.K. Brown Military Collection)

approaching Nyenschantz on 2 May 1703, but the Russians answered them with two shots from the fortress they had just seized "so that on those ships they did not become aware of the fall of the town."[126] The besieged Dorpat issued signals each morning and evening – each consisting of two rockets and two cannon shots.[127]

8 June

At around 2:00 p.m. in the afternoon, in the fortress they heard two cannon shots from the Livonian side of the Narova river. This was the Swedish signal, and it augured that the long-awaited Schlippenbach was approaching to relieve Narva. Just as back in 1700, salvation from the Muscovite siege seemed nigh.

Despite the abundant information that had been obtained thus far from captured peasants, citizens, soldiers and even Captain Staël, the besiegers required "the capture of several good officers, so as to receive a summary of the genuine conditions [in the fortress], because it was impossible to rely on the information gleaned from simple prisoners and deserters." It was known that the garrison was awaiting reinforcements, and that the commandant was eagerly making large sorties (not long before this, on 1 June, Horn had sent out 100 cavalry and 1,200 soldiers against 600 Russian dragoons). Obviously, this combination of circumstances indeed led Menshikov to the thought of simulating the arrival of reinforcements, in order to provoke the garrison into making a large sortie headed by senior officers, and to lead them into a trap.

---

126   Von Huyssen, "Zhurnal Petra I s 1695 po 1709", p. 338.
127   Gostev, "Teksty pervykh instruktsii", p. 40.

In order to imitate the Swedes, Russian regiments that wore uniforms of Swedish colours were selected: the Semenovsky Life Guard Regiment wearing coats of its traditional cornflower blue colour; the Ingermanland soldier regiment in their grey coats; Gorbov's dragoon regiment in its blue cloaks and white trimmed hats; and Astafiev's dragoon regiment dressed in blue coats and hats. Five regimental cannons were attached to this force. Under their white, blue and yellow flags, from a distance these troops fully resembled a Swedish force. According to Kurakin, the similarity was increased by the fact that the fire was conducted according to the Swedish exercise (manual of arms); apparently, the Semenovsky and Ingermanland troops were arrayed in four ranks according to Swedish 1701 regulations, rather than the six-rank formation that was operational at that time in the Russian Army's 1699 "Brief Drill Manual". Tsar Peter himself played the role of General Schlippenbach.

Having stealthily moved to the stone Church of Saint Peter in the Tervaijoga district at about five kilometres distant from the Russian camp, in the second hour of the afternoon "the sham Swedish force" approached from the direction of Reval (the direction from where they expected Schlippenbach's reinforcements) and brushed aside the forward Muscovite outpost. Approaching to within direct line of sight from the fortress, the "Swedes" gave the besieged fortress the signal of two cannon discharges, and the garrison replied with the same signal. Having approached closer and brushed aside the second outpost of the besiegers, the "reinforcement" gave the next signal of four cannon shots and received the same answer. With the help of the given signals, they were extending an invitation to the spectators – Horn was watching from the upper story of his house, and on the city walls "not only all the people, but even little children with helpless delight were running out with uplifted hands to catch sight and to wish blessings and good fortune a thousand times to the long awaited for General Schlippenbach." In the city there was "such joy and happiness for that sham reinforcement, that bells began ringing in all the churches and tables were set out along the streets with food and drink, and everyone was running to the city walls for a look." It was time now to begin the performance.

Menshikov's and Repnin's regiments hastily marched out of the camp and arrayed in two combat lines in an open space opposite Peter's "Swedes". The two lines began to close with firing (they were firing wadding from the muskets, while the cannon's rounds were fired over the heads of the opposing side). Then the "Swedish" right wing (this flank was closer to the city, so on this flank the most entertaining part of the masquerade should be shown) attacked, forcing the Muscovite left wing, having put up a certain resistance, began to retreat; the commandant and the citizens of the city could clearly see from the walls, that the "Swedish" formation was strictly conducting concise volley fire, while the Russians were fleeing in disorder, removing their outposts and striking tents in the camp, and hitching up horses for a general retreat. This display, which continued for an hour and a half, fully convinced the commandant that the reinforcement was breaking through to his aid, and that it was necessary to sally forth to meet it. Cavalry and infantry were sent out beyond the walls of the fortress (800 infantry under Colonel Lode, 150 cavalry under Lieutenant Colonel Macquard, and Lieutenant Colonel Kinnert's four cannons). Meanwhile the infantry of "both friendly adversaries" were firing at each other with blank cartridges, and the "Swedes" were slowly driving the Russians back ever more closely to the city, where they might be able to attack the sortie more advantageously and cut it off from the fortress. Beforehand, at night, von Rönne's dragoons and the Preobrazhensky Regiment had been placed in ambush in the woods and orchards in the proximity of the city. Everything was ready to spring the trap: "in a manner with which it would be most convenient to pull off the large comedy and grand unexpected victory of this entire little theatrical display."

Mounted officers from the "phoney Swedes" led by Colonel Arnstedt, a representative of the Polish Court, rode out to meet the garrison's sortie, as if inviting the garrison's officers to join them (after all, the whole point of the drama consisted in capturing them). In fact, Swedish cavalry officers headed by Lieutenant Colonel Marquard, separating from the main mass of troops, hurried out to meet them. The meeting officers "congratulated each other … and hugged and kissed, and behaved so affably, it was as if they had become fast friends." Having embraced Marquard, Arnstedt grabbed hold of his sword and together with Gorbov captured him without resistance.[128] The same thing happened with two lieutenants, who in their joy rode directly into the formation of Russian dragoons of Gorbov's regiment in their blue cloaks. Even though the Russians were strictly ordered not to make a commotion, so as to not frighten the Swedes, they were unsuccessful in fooling the entire sortie party – Rottmeister Lindkrantz did not allow himself to be disarmed. As a Russian source stated, "a drunken Swedish officer … shot himself with a pistol in such a desperate manner that frightened off anyone from approaching."

It was time to lay the cards on the table, so Gorbov's dragoons charged the Swedes. From the fortress, cannons spoke up. Having heard the opening cannonade, von Rönne's dragoons and the Novgorod noble horsemen leaped out of ambush in the bushes and also attacked the Swedish party. The Swedish cavalry had drifted away from the fortress, so they were cut off and smashed, and their remnants were chased back to the moat and the fortress gates. The Russian cavalry then had a go at the infantry, but Colonel Lode had time to lead his troops back into the fortress together with the artillery, which had been delayed and had thus not made it too far from the fortress. In addition to the cavalry troopers and soldiers, a lot of citizens and peasants, who had hurried out of the fortress in the wake of the sortie in hope of looting on the battlefield, were caught up in the pursuit (back in November 1700, the civilians had taken part in the plundering of the Russian camp). Separate participants of this sortie managed to get away; Quartermeister Schütz hid in the woods, set out in the direction of Reval on foot, and reached Schlippenbach, who sent him on to the king. Lieutenant Colonel Friedrich Marquard, Rottmeister Konau, and cornets Abram Guld, Dunker and Andreas Pippenstock were all

---

128 All of the Russian sources, Kelch and the citizen diaries write about the capture of Lieutenant Colonel Marquard in the masquerade battle; Adlerfeld and Nordberg write instead the Colonel Morath was captured, but this is mistaken; Morath was captured with the fall of the city.

Mounted officers during the siege of Augsburg in 1703 by Franco-Bavarian troops. (Georg Philipp Rugendas 1666-1742, Augsburg, 1703, Anne S.K. Brown Military Collection)

taken prisoner, and detailed testimony was taken from them about Narva's defences. Lower army ranks were also captured – cavalry and soldiers, as well as ordinary townsfolk – a tailor, a cook, a brewer, bakers and servants – a total of 46 men. Bodies of the fallen remained lying on the battlefield, in "no-man's land" and were to be taken away now.

In the Russian camp, they were celebrating the successful military subterfuge, or the "fake battle", as Fedor Zybin, who was one of the participants in it from von Rönne's dragoon regiment, termed it. On this subject, Tsar Peter wrote: "The fools tricked the intelligents" thanks to the fact that the Swedes had such a "mountain of pride standing before their eyes, through which they were unable to see this fraud"; in response, Aleksandr Vasilievich Kikin praised the fabrication and its author: "Who displayed this invention, showed that his noble head is not an empty kettle." An epigram was also written about this event, in which the capture of the officers was compared to the ancient story about the rape of the Sabine women by the Romans:

The Romans boast of taking Sabine women in jest;
Baa, the gender is weak and the feat is not brave.
Here the Russians take lions jest,
Such predatory adversaries, but the feat is great.

Having been conned, Horn sent encoded letters to Riga and Reval, and in order to avoid new confusion over a "fake reinforcement", asked to report new signals to him, according to which he could reliably identify the approach of

Swedish reinforcements. The commandant had decided to defend to the last and ordered the sending out of patrols to burn all the buildings, trees and bushes in the environs, which might serve as cover for the besiegers. On the same day Lieutenant Wilbrandt was sent out with a unit of 40 infantrymen to the outskirts in order to destroy the chimneys there that remained after the destruction of the buildings. However, it ventured too far; his men were encircled by Russians and slaughtered, while the officer barely managed to save himself.[129]

Menshikov had proposed for the Tsar's signature a set of instructions entitled "The articles for the time of a military campaign", which was first published in 1703 and which contained stipulations for the conduct of the troops in combat and on the march. During a battle or an assault, it was forbidden to raise a clamour (otherwise commands could not be heard), to leave ranks in order to carry away the wounded (non-combatants were assigned for this) or for purposes of looting (prior to receiving permission from a superior). On the march it was banned without orders to destroy or burn buildings, break windows, and so forth.[130]

What Were the Uniform Colours?

A soldier executing the command "Ram down your charge!". The Tsarist soldiers at Narva in 1700 were dressed in approximately the same way, in East European dress and caps. (Artist unknown, Russia, 1698, from *Military regulations, compiled and dedicated to Peter the Great by General Weide in 1698,* Saint Petersburg, 1841).

Why in the Russian army did the regiments wear uniforms with Swedish colours? The Semenovsky Guards Regiment traditionally wore cornflower blue coats with red sleeve cuffs. In the Swedish army blue and yellow uniform was more widespread or more common, but blue and red uniforms were also encountered, for example, the garrison regiment of Horn himself wore such colours. Many militia and third-line Swedish regiments wore uniforms made from a cheap grey cloth with colourful blue or yellow cuffs. The Russian Ingermanlandsky infantry regiment was created in 1703 as the personal regiment of Ingermanland's governor A.D. Menshikov. It seems somewhat strange that this regiment, one of the Tsar's favourite, practically on the level of a Guards regiment, was dressed in such a cheap uniform. However, Kurakin's report about the grey coats so far remains the only mention about the colours of the Ingermanlandsky soldiers of that time. According to Swedish information, the "redressed Russians" were all dressed in blue. Ivan Grigorievich Kartashov, a dragoon of Gorbov's regiment and a

129   *Pokhodnyi zhurnal 1704 goda,* pp. 121–125; Von Huyssen, pp. 398–401; Adlerfeld, Vol. 1, p. 307 and 309; Vol. 2, pp. 7–9; Archiv., pp. 247-249; Pib, Vol. 3, pp. 92, 637; Volynsky, Book 1, p. 280; Tatarnikov (ed.), *Ofitserskie skazki,* Vol. 1, p. 891; Palli, pp. 251–252, 255.
130   PiB, Vol. 3, pp. 77–79; Volynsky, Book 1, pp. 198–199.

participant in the action recalled that "it was ordered to give our regiment cornflower blue coats and cornflower blue cloaks from the infantry regiments, and we were made out to be a Swedish dragoon regiment."[131] This means his regiment had a uniform of some different colour, but blue tunics and capes were available in the infantry regiments.

A green and red uniform was characteristic for the Russian infantry; in other countries, such a colouration was rarely encountered. However, by the time of the siege of Narva, the Tsarist regiments were dressed in various colours; no single regulation regarding the uniforms existed; and there was no success in observing uniformity in colouring because of complexities with the supplies of a monochromatic cloth. Few documents about supplying the Russian regiments in the initial stage of the war have been preserved, so the observations of the enemy about the appearance of the Russian troops are particularly valuable. According to the testimony of a Swedish officer, who spent time in the Russian camp on the Emajõgi River in May 1704, in Sheremetev's infantry there were "German officers and men well dressed in red and blue."[132] The Russian dragoons who arrived at the very walls of Narva in July 1703 wore red uniforms that were easily visible from afar.[133] A Narva resident described the Russian troops after Narva's capture. All the troops were dressed in German attire; certain regiments were dressed in the Swedish manner; many officers wore wigs; one regiment of Guards foot soldiers wore green coats with red cuffs, red waistcoats with copper buttons, another was wearing blue coats. A regiment of "Guards cavalry" mounted on grey horses (likely, B.P. Sheremetev's select dragoon squadron) wore yellow coats with green velvet cuffs and waistcoats, and its yellow karpus headgear was decorated with green velvet. Each regiment had a company of grenadiers with bearskin caps; the uniforms were either green and red, blue and red, entirely red, white and red, or yellow.[134]

It is believed that the Russian Guardsmen were the first in the Russian army to begin to receive Western (French) uniforms at the end of 1702, after the fall of Nöteborg. In Kelch's *History of Livonia* it was recorded that almost the entire Russian army at Dorpat was dressed in the German manner, and the same thing was

Dutch infantrymen. Peter redressed his army in a European (French or German) uniform after 1702. (Artist unknown; The Netherlands, 1702-1712, Royal Collection Trust)

131 Tatarnikov (ed.), *Ofitserskie skazki*, Vol. 2, p. 1402.

132 Skytte's letters in the Defensionskommissien, 1704, RA ÄK 243, Vol. 120. Reported by Bengt Nilsson.

133 Horn's letter from 16 July 1703. RA ÄK 243, Vol. 120. Reported by Bengt Nilsson. In von Werden's unit, which pursued the Swedish cavalry to the very walls of Narva on 14 July 1703, were dragoons from G. Volonsky's, I. Ignatiev's, P. Meshchersky's and V. Grigorov's regiments (see Volynsky, Book 1, p. 191).

134 See Appendix 3.

A soldier's uniform.
(Artist unknown; The
Netherlands, end of the
17th century, Collection
Rijksmuseum, Amsterdam)

noted about the regiments at Narva from the testimony of a different foreign eyewitness.[135] However, judging from the fact that the Englishman Whitworth in January 1705 in Lithuania observed an infantry regiment (apparently, from Repnin's corps) in national costume (while the officers were in German dress), the shift to the German uniform during the Siege of Narva still had not had time to be completed and certain regiments were continuing to wear Eastern (Russian or Hungarian) attire.[136]

9 June

A Russian drummer delivered a letter to Horn, who promised to give a reply on the following day.[137]

10 June

The Tsar was going to leave the siege camp for a time and left instructions for the senior general A.I. Repnin for while he was absent: Repnin was to construct a line of countervallation from river to river with redoubts; to build *kettles* – mortar batteries for 20 pieces and batteries with platforms for 30 breaching cannons; to make ready a large quantity of fascines and gabions; and in the event of the arrival of Swedish reinforcements to locate a field for the battle and to draw and distribute to each colonel a scheme of the order of battle.[138]

135 Kelch, C., *Lieflandische Historia oder Kriegs- und Friedens-Geschichte. Continuation* (1690–1706), Dorpat, 1875, p. 280; Names of the Russian Generalls, who commanded at the Siege of Narva, 1704, and Specification of the Regiments employed in the Siege of Narva (The University of Nottingham. Manuscripts and Special Collections. Letters and papers of Robert Harley, 1st Earl of Oxford), Pw2 Hy 1236.

136 Letin, S.A., "Sluzhiloe plat'e ot Petra Velikogo" ["Service attire from Peter the Great"] *Rodina*, No. 11 (2000), p. 20. Sbornik IRIO, Vol. 39 (Saint Petersburg, 1884), p. 19.

137 Adlerfeld, Vol. 2, p. 9.

138 PiB, Vol. 3, pp. 87–88.

The moving of siege artillery into position.
(Artist unknown; in Hans Friedrich von Fleming, *Der Vollkommene Teutsche Soldat*, Leipzig, 1726)

A Russian drummer returned to the fortress and received the promised response letter. In order to keep watch over the movements of the besiegers, Horn sent a portion of his infantry under Colonel Rebinder to a counterscarp. One peasant under the cover of fog escaped out of the fortress and reported that the enemy had received significant reinforcement, and that many residents from Vasknarva[139] and neighbouring places had been marched away into captivity. At midnight the Russians began to dig retrenchments from Wäpskyla through Goldenhof (the hill to the west of Narva) up to the road to Joala – almost those same places where their line was in the previous siege.[140]

On this same day Sheremetev wrote to the Tsar about the finally-begun siege of Dorpat. A "note" that had been distributed by the Swedish administration had fallen into the Field Marshal's hands: it spoke of the imminent arrival of 6,000 troops from Stockholm. However, even the local population did not have much faith in this leaflet.[141]

11 June

The Tsar together with A.D. Menshikov and G.I. Golovkin set out from Narva to Saint Petersburg in order to dispatch a supply train with artillery and other military supplies from there in the soonest possible time. At the same time, a drummer was sent from General Repnin, who had been entrusted with temporary command over the Tsarist forces, to Commandant Horn, with

---

139 Vasknarva, German Neuschloss – a village with a castle of the Teutonic Order on the Livonian bank of the Narova River where it flows out of Lake *Peipus*. The Russian name for Vasknarva – Syrenets or Syrensk – belonged also to the Russian village on the opposite bank.
140 Adlerfeld, Vol. 2, p. 9.
141 *Severnaia voina 1700–1721 gg.* [*The Northern War of 1700–1721*], Vol. 1 (Moscow, 2009), p. 206.

a proposal for a short truce in order to gather the bodies of the dead from no-man's land, who had been killed in the fighting on 8 June. That evening a messenger from Sheremetev galloped into the Russian Narva camp with news of the initiation of the siege of Dorpat. He caught up with the Tsar the next day at Jamburg.[142]

From captured officers it became known that Schlippenbach was standing around Rakvere with 3,000 cavalry and was waiting for another 6,000 cavalry to reinforce him from Riga, Pernau and Reval; the general had an order from King Charles XII to go to Narva's relief at any cost. Therefore, Colonel von Rönne set out from the Russian siege camp with six dragoon regiments (von Rönne's, Pflug's, Gorbov's, Astafiev's, Morel de Carriere's and Souvas') and infantry mounted on horses and wagons (500 men from the Ingermanlandsky Regiment, the Butyrsky Regiment and 30 grenadiers each from both Guards regiments), with orders to locate and attack Schlippenbach. In place of the departing dragoon regiments, infantry was posted around the city "in small entrenchments in the nearby suitable locations" in order to blockade the place.

12 June

A trumpeter set out from the fortress to the Russians with a request to allow the burial of those killed in the recent combat; permission was not granted, referring to the absence on this day of the commanding general. The besieged observed how the Russians were continuing their work both day and night with great effort.[143]

13 June

Horn dispatched a trumpeter to Repnin with a response, in which he agreed upon the collection of the corpses on the following day between 8:00 and 9:00 in the morning. Money and clothing were sent along with the trumpeter for the Swedish officers that had been captured in the battle on 8 June; the items were passed along, but the messenger was not allowed into the Russian camp because of the fact that so far, no Russian truce-bearer had been allowed into the city. The Russians started work to build the countervallation.[144]

What were the Lines of Circumvallation and Countervallation? The 1700 Battle of Narva

Having taken position around a fortress, a besieging army was subjected to danger from two directions: the garrison's sorties from within the fortress; and an enemy's relieving army, i.e. reinforcement or *succour*, which might approach to attempt to lift the siege and to relieve the garrison. Lines of fieldworks provided cover for the positions of the besieging army and encircled the fortress from every direction – their construction was a common practice

---

142 *Pokhodnyi zhurnal 1704 goda,* pp. 43–45.
143 Adlerfeld, Vol. 2, p. 9.
144 *Pokhodnyi zhurnal 1704 goda,* p. 45; Adlerfeld, Vol. 2, p. 9.

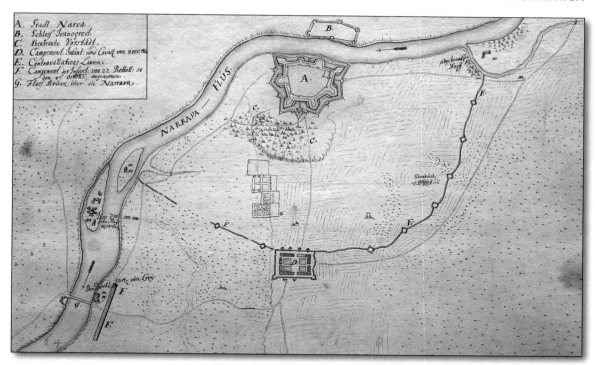

A. Stadt Narva.
B. Schloss Ivanogrod.
C. Abcebrante Vorstädt.
D. Campement Infant: und Cavall: von 8000 m.
E. Contravallations Linien.
F. Campement der Infant: von 22 Batall: so
    den 4 Octob: angecommen.
G. Floß Brücken über die Narrava.

The plan of the siege of Narva as of 24 September 1700. In comparison with other known plans, the given document shows the condition of the siege works as of 4 October [New Style calendar], when the Tsar himself arrived at the siege corps with Guards and infantry regiments. By this time only the countervallation line and Trubetskoy's camp had been built; the circumvallation line and approach trenches hadn't been started yet. In addition, on the map the quarters of Herzog de Croy have been marked, but he arrived at the army only in November. A copy of this map also exists in the Hessen State Archive in Marburg (Hessisches Staatsarchiv Marburg). (Artist unknown, Library of the Russian Academy of Sciences, Department of Manuscripts)

in the European sieges of the 17th century. The countervallation line – continuous retrenchment facing the besieged fortress – served as a defence against sortie attempts. A circumvallation line just as strong and extended was erected to provide security against relieving forces.

Ernst Borgsdorf, an Austrian engineer, who took part in the capture Azov, presented to Tsar Peter in 1696 and 1697 two of his books about the attack and defence of a fortress. In Europe there were many such treatises, but Borgsdorf's books, which were published in Moscow in 1708 and 1709, became the first works in the Russian language on military engineering. According to Borgsdorf, the "circumvallation or encircling line" was built with its rear to the fortress and its face to the field at least 3.6 kilometres outside the fortress; this line would contain all of the besieging army's cavalry, in order to give it the opportunity to attack an approaching enemy force, and infantry that was deployed in intervals between the cavalry. The circumvallation line should be strengthened with bastions and ravelins, which would protect the openings in the wall that were necessary for troops to go out in the field. At a space 700 to 1,000 metres closer to the fortress and facing it, a countervallation line would be built – it was defended by infantry and was strengthened with square redoubts facing the field with an angle.

Borgsdorf also specified that the area between the countervallation and circumvallation lines would hold "the field commander with his main encampment; a place for foreign ambassadors and sirs; an artillery train; a market area with canteens and shops where all kind of goods could be sold; supplies; a wagon park; a place for butchers and tavern keepers; a lower generals' canton and commissariat; an encampment for engineers and

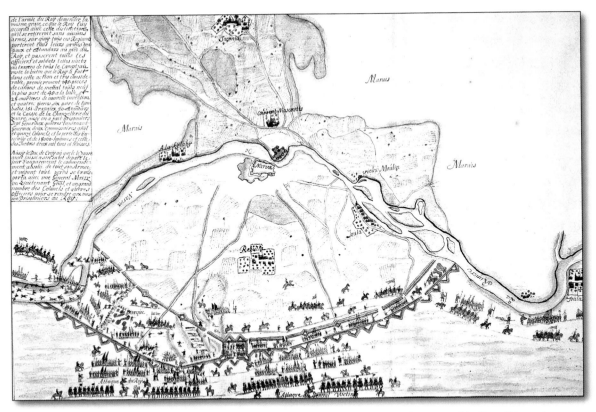

Plan of the town of Narva and the circumvallation and countervallation lines, raised by the troops of the Tsar of Muscovites. The Russians' extended siege lines: the countervallation line, facing the fortress and strengthened by redoubts; the circumvallation line, facing outward and strengthened by bastions and redans. Two Swedish columns are storming these retrenchments; the concentration of attacking troops in the breakthrough sectors wouldn't leave any chance for the defenders of even an experienced army. The outcome was predictable: in the western sector, the Russian troops fled in panic toward the bridge under a covering screen of the Guards; in the eastern sector, Sheremetev's feudal cavalry, that was brought within the lines before the battle, withdrew along the bank upriver and contrary to the popular belief did not drown in the Narova in attempt to cross it. The Russian generals together with their regiments, cut off from each other, entered negotiations with the foe. (Author unknown, 1700, Österreichische Nationalbibliothek)

miners; and military stockpiles of gunpowder, cannon and musket balls, slow match and all sorts of firearms supplies."[145]

The period's most famous French engineer, Marshall Vauban, described in detail not only the construction, but the defence of the lines. For example, he counselled to furnish the wall and ditch with a palisade and discussed how to position it most advantageously. A palisade that was dug in directly next to the parapet was ineffective since it might become cover for the attackers against the fire of the line's defenders. Palings erected in the middle of the ditch would not stop the adversary, since it would be possible to fill the ditch quickly "by tossing a large number of fascines" into it. A palisade could best detain the attackers if it was placed in the field at a distance of 15 to 30 paces

---

145 Borgsdorf, E.F., *Poverennye voinskie pravila kako nepriiatelskie kreposti siloiu brati* [*Trusted military precepts regarding how to take a hostile fortress by force*] (Moscow, 1709), pp. 13–14.

from the ditch. Vauban counselled to dig the stakes into the ground to a depth of one metre and at an angle of 45 degrees. It would be difficult to chop apart or pull such palisades from the ground, and the attacking force would be forced "to stand so close to the lines for some time, and to endure the fierce fire from those lines at such a short distance." Incidentally, having described the ideal palisade, Vauban advises that "it would be quite difficult, almost impossible, to fortify a line with such means": the construction of a palisade along the entire circumvallation would require an enormous amount of building materials and a lengthy amount of time. In practice the building of a line should be done as quickly as possible, and Vauban agreed that it was possible to do without a palisade, only if there was a solid parapet with two banquettes.[146] Further the French engineer wrote about the need to adapt to the terrain and to anchor a line on nearby woods, rivers, swamps, lakes, deep gullies and ravines, and about the Dutch experience of the 16th and 17th centuries in strengthening siege lines with formidable earthen "fortlets" and fieldworks.[147]

Having learned of the approach of a relieving force, the besieger had to distribute his regiments to sectors of defence of the line. A reserve should be kept, ready to go to the aid of a threatened sector; cavalry was more suitable for this role thanks to its greater mobility and capability to fire from horseback. Ammunition would be distributed to the infantry, cannons would be mounted on the parapets, and patrols and pickets would be sent out into the field at night in order to give notice of the enemy's approach.[148] It would be possible to delay the attacking enemy on the approaches to the line with the help of "beacons" – enormous fires built from two to three wagons of dry timber and straw, which were piled up in the field at a distance of 40 to 50 paces from the ditch opposite the salient angles and opposite the middle of the curtain wall. When the direction of attack became known and the adversary had closed to within a third of the range of a cannon shot, two or three soldiers, assigned to each "beacon", were to ignite it and head back into the fortification. The burning bonfires would hinder the attackers and allow targeted fire at them even in the darkness of night.[149]

In order to repulse an attack, it was recommended to deploy infantry in two lines along the parapet, and position one or two lines of cavalry behind them. Forces were to be shifted from distant, secure sectors of the camp. Vauban summarised, "When the besieger has time to get ready in his lines in such fashion, then it becomes almost impossible to believe that a relief force can take those lines" – leaving the prosaic realities of war, when a defender might not be able to organise a fitting defence of the lines, to check the purity of his theoretical exposition.[150]

Vauban demonstrated his contradictory attitude towards circumvallation lines with the siege of Turin in 1706. In one chapter of his book, he cites it

---

146 Vauban, pp. 145–146.
147 Vauban, p. 146.
148 *Ibid.*
149 Vauban, pp. 147, 153.
150 *Ibid.*, p. 150.

as an example of the impregnability of the line – Prince Eugene of Savoy's relieving force was unable to breach the line with a head-on attack, even despite the fortification's poor construction and weak interior force, as well as disagreements in the French command.[151] In a different place in an example of the same siege he shows that no precautions whatsoever in the layout of the lines can guarantee absolute security in the event of an attack, because the line was eventually breached in a weak sector and as a result the siege of Turin was lifted.[152] Apparently, Vauban nevertheless believed fortified lines were a bad defence for a besieging army. They presented an excessively extended position and required too much strength for a defence, while part of the siege corps was busy with attacking the fortress, the carrying out of patrols and other routine tasks. As a result, the circumvallation proved inadequately defended, and the adversary inevitably broke through it.[153]

A different military author of that same period, the French General Marquis Antoine de Pas de Feuquières, dedicated an entire chapter to the question of defending circumvallation lines, and relaying on examples from the wars of his epoch, came to the conclusion that an army should never wait for an adversary in lines of circumvallation, since encompassed in fortifications, the army would be restricted in its movements, while the enemy was free to examine the defences and choose a point of attack while hiding his real intentions under the cover of night and by means of feigned attacks.[154] Yet another French commander and well-known author of the first half of the 18th century – Maurice de Saxe – regarded the defence of lines sceptically, where the attention of each soldier was occupied only with firing, but as soon as the enemy reached the parapet, the men ceased to defend themselves. He wrote, "I scarcely remember a single instance of lines or retrenchments having been assaulted, and not carried."[155]

Like much else in the military sphere of that era, they tried to invent a rational basis for the disposition of the defenders behind the parapet and the organisation of their fire. If in a field battle several ranks of men, the first of which were kneeling, could conduct fire simultaneously, whereas when firing from a parapet or an enclosure the first row of men could only fire while standing. In the 1720s and 1730s, means of conducting trench or parapet fire were formulated, though doubtlessly these were known even earlier. In them, the soldiers of the first rank would fire from behind the parapet and then move to the rear of the formation (through intervals in the ranks or around the flanks), while the next rank stepped forward to take their place. When conducting fire, it was advised to aim low, so that the bullets did not fly over the enemy's heads, but in this case, it was necessary to hammer down the bullets with a ramrod, otherwise the bullet would roll out of the

151 *Ibid.*, pp. 150–151.
152 *Ibid.*, p. 147.
153 Vauban, pp. 29, 30 and 153.
154 Feuquières, A., *Memoirs historical and military ...* (London, 1735–1736), Vol. 1, p. 407.
155 Saxe, M., *Reveries, or memoirs concerning the art of war* (Edinburgh, 1776), pp. 189, 191–192.

tilted barrels.[156] A different document argued that the movement of the ranks would only cause disorder and that it was better to let the front rank remain in place and conduct fire in volleys or successively, while the rear ranks reloaded the muskets.[157] All of these lines of reasoning were written according to the results of the wars of the early 18th century; however, nothing was said about trench fire in the Tsarist manuals of arms, and the Russian infantry was not taught it.

Vauban also formulated recommendations regarding the attack against lines. An army which was moving to the relief of a besieged fortress should have in supply a sufficient amount of "ordinary necessities" (entrenching tools and artillery), as well as of "emergency needs" – fascines, required for filling the ditch of a fortified line. Vauban warned against a hasty attack upon a line; the relieving force should, "approaching little by little", take up position about a mile away, dig a retrenchment, attentively study the enemy's positions, and prepare a route for the attack; it was necessary to keep the besieged garrison informed about its actions and to coordinate joint actions against the enemy. In this fashion the besieging force would itself end up in the position of the besieged.[158]

When matters culminated in an attack, then it was conducted in daytime without any trickery – the troops should be arranged in two lines of infantry and two or three lines of cavalry and approach the point of attack in that formation. The soldiers carried fascines in order to fill the ditch; several detachments could be sent ahead "in order to absorb the initial fire".[159] A night-time attack ("early in the morning before the rising of the sun") was more favourable, because the darkness allowed a concealed approach to the point of attack, as well as to confuse the enemy with several feigned attacks. Vauban believed that "when you do not know the genuine intention of the enemy, you will be equally on guard from every direction" (which means you will evenly distribute your forces along the entire fortified line), then such a defence will undoubtedly be breached. For a successful attack, the assaulting units will follow one after the other, thereby ensuring a numerical superiority over the defenders at the designated sector of the front. The attackers were advised to close right up to the line, and from there drive the defenders out of it with intense fire and allow labourers to destroy the parapet for the free entry of troops into the breach.[160]

In the autumn of 1700 during the first Narva campaign, the besiegers built an entrenchment "so that the army was positioned between two

156 Bland, pp. 83–86; *A Treatise of Military Discipline; which is Laid down and Explained The Duty of the Officer and Soldier, Thro' the several Branches of Service* (London, 1757), pp. 48–49; Kane, R., *Campaigns of King William and Queen Anne from 1689 to 1712* (Dublin, 1748), p. 118.
157 Tatarnikov, K.V., *Stroevye ustavy, instruktsii i nastavleniia russkoi armii XVIII veka. Sbornik materialov v 2 tomakh* [*Drill regulations, instructions and guidelines of the Russian Army of the XVIII century. Collection of materials in 2 volumes*], Vol. 1 (Moscow, 2010), p. 140.
158 Vauban, p. 149.
159 *Ibid.*, p. 150.
160 *Ibid.*, p. 151.

ditches."[161] In full correspondence with the recommendation of Borgsdorf and the others, these were ramparts with redoubts, bastions and ravelins; the breastworks were jutted with stakes, and *chevaux-de-frise* were placed atop the ramparts. Distinct from the ideal "book" arrangement, the lines around Narva had to be constructed in uneven topography with swamps and hills, and the space between the circumvallation and countervallation lines was uneven – on the left flank the troops ended up squeezed into a narrow space between the lines. The besieging body was standing in the positions for a long time in a chilly season of the year; the camp consisted of tents, barracks, dugouts, cabins and huts and contained a large artillery park, the encampment and all of the field gear for a more than 30,000-man army. The siege lasted from September to November, and the chilly weather and rains only aggravated the hardships of positional warfare. One soldier wrote home in Pskov: "We are standing in Rugodiv for the fourth week in a row and we are dying from the cold and hunger …"; another took heart: "… everything you might want is scarce in our regiment, but I won't lament over my day-to-day life", but both men asked their families to send them warm clothing and victuals from home.[162] A member of Sheremetev's feudal cavalry in his chronicle reported on the poor weather in those days that preceded the Battle of Narva ("rain fell constantly over all those days and nights"), and about the burdens of camp life in such conditions: "In the camp the troopers endured much hardship because the mud was as high as a man's knees and a horse's belly; the ground was clay and the rains heavy, and it flooded and caused great misery for the men."[163]

When the Swedish relief force was approaching Narva and Tsar Peter had departed, all of his generals were made subordinate to Field Marshal Duke Charles Eugène de Croy. Thus, just a day before the battle, a man who was unfamiliar with his subordinates took control of the army. Nevertheless, de Croy made the necessary dispositions – half of the regiments that night remained under arms, an inspection was scheduled for the morning, each man was supposed to have 24 rounds in his cartridge box and was not allowed to open fire at a range greater than 20–30 paces. In addition, an order was made to send a mounted patrol of 100 men into the field outside the retrenchment; however, this order was not carried out, so the Swedish Major General Johan Ribbing was able to approach unhindered and measure the depth of the ditch. On the morning of 19 November at a signal of three cannon shots, the Russian army took position along the circumvallation line, the drums beat a march, and banners were unfurled. The Duke rode along his troops and realised that for a reliable defence of the entire perimeter he

161 Allart, No. 1, p. 12.
162 Kozlov, S.A, "Okopnye pis'ma russkikh soldat 1700 g."// Istoriia Rossii do XX veka. Novye podxody k izucheniiu. Kurs lektsii. ["Trench letters of Russian soldiers of 1700"// History of Russia up to the 20th century. New approaches to study. Lecture course.] (Saint Petersburg, 2008), pp. 201, 202, 206. See also: Dadykin, M.M. and Bazarov, T.A., "Pis'ma russkikh soldat iz-pod Narvy 1700 g." ["Letters of Russian soldiers from Narva 1700"] (according to materials of the Government Archive in Stockholm), as found in *Readings from Men'shikov – 2008. Reading materials*. 6th ed. (Saint Petersburg, 2008).
163 "Chronicle of 1700", p. 142.

would need at least 70,000 men, while he had only 20,000 men under his command. According to the army's General-Engineer Ludwig Nikolai Allart, all of the regiments deployed in one line without any reserves; in order to take up a larger front, instead of the regulation formation six ranks deep, the men had to arrange in two or three ranks.

The cannons on both sides opened up an ineffective fire at a range of up to 1,500 paces; the Swedish battalions and squadrons took formation and readjusted their lines in sight of the Russians and the cavalry was bringing up fascines, but nothing happened until 1:00 in the afternoon. The Russians managed to capture one Swedish dragoon, and according to the number of regiments that he reported (16 regiments of infantry and 16 of cavalry), they assumed that the entire King's army had to consist of at least 25,000 men, and the small force that was visible was taken as a vanguard, which would not undertake any independent actions. It turned out that these 8,000 men were in fact King Charles XII's entire army; his battalions and squadrons were thin in numbers, but he was ready to hurl them into battle.[164]

According to the chronicle, Sheremetev's cavalry was located in the field and received an order to return to the fortifications, which was carried out unwillingly. Meanwhile Charles XII examined the Russian line and noted two points of attack, having divided his small army into several columns. Each column consisted of infantry battalions that were deployed one behind the other, with a platoon of grenadiers at the point of the attack. The cavalry squadrons were supporting the infantry and stood ready to enter a breakthrough. The signal to attack was given at 2:00 in the afternoon with two shots. The combat cry "With God's help!" rang out above the Swedish army, and the regiments advanced towards the Russian positions. At this moment the weather sharply deteriorated – heavy snow and sleet began falling, visibility dropped to 30 metres, a strong wind blew in the Russians' faces and blinded them to the attackers until they had approached the edge of the moat and had ended up right under the cannons of the Russian batteries.

The extremely rare testimony from the ranks of the Russian army (the Chronicle of 1700) together with General Allart's diary and Adlerfeld's history allows us to look at the course of the battle through

According to Vauban, two lines of infantry and a cavalry reserves should defend the circumvallation line. (Artist unknown; in S. Vauban, *Kniga o atake i oborone krepostei* 'Book about the attack and defense of fortresses', Saint Petersburg, 1744)

Cross section of the right flank's circumvallation line. This image of the Russian positions outside of Narva is based on General von Hallart's notes and sketching; he was responsible for providing engineer support for the siege of 1700. (L.N. Hallart, *Das Tagebuch des Generals von Hallart uber die Belagerung und Schlacht von Narva, 1700* Reval, 1894)

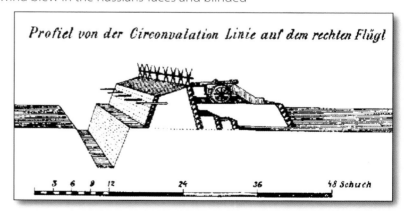

164 Allart, pp. 56–57; Allart, No. 2, p. 125 and 127; Petrov, A., "Narvskaia operatsiia", *Voennyi sbornik*, No. 7 (1872), pp. 22, 27, 28.

PETER THE GREAT'S REVENGE

The Russian camp in cross section. A detail of the etching "The relieving of Narva and the defeat of the Muscovites." The author of the most detailed map of the Battle of Narva Zacharias Wolf was a Swedish military engineer and a contemporary of the events. His work, in particular, is valuable for its most rare depiction of the Russian tents and arms bell tents; this fragment was later published in Adlerfeld's work. The thin line of infantry along the breastwork is noteworthy. (Zacharias Wolf 1667-1726, Sweden, www.raremaps.com)

the eyes of direct participants. At the moment of attack, the Chronicle informs, many soldiers were located in the works and trenches outside the fortress; behind the breastwork the regiments were standing in six ranks in some places, three ranks in other places, and in places just a single rank. The Swedes were attacking the Belgorod *streltsy* and Prince Trubetskoy's camp in a column ("in a rectangular formation"). Under musket and cannon fire, Swedes, disdaining their losses, "have been stabbed on the rampart with long lances", were filling the ditch with fascines, clambering up the rampart and pulling apart the *chevaux-de-frise*, in order to clear a path for the battalions and squadrons: "Soldiers with fusils were moving in front, followed by companies with long lances, and cavalry behind them: the forward companies were firing in advance, then lances were stabbing, and the cavalry was hacking up and plundering the tents of the monarch in the Trubetskoy camp."[165] The chronicle gives a picture of confusion and flight – the soldiers were standing on the rampart and watching the Swedes, but offered no resistance and fled together with their commanders, while the Swedes fired at their backs and advanced into the depth of the retrenchments.[166]

The attack was conducted so valiantly and successfully, that the Swedish infantry was able to clear a passage in less than a quarter of an hour, and the cavalry poured into the retrenchments. The Russian forces, torn apart from each other by the Swedish columns, were deprived of unitary command, and having lost the initiative, began to seek salvation. On the Russian left flank, the space between the circumvallation and countervallation lines was filled with barracks and huts that served as sleeping accommodation for the soldiers of Weide's division; now these structures hindered the ability of both armies to manoeuvre, but they let the Russians consolidate and stop the Swedish advance. General Weide's infantry began barricading the passages with wagons and *chevaux-de-frise*, and "firing with great cries and yells". Here the victors' attack was stopped, and the soldiers together with the Smolensk nobles and the Moscow and Novgorod feudal horse companies held their lines, having fenced themselves off from the point of breakthrough with *chevaux-*

---

165 "Chronicle of 1700", p. 147.
166 *Ibid.*

de-frise. However, the combat in this sector did not immediately take on a positional character. A counter-attack was implemented on Weide's flank, which brought temporary success; it was reflected in the autobiography of Major Avraam Korret of Alexander Gordon's regiment. When the Swedes burst into the line and, having bypassed a redoubt of the countervallation line, reached the positions of Gordon's regiment, at an order from General Weide, Korret and 20 soldiers broke through to the redoubt, turned the cannons around, and began to fire into the enemy's flank. This threw the Swedes into disarray, and Weide's regiments counter-attacked and drove them back along the line as far as the positions of Devson's regiment, which is to say, back to Trubetskoy's camp.[167] This episode, incidentally, had no effect on the overall outcome of the battle.

The remaining Russian regiments started fleeing along the fortifications to the right flank, where there was a bridge across the Narova River to the eastern bank. On that side

A soldier executes the command "Open your pans!". (Artist unknown; Russia, 1698; in Adam Weide, *Voinsky ustav, sostavlennyi i posviashchennyi Petru Velikomu generalom Weide v 1698*, Saint Petersburg, 1841)

of the river was the Tsar's headquarters on the coastal island of Kamperholm. Some of the Russian soldiers attempted to escape from the fortifications, but they were chased back by Charles XII's dragoons and drabants. "The accursed Swedes and miscellaneous Germans" seized the Grand Battery with its multitude of cannons, powder, cannonballs and bombs, the nobles' tents, the treasury and the campaign chapel. Here the scene of panicked flight grew worse because the crowd had been pressed back to the river: "The soldiers all ran down to the river and were sinking, the nobles as well … and the commanders on their mounts rode straight into the river and were swimming across it. Many men drowned in the Narova, having fallen from the steep banks after being pushed by the crowd. From the musket fire, the bullets were striking the river like raindrops. Other men were running across the bridge until it collapsed."[168] Here the Swedish attacks were stopped by two Guards regiments – the Preobrazhensky and Semenovsky. They were positioned on the extreme right flank, and apparently suffered less from the enemy's initial attacks and maintained their order for a longer time, although in the battle they nevertheless lost some of their flags. Both regiments under the command of their "lower ranked superiors and sergeants" threw up barricades and despite the fierce fire from the pressing Swedes, held their final line of defence. In the words of the Chronicle, they repulsed the enemy with fire and even won back the Grand Battery, the Tsar's tent and the treasury.[169]

---

167 Tatarnikov (ed.), *Ofitserskie skazki pervoi chetverti XVIII veka*, Vol. 1, p. 1169.
168 *Ibid.*, p. 148.
169 "Chronicle of 1700", p. 150.

The heavy fire continued in the descending darkness, which added to the chaos on the congested field of battle. At some moment the Swedish king with his cavaliers hurried off to the sound of battle and accidentally rode into the quagmire of a swamp; he was hauled out, and in one riding boot and without his sword, Charles continued to direct his troops energetically.[170] Two Swedish battalions in the darkness exchanged volleys of fire until they realised they were firing at friendly forces. Unexpectedly for the Swedes, the desperate resistance on the part of remnants of the shattered Russian army forced a halt to the battle. Since a large part of the Russian camp and the supplies therein had fallen to the victors, the exhausted and famished soldiers were diverted by plundering the camp and drinking the wine that they found.

Even before the fighting ended, the Russian commander-in-chief Duke Croy, General Allart and Colonel Blomberg of the Preobrazhensky Regiment surrendered to the enemy. With the cessation of the fighting, the Russian generals that remained on the right flank – Iurii Fedorovich Dolgorukov, Avtomon Mikhailovich Golovin, Prince Ivan Iurievich Trubetskoy, Prince Aleksandr Archilovich Imeretinsky and Ivan Ivanovich Buturlin entered into negotiations and reached an agreement regarding the free departure from the battlefield. Meanwhile on the left flank, the wounded General Adam Adamovich Weide was also forced to capitulate under the conditions of leaving without a weapon. By morning the Guards had freely crossed the bridge, but other regiments were disarmed and plundered, and in violation of his verbal promise, the Swedish king took prisoner all of the generals and a large number of subordinate officers. This was the worst defeat for the Russian army in the "Narva confusion"; if the cannons, weapons and flags could be purchased and replaced relatively quickly, it would take a long time for the Tsar to replenish the deficit of experienced command cadres.

Thus, the Russian command doubtless made a number of mistakes in the organisation of the defence in the battle of Narva – the approaches to the fortifications were not guarded by surveillance patrols, the troops were left without reserves and without the possibility of rendering support to threatened sectors. One can speculate how successfully the Russian army might have dealt with the Swedes on an open field, but the adopted tactic of a passive defence behind the ramparts of the circumvallation line was an inherent defect, which could not but tell on the outcome of the battle.

The official version, offered up in the "Ob'iavlenie s rossiiskoi storony o batalii s shvedami pri Narve" ["Announcement from the Russian side about the battle with the Swedes at Narva"] argues as the reason for the defeat that "the entrenchments covered an extremely large area and there were not enough men to occupy them." This appears to be the most well-founded explanation for the defeat. It was also written that a turncoat, the captain of the Preobrazhensky Regiment's bombardier company Johan Gumert had pointed out to the Swedes the weakest sector of the line, which was being defended by less combat-capable troops (the *streltsy*). However, there is a lot

---

170 Adlerfeld, Vol. 1, pp. 53–55.

of doubt about this – in the first place, Gumert had deserted to the fortress, and not to Charles XII's field army; secondly, he had deserted the army 10 days before the battle and was not able to deliver any fresh information about how the regiments were arrayed on 19 November; thirdly, the attack of the Swedish columns struck not only the *streltsy*, but also the regular regiments; in addition, a comparison of the combat capabilities of the old and new regiments at that moment was not in favour of the latter.[171] In the Tsar's "Journal or the daily notes", the inexperience of the troops was called the main reason for the defeat; however, the lessons regarding engineering were heeded: from then onwards, such powerful earthen fortifications were no longer built during sieges. Countervallation lines could still be constructed against sorties out of the fortress, but in place of the circumvallation line, only a line of *chevaux-de-frise* was contemplated in 1704. Instead they prepared to give a field battle in order to meet the probable Swedish relief force.

14 June

A ceasefire was announced for the search and removal of corpses; eight soldiers with cavalry Captain Kalantin headed out of the fortress, while just as many men emerged from the siege camp under the leadership of a non-commissioned officer. Two Russian and eight Swedish bodies were found; there were more of them left after the battle, but since then, likely the majority of them had been carried back into the city during the night-time hours. There was no firing during the searches; in addition to the agreed-upon number of labourers at the place of the searches, other Russians approached the city from the opposite side as well.[172]

---

171 *Severnaia voina 1700–1721. K 300-letiiu Poltavskoi pobedy. Sbornik dokumentov* [*Northern War of 1700–1721. On the 300th anniversary of the Poltava victory. A collection of documents*] (Moscow, 2009), Vol. 1, pp. 74–75.

172 *Pokhodny zhurnal 1704 goda*, p. 46; Adlerfeld, Vol. 2, p. 10.

2

The Formal Siege

15 June

On the night of 15–16 June, the besiegers began to dig approach trenches towards Narva along the riverbank from the direction of the sea, near Rottenhan, Swedish Colonel Stelen's manor house, not far from the place where a bombardiers' battery had stood in 1700. On the first night, 36 metres of approach trenches were dug, 600 metres distant from the moat of the fortress. The labourers were subject to heavy fire from cannons and mortars; six soldiers were killed and all of the buildings and orchards in the immediate environs were burned down. From the city a scout set out in a boat in order to examine the approach trenches, but during the attempt to capture him he was able to paddle back to the city.[1]

The opening of trenches. A fragment. The series of six etchings by J. Rigaud show the successive stages of a formal attack against a city on the example of the siege of Barcelona in 1714. The fragment shows the moment of initiating trench work – on the left, a pile of prepared fascines is visible; a file of infantrymen carrying tools is moving. Workers with picks and shovels have recently started work but still haven't made much progress. Along both sides of the trenches, the pickets of the infantry screen are visible – the trench guard. In the foreground, a soldier wounded when starting the trench is being carried away. (Jacques Rigaud 1681-1754, France, 1732, Anne S.K. Brown Military Collection)

---

1   *Pokhodnyi zhurnal 1704 goda*, pp. 46–47; Archiv., p. 251; Adlerfeld, Vol. 2, p. 10.

Meanwhile: The Battle Near Rakvere in the Reval Woods

A cavalry clash.
(Georg Philipp Rugendas I 1666-1742, Augsburg, 1740s, Anne S.K. Brown Military Collection)

Major General Schlippenbach's three mounted regiments numbering up to 1,400 men were located in Rakvere. This town with a castle in the preceding year of 1703 had been already occupied by Sheremetev's troops – back then the Swedes had retreated without offering resistance, having first put the torch to a stockpile of dragoon saddles and having smashed barrels of wine, though the Russians managed to acquire a large quantity of grain, meat, lard, herring, tobacco and salt. Sheremetev and his men remained in Rakvere between 5 and 9 September 1703, but then burned down the entire town and surroundings and headed to Paide and Viljandi, which were subjected to the same fate.[2]

The Wesenberg (Rakovor or Rakvere) Castle and its immediate surroundings; views from the north and south.
(Sweden, 1683, Krigsarkivets kartsamlingar)

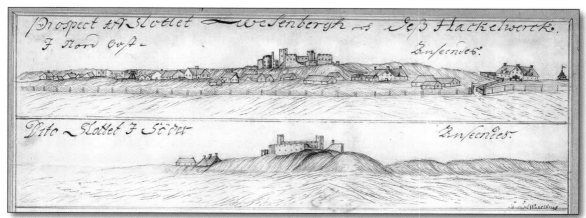

---

2   Sheremetev's war campaign diary, 1701–1705, pp. 139–141.

PETER THE GREAT'S REVENGE

The pursuit of General von Schlippenbach (right) and the capture of Colonel Wachtmeister (next page) on 15 June 1704.
(Aleksei Vladimirovich Temnikov, Vladimir, 2016)

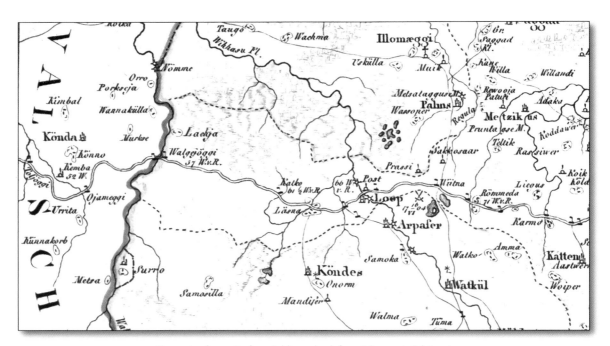

The route of pursuit of von Schlippenbach from Arbavere to Telejoggi.
Fragment of Atlas of Livonia. With the crossed swords, the cartographer has marked the presumed place of the first encounter between von Rönne's dragoons and von Schlippenbach's rear guard.
(Ludvig August Mellin 1754-1831, Russia, 1790s Library of Congress)

Now, having learned of the approach of Colonel von Rönne's force, Schlippenbach decided to make a retreat in the direction of Reval, and the Russians once again took the town without any fighting. Von Rönne went in pursuit of Schlippenbach, who was encamped in and around the village of Lesna. The first contact occurred on 15 June at 4:00 in the morning somewhere between the villages of Lobu and Arbavere:[3] the Swedish rearguard was driven back and together with Schlippenbach's entire force withdrew behind the Loksa [Valgejögi] River. Altogether over that day, more than six rivers were crossed; the Russians continued to pursue and harry the retreating Swedish troops with constant fire. In the defile (narrow passage) at Telejoggi (known as *Serebriannaia Myza* [Silver Manor] by the Russians), Schlippenbach stopped in order to give battle.[4] The General ordered the dragoons of his regiment to dismount and set up an ambush, but even here they were unable to slow the Russians. The foremost Russian unit of 500 horsemen under Colonel Pflug attacked, "but the Swedes did not give us proper battle" and went into a disordered flight. Schlippenbach himself galloped away to Reval with 200 troopers, while the rest of his force was scattered through the woods, slaughtered or taken prisoner. The Swedish infantry regiments, numbering approximately 2,000 men and four cannons, which had been sent to reinforce Schlippenbach and might have proved useful for him in the battle against von Rönne, had been stopped in Kaspervike (Käsmu) at his order. The victors captured the extra horses belonging to the Swedish commander and officers,

---

3   Today, these three villages are known as Läsna, Loobu and Arbavere, which lie 30 kilometres to the north-west of Rakvere.

4   According to Nordberg, it was the defile between Wittena and Tellejoggi. Not marked on modern maps, on Mellin's map, Tellejogi (or Toljoggi) is marked approximately where modern Road 260 crosses the Kalme oja River. The Russian participants in the battle called this place "Serebrianaia myza" (Silver Manor) (*Ofitserskie skazki*, Vol. 1, pp. 67, 507, 907 and others).

The country homes and gardens on the bank of the Narova River, among which the Preobrazhensky bombardiers positioned their mortars. Fragment of a map of the siege of 1700. (L.N. Hallart, *Das Tagebuch des Generals von Hallart uber die Belagerung und Schlacht von Narva, 1700*, Reval, 1894)

two 6-pound cannons, 50 dragoons and nine officers; Captain Ivan Vasilievich Podymov of the Astafiev Dragoons captured a colonel of the Estonian squadron of nobles Baron Friedrich Wachtmeister.[5] The news about this victory reached the Russian camp at Narva on 18 June.

16 June

Colonel Herman von Fersen was dispatched from the fortress into the immediate surroundings with 800 infantrymen; he had been given the mission to destroy the buildings and orchards, so that they would no longer provide cover for the enemy. The Swedish sortie approached to the new Russian trenches to within pistol range, and the soldiers in the trenches opened fire at it. The Swedes retreated, having lost four men wounded, and then "burned the wooden buildings on the immediate outskirts of the town opposite those approaches" and headed back into Narva.[6]

On this same day, Swedish cavalrymen headed out of Ivangorod, where they dismounted to let their horses graze. On that bank of the Narova River, the besiegers had only small mounted patrols in order to keep the city blockaded. Several volunteers from P.M. Apraxin's cavalry suddenly attacked and chased the Swedes back into the city without combat; in doing so, one Narva corporal, who had not had time to mount his horse, was taken prisoner.[7]

Why the Destruction of the City Suburbs by the Besieged?

Everything that might serve as cover for the attackers and which hindered lines of sight and fire from the fortress complicated the defence. Over the years of peace, gardens, fences, ditches, homes, barns, root cellars and other

---

5   *Pokhodnyi zhurnal 1704 goda*, pp. 48–49; Adlerfeld, Vol. 1, p. 309; Nordberg, Vol. 1, pp. 524–525; Volynsky, Book 4, p. 185.
6   Adlerfeld, Vol. 2, p. 10; *Pokhodnyi zhurnal 1704 goda*, p. 47.
7   *Pokhodnyi zhurnal 1704 goda*, p. 47.

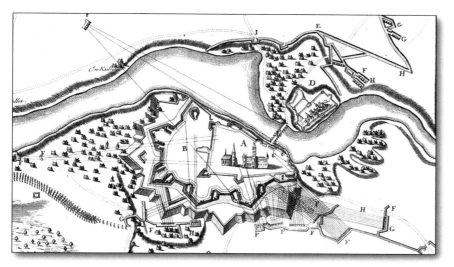

The extensive surroundings of Narva and Ivangorod, which the Swedes had been destroying in the sieges of 1700 and 1704. Fragment of the etching "The relieving of Narva and the defeat of the Muscovites". (Zacharias Wolf 1667-1726, Sweden, www.raremaps.com)

structures grew up around the city. Vauban insisted: "The governor-general of that fortress should check to see that there is nothing under the guns of the city, behind which the enemy would be impossible to see; he should order all ditches to be filled, all woods around to be cut down entirely, and to level highpoints wherever possible."[8]

After the capture of Nöteborg in October 1702, Petrine troops halted offensive operations, although in the nearest Swedish city of Nyenschantz, a "Muscovite" attack was expected from day to day. The nearby appearance of a Russian horse patrol prompted genuine panic – the outposts fled into the city, General Kronhjort's field army withdrew to the north, and the commandant ordered to put the torch to the settlements around the fortified city as well as to destroy four months' worth of provisions. Thereby, the city was burned down by the Swedes more than half a year before the day when the Russians actually arrived to set siege to the Nyenschantz fortress at the mouth of the Neva River. In 1704 the Dorpat commandant Karl Gustav Skytte ordered the burning down of the suburbs and when the siege was already in progress, setting an example, he ordered for his own suburban home to be set on fire first.[9]

Maps depicting the first siege of Narva show a large settled area of farmsteads and country houses to the west of the city, which the Swedes began to burn, while the Russians, on the contrary, tried to defend from the start of combat operations.[10] General Trubetskoy reported to the Tsar on 15 September 1700: "The Swedes at night are secretly setting fire to surrounding farmsteads, no matter how we try to keep them safe."[11] In July 1703 it became known to Sheremetev from "fleeing citizens, deserters and informants" that the Swedes, when leaving Narva, were "tearing down a mansion building

8   Vauban, p. 165.
9   Adlerfeld, Vol. 1, p. 332; Laidre, p. 116.
10   *Severnaia voina 1700–1721*, p. 56.
11   Ustrialov, Vol. 4, Part 2, p. 155.

close to the city".[12] Thus, according to the cruel demands of military necessity, the Swedes themselves were implementing a scorched earth policy, so in 1704 Narva was surrounded by burned homes, smashed fences and cut down orchards – all thanks to the garrison.

17 June

The besiegers continued the trenchworks energetically; over the night, they advanced another 300 metres towards the moat. Swedes next to the village of Joala spotted several boats that the Russians were using to deliver cannons.[13]

Von Rönne delivered 117 prisoners from Rakvere and reported that he was continuing to pursue Schlippenbach.[14]

Who Was Wolmar Anton von Schlippenbach?

Major General Wolmar Anton von Schlippenbach was born in 1653. From 1674, he served as a lieutenant in a dragoon regiment and participated in the war with Brandenburg. With the start of the Northern War, he recruited a Livonian dragoon regiment and became its colonel. In November 1700 he crushed a Russian unit on Lake *Peipus*. In February 1701 he took part in the unsuccessful attack against the Pskov-Pechersky Monastery, but in autumn of the same year he gained a victory over the Russians at Röuge in Estonia and was promoted to the rank of major general. He was appointed to take overall command of the troops for the defence of Livonia. Schlippenbach suffered defeats against Sheremetev in the battles at Erastfer (present-day Erastvere) in 1701 and Hummelshof in 1702.

18 June

The Swedes brought out several 3-pound cannons from the city and put them in action against the Russian approaches from the direction of Bahrberg.[15] From von Rönne arrived the news about the defeat of Schlippenbach just two miles beyond Rakvere on 15 June.[16] Repnin passed this news along to Menshikov and asked what to do with the prisoners that had arrived, who "would be needlessly consuming bread" and diverting soldiers to guard them.[17]

19 June

The Russians made attempts to drive cattle away from both Narva and Ivangorod, but everywhere they were hindered by shots from the fortress. On this same day Horn sent infantry with two field cannons on a foray in front of the Gloria Bastion, where the besiegers were directly closing to the Segelberg

---

12   Sheremetev's war campaign diary 1701–1705, p. 135.
13   Adlerfeld, Vol. 2, p. 10; *Pokhodnyi zhurnal 1704 goda*, p. 48.
14   *Pokhodnyi zhurnal 1704 goda*, p. 48.
15   Bahrberg is mentioned in the diary of Narva's resident, but its location is unknown.
16   Archiv., p. 252; *Pokhodnyi zhurnal 1704 goda*, pp. 48–49.
17   Volynsky, Book 3, p. 303.

Hill.[18] Approaching unnoticed and aiming their cannons, the Swedes gave a salvo and saw that several men fell, while the rest fled from the trench. All day long the garrison conducted lively fire from mortars and large cannons.[19]

20 June

Soldiers of the Preobrazhensky Regiment left a trench, made their way through the orchards closer to the city, and spotted a small depression, "a pit", opposite the Victoria Bastion next to the river, 200 metres from the moat (this might have been an old root cellar or a garrison training artillery emplacement, which are mentioned in Swedish sources). A Swedish forward picket was sitting in it. At midday the Preobrazhensky volunteers attacked this outpost, killed six of the defenders, drove off the rest, and took the pit, encircling it with gabions and strengthening it as an approach – from this position, it was now possible to reach the bastion with musket fire.[20] While the Russians were preventing the Swedes from destroying the furnaces and chimneys outside the city, the besieged troops were constantly harassing them

Powder charges in pots, bottles and bags could serve as an alternative to grenades. (Mallet Manesson, *Les Travaux de Mars Ou L'Art de Guerre*, Vol. 3 La Haye, 1696)

with continuous musket fire and a multitude of grenades; the Russians responded with the same and killed several of the defenders. Because of the strength of the enemy fire, Horn directed that evening that no one make an appearance on the walls. On this same day, a Russian drummer arrived in the fortress with a letter from Colonel Marquard and from other officers, who had been captured on 8 June.[21]

Outside of Narva, the Polish grand ambassador Tomasz Dzialyński, the Chełm *wojewoda* (military commander), arrived in the besieger's camp. He had come in order to conclude agreements in the name of the Reczpospolita. The point was that the allied ententes of 1699 and 1701 had been concluded with the Polish King Augustus, not with Poland; in fact, these were only Russian–Saxon pacts (Augustus was the hereditary Saxon prince-elector and elected Polish king). Now, in 1704, the Swedish army was manoeuvring through Poland, and the republic's aristocracy was divided into two camps – opponents of Augustus had decided to elect a new king, that would be supported by Sweden. Thus, for Tsar Peter it was important to establish

18 Adlerfeld's book mentions the Segelberg hill, which was apparently an elevated sector of the bank of the Narova River next to the Victoria Bastion.
19 Adlerfeld, Vol. 2, p. 10.
20 *Pokhodnyi zhurnal 1704 goda*, pp. 51–52.
21 Adlerfeld, Vol. 2, pp. 10–11.

A coach with a cavalry escort. (Adam Frans van der Muelen 1632-1690, France, 1685, Anne S.K. Brown Military Collection)

relations not only with King Augustus, but also with the senators. The Poles were pressing for the provision of Russian forces and money for the struggle with the Swedes. Ambassadorial tents had previously been pitched on the Ivangorod side of the river a half a verst from the camp. Colonel Busch's soldier regiment was formed up for the meeting in blue German dress. Upon the ceremonial arrival of the Polish "train", three carriages carrying the embassy secretaries were moving in front, followed by several nobles in Polish dress riding on horseback; behind them were two trumpeters and 14 footmen in French dress, followed by the ambassador himself riding in a coach with gilded carving and "entirely glass windows". Two Haiduks with axes rode on either side of the coach, and following the coach were seven exquisitely saddled horses of the ambassador. Closing up the rear were 26 cavalry in grey uniforms. Two bulls had been sent to the ambassador from F.A. Golovin, and a company of soldiers with a flag had been posted on sentry at the embassy tent. On this formality, the protocols were observed. Subsequently there took place a series of meetings with F.A. Golovin and P.P. Shafirov on 4, 6, 11, 15 and 24 June, which culminated in the signing of an allied pact already after the siege ended.[22]

The Swedish naval squadron that was sitting off the Narova estuary departed; Shchepotev wrote the Tsar that at midday, the vice admiral's ship gave a signal from cannons, raised a white flag, and all 12 ships sailed off with a following breeze to the east, in the direction of the mouths of the Luga or Neva Rivers.[23]

21 June

The besieged Swedish troops tried to drive the Russians out of the "newly occupied natural entrenchments" just outside the Victoria Bastion. A schute armed with cannons approached along the river from the direction of the city, while infantry and cavalry sortied out of the fortress on land. However, the Russians had set up regimental cannons at the new position, and with artillery fire and musket volleys forced the attackers to retreat. In the afternoon, Baron Ogilvy arrived in the camp from Moscow.[24]

---

22   *Pokhodnyi zhurnal 1704 goda*, pp. 52–53.
23   NIA SPbII RAN, F. 270, Op. 1, D. 41, l. 48.
24   *Pokhodnyi zhurnal 1704 goda*, pp. 52–53.

In order to initiate a full-scale assault on the fortress, the siege force was still waiting for the delivery of siege artillery from Petersburg and Pskov. F.A. Golovin reported about this in a letter to the ambassador in Warsaw Grigorii Fedorovich Dolgoruky.[25]

Who Was Georg Benedikt Ogilvy?

Baron Georg Benedikt Ogilvy was born in 1644. A Scotsman, from youth he served in the Austrian service and took part in the wars of the Holy Roman Empire against the Turks and Frenchmen. After the capture in 1700 of many generals and senior officers, the Russian government was in acute need of experienced commanders and initiated a fresh campaign to attract foreign military specialists who had knowledge of Slavic languages. With the mediation of a secret advisor, Johan Patkul, at the end of 1702 Ogilvy signed an agreement with the Tsar's ambassador in Vienna Petr Alekseevich Golitsyn about transferring to Russian service in the rank of Lieutenant General-Field Marshal. His travel to Russia was postponed for a long time under the pretext of the non-payment of an advance fee and the absence of permission from the Imperial Military Board.[26] Ogilvy arrived in Moscow on 5 May 1704 and headed to the camp near Narva from there. Under the terms of the agreement, in his new rank Ogilvy yielded only to the Russian field marshal (who at that moment was the boyar Boris Petrovich Sheremetev), but the field marshal was not supposed to interfere in Ogilvy's orders. Patkul recommended him as "one of the outstanding infantry generals, and he speaks the Czech language."[27] Upon first meeting, he was also liked by the members of the Russian command; F.A. Golovin on 22 June wrote the Tsar, "It seems that he is a quite a fellow … I think that you will be satisfied."[28] Menshikov on 7 July characterised him in the following manner: "Extremely skilful in everything and is gamely adventurous."[29] Ogilvy himself, obviously, assumed that only the Tsar and Sheremetev outranked him, so in his correspondence he looked at Menshikov as a junior: "my son"; possibly, this served as the basis for the future animus on the part of the Ingermanland governor-general, who was himself an influential close associate of the Tsar.

22 June
The Russians continued their trenchworks below the Segelberg Hill next to Lyfvenkulla[30] between the slopes of two hills. They were extending their line towards the Victoria Bastion.[31]

---

25   PiB, Vol. 3, p. 629.
26   See PiB, Vol. 2, pp. 264–266 and 682–685.
27   Ustrialov, *Istoriia tsarstvovaniia Petra Velikogo*, Vol. 4, Part 2, p. 253.
28   Volynsky, Book 3, p. 72.
29   PiB, Vol. 3, p. 641.
30   A place apparently in the environs to the north of Narva.
31   Adlerfeld, Vol. 2, p. 11.

A military wagon train. (Adam Frans van der Muelen,1632-1690, France, 1685, Anne S.K. Brown Military Collection)

23 June

Peter Apraxin's corps, which had thus far been positioned in earthworks at the mouth of the Narova River, left one regiment there in order to blockade from the sea, and with the rest of his troops moved and set up camp outside of Ivangorod. From there he was ordered to dig approaches towards the fortress, "having searched for a suitable place". The Swedes watched how in the evening a large mass of infantry with a multitude of loaded wagons marched past the Rudhofsberg Hill from the mouth of the Narova.[32] On the Narva side, the Russians were continuing to dig trenches along the river. The Narova River was securely blocked by artillery in two places: downstream from the fortress stood batteries of seven and 10 cannons on both sides of the river, and closer to the sea were batteries of six and 17 guns at Kutterkuhl.[33]

24 June

The besieged watched as a large amount of cargo was brought up to the Russian camp. The besiegers were now working directly below the Fama Bastion. The Danish envoy Paul Heinz and the Prussian Georg Johann von Keyserling arrived from Moscow. Denmark formally remained a member

---

32   Adlerfeld has it as Rudhofsberg, which was apparently a hill at Ratshof to the south-east of Ivangorod; incidentally, a point with the same name of Ratshof was shown on maps in the area of the Russian lines to the north-west of Narva.

33   *Pokhodnyi zhurnal 1704 goda*, p. 53; Adlerfeld, Vol. 2, p. 11; Archiv., pp. 285–286.

of the Northern Alliance and negotiations were continuing regarding its entry into the war, while Peter and Augustus were also striving to draw Prussia into the war on their side even though Prussian troops had been hired as mercenaries by Holland and the Emperor for the war in Europe.[34] Thus, since the Tsar and the head of his foreign policy office F.A. Golovin were at Narva, during the siege a rather large diplomatic corps gathered in the Russian camp. In addition to Heinz and von Keyserling, the previously mentioned Saxon representative Arnstedt and the Polish grand ambassador Działiński made visits there, as well as the Lithuanian minister plenipotentiary of the Vilnius canon Mikhail Belozor, the Dutch minister plenipotentiary Van der Hulst and the British consul Charles Goodfellow.[35]

25 June
The Russians continued their work on the approaches on the Ivangorod side. At the same time, they made attempts to drive away cattle, but were prevented from doing so by cannons mounted on the walls.[36]

What Was the Trenchwork?

The trenches leading to the fortress were called approaches. In the Russian documents regarding the construction of approaches, one can also encounter the expression "to build *schantzen*" (German for fortifications) but depending on the context the *schantzen* were also called fieldworks, batteries or other earthworks. The construction of siege works rested on the infantry. A specific number of soldiers from each of the army's battalions were assigned each day to the work: for example, on 9 July – 20 soldiers each with a corporal, on 21 July – 320 men, 10 from each battalion, on 22 July – no one was sent to work, on 30 July, 20 men from each battalion (a total of 600 men) were assigned to night work, on 3 August – 33 men from each battalion (a total of 990 men), and on 7 August – 31 men each for a total of 992 men. Lieutenants and captains were located with the labourers, from four to 10 depending on the total number of soldiers, as well as senior officers – a major or lieutenant colonel. An on-duty general was responsible for the troops in the trenches, who then yielded his post to the next chief. The General-Engineer of the army, the Frenchman Lambert de Guerin, and the engineers subordinate to him

An engineer traces out a line of trenches.
The book *Abbildung Der Gemein-Nutzlichen Haupt-Stande Von denen Regenten Und ihren So in Friedens- als Kriegs-Zeiten* contains a description and picture of a multitude of professions and trades. The given etching shows an engineer's primary tools: a draft board and case, a protractor, a compass, a caliper, a gauge, and also survey pegs, twine and a mallet. (Christoff Weigel 1654-1725, Regensburg, 1698, Sächsische Landesbibliothek – Stats- und Universitätsbibliothek)

---

34   *Pokhodnyi zhurnal 1704 goda*, p. 53; Von Huyssen, p. 411; Adlerfeld, Vol. 2, p. 11.
35   Kurakin, B.I., "Russko-shvedskaia voina. Zapiski. 1700–1710"//Arkhiv kn. F.A. Kurakina, Book 1, p. 298.
36   Adlerfeld, Vol. 2, p. 11.

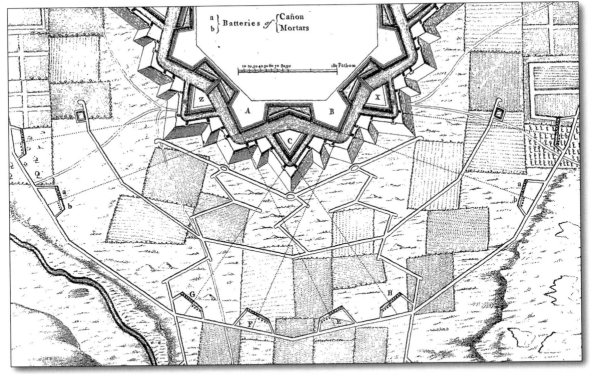

The fall of the city of Ath in 1697, Vauban's perfect siege.
The schematic drawings from Vauban's book were repeatedly used by many European authors, including the English Professor John Muller. This plan was unfailingly used as an illustration of the perfect Vauban siege – with the use of three parallels and zigzag approach trenches leading to the fortress. The configuration of the Russian trenches at Narva was different: in step with the progress, square redoubts were erected as strong points (the pre-Vauban practice). The approaches were started relatively not far from the attacked front, apparently due to the cover of the remnants of buildings on the outskirts and ground undulations. The feigned attack toward the Fortuna and Triumph Bastions was linked by trenches with the main attack, and this line of communication ran around the entire fortress. It is possible that the besiegers had enough time to busy themselves with such superfluous works while waiting for the arrival of the artillery. (Artist unknown, J. Muller, *The Attack and Defence of Fortified Places* London, 1757)

– the Italian Andre de Brilli and the Mecklenburger Mark Heinson assumed general direction over the trench works. The artillery Lieutenant Colonel Johan Gunter also built approach trenches and batteries.

In order to find cover from enemy fire, the work was conducted at night; the gathering of the soldiers with firearms and fascines was set for 4:00 in the afternoon before the front of the Preobrazhensky Regiment's camp; during the work, the weapons were laid aside, and the tools for the workers – 1,000 shovels and pickaxes each – were continually located in the trenches; at the completion of each night's work, the labourers could leave the trenches only at the order of the commander in charge. It was recommended to the engineers to mark the line of the approach trenches with stakes, to which bundles of straw would be attached in daylight hours and smouldering fuses in night-time hours to serve as guide markers. If the soil allowed, then fascines would be laid out along the designated line, which would serve as braces for the removed earth – the result would be a dirt breastwork for the trench. Taking advantage of the darkness, the men would work at full height.

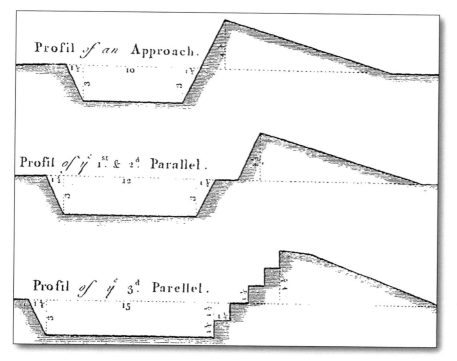

A cross-section of the trenches.
According to Vauban, the approach trenches had a simple earthen breastwork; the first and second parallels – a foot step (banquette) for conducting fire when repelling sorties, and the third parallel – steps, since the soldiers would go over the top when launching the assault. Outside of Narva and Ivangorod, these trenchworks looked differently, because it was difficult to penetrate the rocky soil and the breastwork was made with large gabions. (J. Muller, *The attack and defence of fortified places*, London, 1757)

With the sunrise, the night shift of diggers would leave, and the day workers would arrive in their place in order to deepen and "touch up" the sector of trenches started during the night. However, in the immediate environs of Narva the ground was so rocky that it was practically impossible to dig trenches; therefore, the trenches were not deepened into the ground, and the breastwork would be built from gabions that were packed with brought-in soil.[37]

Vauban described in detail why the work in the trenches was dangerous – a cannonball might penetrate the weak breastwork or fly along the length of the trench; musket rounds would be whistling overhead and ricocheting off the rear wall; and the closer to the moat, the more harm that tossed grenades would deliver. Borgsdorf added that not only were the shots dangerous, but also the fragments and chips sent flying by the cannon and musket balls when striking the breastwork of the trench, so earth bulwarks were considered more preferable to wooden or stone.[38] Somewhere in the entrenchments near Narva, memoirist Major Grigorii Petrovich Chernyshev was wounded in the left shoulder by a grenade fragment.[39]

37 RGVIA, F. 2584, Op. 1, D. 6, l. 1, 2, 4–7; Vauban, pp. 36-38; Borgsdorf, E.A., *Precepts*, pp. 16–17

38 Borgsdorf, *Precepts*, p. 16.

39 Chernyshev, G.P., *Zapiski G.P. Chernyshev* [*Notes of G.P. Chernyshev*] (*Russkaia starina*, 1872), Vol. 5, no. 6, p. 793.

PETER THE GREAT'S REVENGE

Entrenching tools in a trench. Fragment of an etching showing Coehorn mortars. The artillery administration delivered 12,299 shovels and spades, 5,686 pickaxes and hoes, and 3,884 axes for the army outside of Narva. The majority of these tools were written off after the siege as broken, so in 1706 James Bruce ordered to make these objects in the Swedish fashion, which was apparently sturdier. Ivan Pososhkov argued that the Swedish style tools were more fragile. (Johannes Meyer 1655-1712, Switzerland, 1711 Zentralbibliothek Zürich)

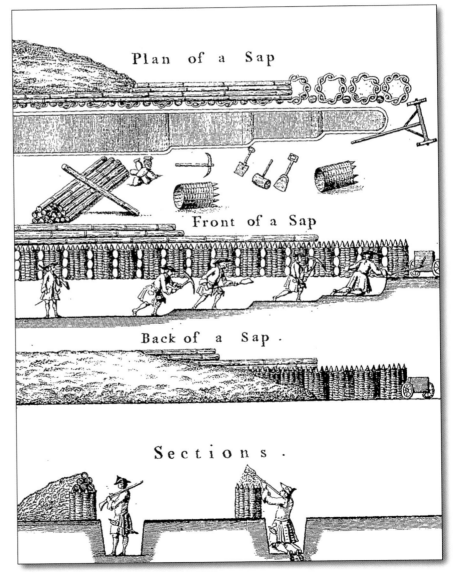

Plan of a Sap

Front of a Sap

Back of a Sap.

Sections.

A sap.
(J. Muller, *The Attack and Defence of Fortified* Places, London, 1757)
An etching from Vauban's book shows the conducting of saps (in the plan, from the rear and front, and in cross-section), the sappers' allocation of duties, and the tools and materials used for making them.

26 June

Corporal Andries Falk crossed over from the Narva garrison into the Russian trenches; under interrogation, he told about the condition of the besieged city, as well as about what prompted him to desert – the fear of an undeserved punishment at the hands of his commander (the lieutenant had worked Falk's horse to death, did not want to compensate for its cost, and was threatening him with rods). That evening, the Tsar returned to the camp from Petersburg.[40]

27 June

At the Tsar's order, command over the entire army at Narva was entrusted to the recently arrived Ogilvy. He inspected the lined-up troops, after which he was announced as a field marshal in front of the generals and officers. That evening the Polish emissary Dzialiński had an audience in front of the Tsar.[41] That night the besiegers were working in the trenches beyond Ratshof, while they were receiving heavy fire from Ivangorod.[42]

Lavr Ingrikov, a servant of the Narva doctor Tugolniksht, left the fortress with his comrades in order to cut grass, but he was grabbed by the Russians outside of Ivangorod. Under interrogation, he talked about the situation in the city. There were little more than 100 cavalrymen left, and their horses were in poor shape because of the lack of fodder. Less bread was being distributed in June than before, and the ration was not enough to satisfy the hunger of the people; peasants that had taken shelter in the city were dying from hunger, since they could not obtain bread – its reserves had been requisitioned from tradesfolk, but even they were enough for only two months of siege. The naval blockade was being blamed for the hunger, because of which the ships loaded with provisions had not been able to get through to Narva since the spring. The civilians were as before hoping that the King would not abandon them in the siege. However, the officers had been informed that Schlippenbach had been defeated and no help would come from him. The residents were gathering in root cellars and

The bell tower of Narva Cathedral; its bells fell silent during the siege. (Otto Kletzl 1897-1945 and Richard Hamman-MacLean, 1908-2000, Estonia, 1940-1941 Bildarchiv Foto Marburg)

---

40   *Pokhodnyi zhurnal 1704 goda*, p. 53; Von Huyssen, p. 412.
41   *Pokhodnyi zhurnal 1704 goda*, p. 54.
42   Adlerfeld, Vol. 2, p. 11.

A column of cavalry led by musicians.
(Georg Philipp Rugendas I 1666-1742, Augsburg, 1740s Anne S.K. Brown Military Collection)

basements in order to find shelter from the bombardments. The church bells "had been removed and buried underground, leaving only small bells behind, but they were wrapped in sheathes and did not ring because of the sorrow". The soldiers, cavalry and dragoons of the garrison were saying among themselves that they would not sit long under siege because of the hunger; the command did not trust them.[43]

28 June

Von Rönne's force returned to Narva after the victory over Schlippenbach on the other side of Rakvere. They entered the camp in formation, with the dragoons in front, followed by the captured prisoners on foot, with the procession of infantry bringing up the rear. That night the Russians continued to dig trenches on the Ivangorod side, below the hill towards the road to Jamburg, and threw up a breastwork there, despite the fire coming from the town and Ivangorod castle. In the daytime, the besiegers were inactive.

Horn wrote to Schlippenbach that half of the people in the garrison were sick from hunger. He added that "the people are increasingly experiencing the subversive desire to flee to the enemy, which especially many of the poor people are desiring because of the hunger."[44]

---

43   Volynsky, Book 3, pp. 19–20.
44   *Pokhodnyi zhurnal 1704 goda*, p. 54; Adlerfeld, Vol. 2, p. 11; Rosen, p. 186.

29 June

On the name day of Saint Peter and Paul, Colonel von Rönne was promoted to Major General "for his many brave and reliable services", after which a celebratory reception for the entire court, ambassadors, envoys, generals and officers was arranged in the tents of the main quarters.[45] The besiegers extended their trench to the road to Jamburg.[46]

Who was Carl Ewald von Rönne?

Baron Carl Ewald von Rönne, born in 1663 in the Courland area, hailed from Mitau (Jelgava). He served 10 years in Sweden, then another 10 years in the Netherlands and took part in the capture of the French fortress of Namur in 1695. He then transferred to service in Saxony and took part in the campaigns towards Riga in 1700 and 1701 as a lieutenant colonel. Von Rönne was hired for Russian service in 1702 by Patkul. As the colonel of a dragoon regiment, he took part in the 1703 campaign, and at the head of his dragoons played the decisive role in the defeat of General Kronhjort on the Sestra River in the fighting on 7 July; he was appointed as the first commandant of the just-founded city of Saint Petersburg.[47]

Baron von Rönne in the rank of Lieutenant General of cavalry.
(Artist unknown, 1705-1709)

30 June

Major General Horn ordered all of Narva's residents to turn over their horses for the needs of the defence. Officers of the garrison were busy with receiving the animals in Ivangorod, and then remained there while waiting for further orders. From the walls of Narva it was clearly visible that the Russians ventured out of their trenches to a spring of water near Ivangorod, and the commandant decided to take advantage of this. He ordered those officers who were now waiting on horseback to head down into a valley below the castle and at a signal from the fortress to charge with sword in hand and cut off the retreat of the Russians into their trenches. However, when the officers with drawn swords sprang from their cover at the discharge of a cannon from one of the bastions, they discovered no more than a single Russian, who upon sight of the riders "threw himself on the ground and chose to die rather than surrender." A trench sentry fired several shots but did not hit anyone, even though he was just 30 paces away from the enemy. According to the Russian siege journal, around midday the Swedes made two sorties out of Ivangorod towards the approach trenches and were driven back with the loss of four men killed and several wounded, while the besiegers lost one man killed and two wounded.

---

45 *Pokhodnyi zhurnal 1704 goda*, p. 54; Von Huyssen, p. 43.
46 Adlerfeld, Vol. 2, p. 12.
47 Volynsky, Book 3, p. 106; *RBS* [*Russian Biographical Dictionary*] (Saint Petersburg, 1913), Vol. 16, p. 57.

As this attempt on the Ivangorod side was unsuccessful, Captain Hochmuth proposed to draw the Russians nearer to the Victoria Bastion; for this purpose, that evening Swedish dragoons disguised as fishermen were dispatched to the river to pretend to be fishing in three small boats. At this time the forward outpost of the besiegers was located between the approaches and the bastion "in a pit and in root cellars on the riverbank". Forty soldiers of the Preobrazhensky Regiment were ensconced in them. In the ensuing exchange of fire with the approaching boats, the Preobrazhensky men did not notice another Swedish unit stealthily left the fortress – this was Lieutenant Eschener with 50 soldiers who had been sent forth by the commandant in order to cut the Russians off from their path of retreat. The "fishermen" with Captain Hochmuth landed on the bank, and the Preobrazhensky soldiers ended up encircled. During the attempt to break through, several men were wounded, killed or drowned in the river, while the Swedes captured the remaining Russians and shepherded them back into the fortress. On their return path the Swedes also burned down a few of the remaining structures in that area. Russian soldiers came running out of the approaches in pursuit of the departing Swedes and to rescue their own. Having advanced more than 500 metres, they caught up with the enemy at the fortress itself and freed those Preobrazhensky men who had not yet been shepherded inside. Then from under the walls of the city, the saviours returned to their trenches with the men they had saved while being fired on with cannonballs and case shot. The Guardsmen's losses amounted to two killed, 18 wounded and 14 missing in action – of the latter category, eight men had been escorted into the fortress. Under Colonel Apoloff's interrogation, the Russian prisoners revealed that Schlippenbach had been crushed, and Colonel Wachtmeister had been captured.[48]

Among the Guardsmen of the Preobrazhensky Regiment there were a lot of nobles, who had enlisted as privates in the winter of 1704, and the siege of Narva became their first combat experience. The participants of the events of this day, Preobrazhensky soldiers Bogdan Petrovich Neliubov and Mikhail Iakovlevich Durov, who later rose to be lieutenants in the Narvsky Regiment, recalled that they were serving under the command of Captain Prince Cherkassky during the Swedish foray, "when the Swedish schutes were coming out of Narva."[49]

The Tsar set out from Narva to meet with Sheremetev at Dorpat. Prior to this, the new commander Ogilvy gave Peter a "reasoning" about how the siege of Narva should be conducted. He considered it dangerous to launch an attack from the left bank – there Narva had its strongest fortifications (the New Town, the Old Town and the castle); from the experience of 1700, it was more difficult there to defend the extended position against a relief force and easier to lose artillery. Therefore, he proposed to transfer the entire army to the right bank, destroying the bridge behind it, cut the communications between Narva and Ivangorod, and for a start, take only Ivangorod. After its capture, it would be possible with cannon fire across the river to create a

48   *Pokhodnyi zhurnal 1704 goda*, pp. 54–56; Adlerfeld, Vol. 2, pp. 12-13.
49   Tatarnikov (ed.), *Ofitserskie skazki pervoi chetverti XVIII veka*, Vol. 2, pp. 1859, 1867.

A sortie on boats and the rescue of captured Preobrazhensky Guardsmen.
(Maksim Vladimirovich Borisov, Moscow, 2016)

breach in the walls of Narva that project towards the Narova and then launch an assault in boats. In the event of an enemy offensive, two bridges should be laid across the Narova, transport should be arranged for withdrawing the cannons, and through the efforts of 10,000 peasants build a fortified line and a road to Jamburg. With the approach of King Charles XII, Sheremetev should quickly send his infantry to join the siege body at Narva, and use the cavalry to delay the Swedish advance on the approaches to the city for two days. Apparently, the quality of the Tsarist troops prompted serious concerns in Ogilvy, and he wanted "to form all of the regiments on the German basis with superior and lower officers, to demonstrate the troops' exploits, and to teach them how to beat the enemy."[50]

1 July

The caravan of small cargo ships loaded with cannonballs, bombs and other combat supplies arrived at the Russian camp at Narva by sea from Petersburg after an eight-day journey. The Swedish fleet standing offshore did not attempt to prevent the passage; two of their schutes approached, but they were driven away by the cannon fire from a single armed Russian ship. With the convoy was a lieutenant of Bordovik's Regiment, Ivan Grigorievich Polivanov, who had experience with naval service at Arkhangelsk; later he recalled: "I was on assignment from Petersburg to travel by sea to Narva with hand grenades, and I had not reached the Luga River, when enemy troops in lifeboats from schutes approached me, and there was a battle."

Ogilvy had studied the routes from Reval to Narva and in order to block the path to the likely Swedish relief force, ordered two fortified lines to be built. Dragoon regiments were told to build the first at Pühajöe, six German miles from Narva, while the second was to be built at Waiwer by 8,000 labourers ("pioneers", as peasants who were rounded up to build earthworks were called at the time in Europe).

What Were the Fortified Lines?

The construction of lengthy lines of defence, as well as the building of entrenchments and fortified camps on the battlefield was a widely employed practice of the European armies of the 17th and early 18th centuries. Despite the fact that certain military theoreticians of that era were critical of field fortifications (an opinion regarding the disadvantage of lines of defence that was seemingly confirmed in practice by the 1700 Battle of Narva), retrenchments were built often and everywhere. For example, extended fortified lines were broadly used on the borders of France to defend against enemy raids in the years of the War of Spanish Succession. In 1708 Eugene de Savoy conducted a siege of the major French city of Lille, while the Duke of Marlborough was screening his ally against external French interference with his "observation" army; preventing them from manoeuvre, the Duke blocked

---

50   Ustrialov, Vol. 4, Part 2, pp. 307–309.

The Russian fortified lines of 1704 at Pühajöe and Vaivara. Fragment of the Atlas of Livonia. Count Mellin showed the approximate configuration of the retrenchments, without going into the nuances of the fortifications; today, in a field to the east of Sillamäe, one can see a line with a bastion and with a redan. The indications of combat with dates on the map assume that both fortified lines relate to the 1700 campaign; however, they were both definitely erected in 1704. The only clash occurred between Sheremetev's detachment and Maidel's Swedish vanguard at the unfortified position at Pühajöe back in 1700. (Ludvig August Mellin 1754-1831, Russia, 1790s, Library of Congress)

the approach passages with entrenchments so strong, that the Frenchmen declined to attack them and were unable to liberate the fortress. It was considered that a well-fortified entrenchment should have a ditch 3.6 metres wide and 2.4 metres deep, and a breastwork of similar proportions with a banquette for the shooters. Every 160 metres along the line redans should be built and cannons should be mounted in them. These sectors of the rampart that project out into the field were necessary for an effective fire defence, since it had been noted that 20 flanking shots inflicted greater damage to attacking troops than 60 frontal shots.[51]

So, Ogilvy's idea to block the sectors between the sea coast and the swamps with an earthen rampart was in keeping with contemporary military thinking. The line closest to Narva was built at a distance of approximately 20

The Art of War, in four parts. Written in French by Four Able Officers of Long Service and Experience, and Translated into English by an English Officer (London, 1707), pp. 219–221.

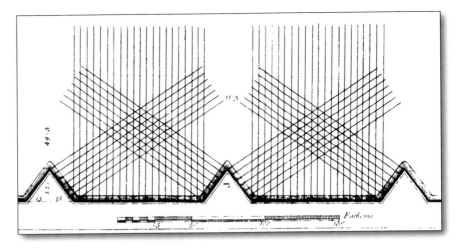

The interlocking zones of fire when defending a retrenchment with redans. (Chevalier de Clairac, *The Field Engineer* London, 1760)

km from the city across the road to Reval; it ran along the Waiwer high ground from the sea coast to the swamp at Auvere to the south. Captain Dupres of the Ingermanlandsky Regiment was sent as an engineer to oversee the work. Since neither the Swedish king nor General Schlippenbach came to Narva's relief, the lines that were constructed by the Russians were not attacked. The Swedes crossed them in a different direction and under different circumstances – at the end of August, the surrendered Swedish garrison of Ivangorod marched off to Reval, and one of the officers noted that the Russians had fortified the passages at Pühajögi and Sillamäe so artfully, that it would have been extremely difficult to storm them. Today one can see the remnants of that line on the eastern outskirts of Sillamäe between the Tallinn highway and the sea coast – the rampart and trench distinctly stand out in relief, and in satellite images a line is visible with several redans and bastions facing to the west.[52]

2 July

The besiegers extended the approaches from the point where the skirmish took place on 30 June upwards to the counterscarp of the Gloria Bastion. Captain Freulich and 80 soldiers were sent out from the fortress to the covered way in order to conduct harassing fire. However, the Russians paid little attention to their fire and, as it seemed, were ready to do the work without regard for losses. A drummer arrived at the fortress with letters.[53]

3 July

At an order from the Tsar, all of the infantry regiments on the Narva side, having formed up, marched to a new place that was one kilometre from the city. There they set up camp along a new line of countervallation; instead of a circumvallation line, the field was fenced off only with *chevaux-de-frise*. The arrangement of the regiments and generals on the new line had been determined by an order from 2 July. On the right flank (with its front

---

52   Tatarnikov (ed.), *Ofitserskie skazki*, Vol. 1, p. 29; Adlerfeld, Vol. 2, p. 26.
53   Adlerfeld, Vol. 2, p. 13.

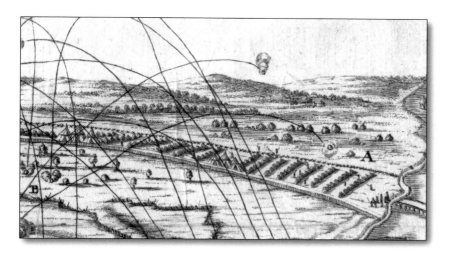

The western flank of the Russian siege camp in 1704. Fragment of the etching "Delineation der Stadt und Vestung Narva, samt des Schlosses Ivangorod". This is a rare depiction of the second siege of Narva, where, at least symbolically the position of the Russian camp is shown, and in particular, its defenses – a breastwork facing the fortress, and *chevaux de frise* facing the field. (Artist unknown, 1700s Krigsarkivet)

towards the field and its back to the city, just as in 1700), were Major General Chambers' regiments (the Preobrazhensky, Semenovsky, Ingermanlandsky and Gordon's); in the centre were Lieutenant General Schönbeck's regiments (under Gulitz, Dediut, Ogilvy, Berner and Ridder); and on the left were Major General Scharf's regiments (under Bovisch, Busch, Cooper, Schönbeck, Chambers and Repnin).[54]

Ogilvy and the generals moved to the new position on 4 July, F.A. Golovin and the chancellery on 8 July. At around midday, Swedish cavalry exited Narva in order to observe the setup of the new camp. The besiegers daily kept 500 dragoons on watch that were concealed in the woods next to the city; on this occasion the Russian sentries pulled back towards the camp, deceiving the Swedes, and then suddenly attacked and drove back the sortie. They pursued the Swedes back to the very counterscarp; several of the Swedish cavalrymen in their haste galloped past the gates and tumbled into the moat. Cannon fire from the fortress stopped the pursuit, and the Russian dragoons, having lost only one horse, withdrew, having in passing driven away horses and cattle, which had been let out of the fortress to graze under the cover of the Swedish cavalry.[55]

From the fortress, the repositioning of the Russian forces was perceived as the arrival of major reinforcements. Around Wäpskyle, the Swedes noticed the preparation of a lot of boats.[56]

What Were *chevaux-de-frise*?

The 'Spanish rider' (from a German term) or *cheval-de-frise* (French; plural *chevaux-de-frise*) was four (more rarely, six) faced beams with sharply pointed stakes; with the help of iron bands and hooks on the ends, the beams were fastened together, and the result was a lengthy obstacle, which could stop

---

54   Arkhiv SPbII RAN, F. 83, Op. 1, D. 292, l. 1 obr.
55   *Pokhodnyi zhurnal 1704 goda*, pp. 57–58.
56   Adlerfeld, Vol. 2, p. 13.

Chevaux de frise (Spanish rider in German or Frisian horse in French) were conceived as an obstacle for cavalry. (Artist unknown, Italy, 17th century Library of Congress)

cavalry and slow down infantry. In fortifications, entrances and breaches were blocked with *chevaux-de-frise*, and they were also placed on earthen ramparts as a supplementary barrier to the attackers; in cities, *chevaux-de-frise* blocked gates, bridges and streets. *Chevaux-de-frise* could be quickly erected, taken apart, or easily shifted in its assembled condition, so the field armies of the allies, which as a rule preferred the defence, actively employed them against the impetuous attacks of Swedish infantry or cavalry charges. In the Petrine army, in various years one infantry company was to have three to eight beams, in each of which 20–24 stakes were set; in order to transport this, the units had wagons to carry the *chevaux-de-frise*. It is known that Menshikov ordered 4,200 Spanish riders to be built and sent to the regiments at Narva: the beams should have a length of 2.5 metres and should have hooks on the ends and 20 spikes (palings) each; 1,200 such *chevaux-de-frise* were prepared in Moscow and Tver'. It is not known when the order was given (obviously, no earlier than the end of May) or when it was fulfilled. In the papers of the Artillery administration, documents are preserved regarding the production of "spears" – iron tips for the *chevaux-de-frise*'s spikes – by the blacksmiths of Moscow and of seven other towns, as well as the hiring of carts by 10 July for delivering 20,000 of these components to Narva.[57] Apparently, during the siege the soldiers had to make *chevaux-de-frise* themselves in field conditions; according to the order from 20 July, the regiments at Narva should produce them in place, preferably from birch trees, according to a model that stood before the camp of the Preobrazhensky Regiment's 1st Battalion. The centralised production of *chevaux-de-frise* dragged on: linden tree beams and maple tree half-pikes were still under construction in February of the following year, 1705.[58]

4 July

The Russians continued to extend the trench along the river 8–10 metres from the bank and were continuously firing muskets at the walls of Narva. From the fortress they watched fresh troops that were arriving in the Russian

---

57   Arkhiv VIMAIViVS, F. 2, Op. 1, D. 3, ll. 291 obr., 308 obr. –312.
58   RGVIA, F. 2584, Op. 1, D. 6, l. 3; Arkhiv VIMAIViVS, F. 2, Op. 1, l. 291 obr., 308 obr. –312; NIA SPbII RAN, F. 270, Op. 1, D. 41, l. 105; Tatarnikov, K.V., *Russkaia polevaia armiia 1700-1730 [Russian field army of 1700–1730]* (Moscow, 2008), pp. 111–112; Ustrialov, Vol. 4, Part 2, p. 306.

camp each day. They could also see a new bridge that was laid across the river at Wäpskyla, and that the number of tents at a place called Sacronia was increasing.[59]

The Tsar wrote Menshikov that after a long journey on boats he had reached Dorpat and discovered that Sheremetev was conducting the siege of that city unsuccessfully: the approach trenches from two directions and the batteries proved useless for an attack; the soldiers were exerting themselves on the works in vain; and 2,000 bombs had been expended pointlessly. Peter considered that the Dorpat bastions were no weaker than Narva's, but he was hoping to start breaching the walls soon and finish it in 7–10 days. He also asked to be notified if it became known that a relief force was approaching, so that he would have time to haul away the artillery and prepare the regiments for battle. A local Chude had been captured around Dorpat, who not long before had been in Reval; he reported that 2,000 cavalry troopers had arrived there from Pernau, as well as infantry and horse aboard 16 ships. Because of this news, the threat of a relief force still existed, and it was decided that it was "extremely necessary" to send a unit on reconnaissance towards Reval.[60]

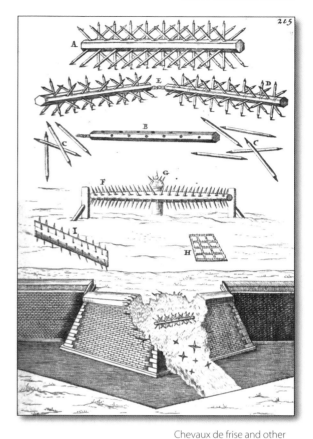

Chevaux de frise and other obstacles with spikes – herisson, hersillon, herse and caltrops – were used as breach obstructions for the attackers. Hexagonally-shaped beams of chevaux de frise continued to be depicted in numerous illustrated military reference books of the 17th and 18th centuries; however, judging from all of the available evidence, in practice simpler quadrangular beams were used. (Romeyn de Hooghe, 1645-1708, France, 1672 A. Manesson Mallet, *Les Travaux de Mars Ou L'art De La Guerre*, Vol. 3 La Haye, 1696)

5 July

The Russians extended their trenches as far as the river from the direction of where the Axel's water mill stood.[61] From the opposite direction, they extended their trenches as far as the road to Lilienback.[62] From the battery positioned at Ratshof, they were firing three-pound cannons at the Swedish labourers at Ivangorod's hornwork and later at the city itself but did little damage.[63]

Colonel Fersen from the Ivangorod hornwork was firing cannons at the place where the Russians were stockpiling the gabions for their trenches.

59   Adlerfeld, Vol. 2, p. 13.
60   PiB, Vol. 3, pp. 94–95.
61   Apparently, this was a water mill on the Ivangorod bank at the Narova rapids. On a 1700 map from an Austrian library, an "old mill" is shown at that location, while on Mellin's map of the 1790s, this figures as "Kramer's mill".
62   Adlerfeld refers to this as "Bleeking", but this place name is not encountered in other sources. Presumably, this appears to be the location of "Lillienbacka" to the north-east of Ivangorod on Swedish maps of 1678 and 1699 (and was later known as Lillienbach).
63   Adlerfeld, Vol. 2, p. 13.

Commandant Horn gave him a reprimand for this and demanded the payment of a ducat for each shot.[64]

The commandant's strange demand is mentioned in the *History of Livonia*. According to Kelch, Horn was threatening the enlisted men with punishment for each musket shot fired without a special order – three white loaves (*weisse Runstucke*) and five pairs of strokes with a rod, and for voluntarily firing a cannon, a penalty of 2, 3, 4 or more riksdaler [Swedish currency of that era] for each shot fired. This ban became known to the besiegers: when the Russians neared the counterscarp, they shouted to the Swedish soldiers lying there: "Don't fire, this will cost you three loaves or ten strokes with a rod." The Russian command supposedly assessed Horn's order as intentional disrespect for the adversary – if you will, the Russians were unworthy of wasting gunpowder on them.[65] Judging from the further mentions in sources, Horn's ban did not mean the complete ceasing of fire on the part of the garrison.

A Hetmanate *companiec* – a mercenary mounted Ukrainian Cossack of the early 18th century.
(Sergei Igorevich Shamenkov; Odessa, 2015)

Meanwhile: the Uprising in Western Ukraine

The news was reporting: "Cossacks have taken Nemirov and are governing there at their own will." After right-bank Ukraine and Kiev had rejoined the Russian state, the Ukrainian lands on the western bank of the Dnepr River remained part of the Reczpospolita, though the Cossacks and peasants continued to rebel against the Polish rulers. In 1702 in the areas of Kiev, Volyn and Podolie a fierce uprising erupted under the leadership of Hetman Samoilo Samus and Colonels Paliy, Iskra and Abazin. The Cossacks were driving out and massacring Polish noble *szlachta* and Jews, took several fortresses, and on the conquered lands were counting on reuniting with the left-bank Ukraine as part of Russia. However, neither Tsar Peter nor Hetman Mazepa were interested at that moment in seizing territory from Poland, which they were trying to make their ally in the war against Sweden. In 1703 the Poles took revenge and drove the rebels out of a number of fortresses, including out of Nemirov, while cruelly suppressing resistance and punishing rebel sympathisers.

Moscow still had no intention to support the uprising, but in connection with the fact that the Swedes had marched into central Poland and

und Einahme von der Russen, nach Aufzeichnungen dasiger Einwohner in Jahre 1704", p. 259.

65   Kelch, pp. 424–425.

a portion of the *szlachta* had risen up against King Augustus, Tsar Peter ordered Mazepa to enter right-bank Ukraine in order to deter the anti-Saxon opposition. Inspired by the arrival of the Hetman's troops, the rebels went on the offensive, in the course of which Semen Paliy took Nemirov from the Poles. Soon the Cossacks yielded the cities of Bila Tserkva [or Belaya Tserkov], Fastov, Korsun and Boguslav to Mazepa's control, and thereby Ivan Stepanovich in fact became "the hetman of both banks of the Dnepr". He arrested the populist Paliy and sent him off to Moscow, and returned Nemirov, "which had been won back from Paliy's obstinate men", to the Polish commandant.[66]

6 July

The besieged garrison reduced their strength on the counterscarp – if previously there was a captain with 80 soldiers constantly located there, now a lieutenant and 30 soldiers were posted there. Each musketeer was supposed to fire 30 bullets over the day. The Russians extended their trench beyond the road to Lillienbacka and strengthened them with gabions from one end to the other. At 2:00 in the morning an alarm was raised on the Ivangorod side, when Swedish soldiers who had been sent out on reconnaissance bumped into a Russian patrol and exchanged fire, losing in the process three men killed and several wounded.[67]

7 July

The trenches on the Ivangorod side were extended as far as a place called Katterumpan, from where the Russians then conducted intense musket fire.[68] On the Narva side, they constructed a redoubt atop the Goldenhof hill. In the daytime, 13 ships arrived from Lake Peipus.[69]

The execution of the command "Charge with your cartridges!". (Artist unknown; Catalonia, 1714, Juan Francisco Ferrer, Exercisio practico y especulativo de el fusilero, y granadero, 1714)

Menshikov wrote the Tsar, who was still at Dorpat, that he and an engineer had examined the Narva fortress for the last several days and had spotted a damaged place in the wall at the Victoria Bastion by the river, where it might be possible to make a breach rapidly. He also reported that information had been received through the Danish envoy regarding the possible arrival of

---

66 Chukhib, T.V., *Kozaki i monarchi. Mizhnarodni vidnosini rann'omodernoï Ukraïns'koï derzhavi 1648–1721 rr.* (Kiev, 2009), pp. 394–404, 433–442; NIA SPbII RAN, F. 270, Op. 1, D. 41, l. 65.
67 Adlerfeld, Vol. 2, p. 14.
68 Adlerfeld has this place called Katterumpan, but it is not encountered in other sources. Judging from the context, this sector of the Ivangorod side of the river was opposite the Victoria and Honour bastions.
69 Adlerfeld, Vol. 2, p. 14.

Cavalry at the preparation of fascines.
Guérard's etching from the military series "L'art militaire ou Les Excercices de Mars, livre à dessiner" depicts troops in woods that are preparing fascines and gabions. The cutting down of the nearby woods and bushes for the army's needs was the indispensable attribute of any siege. (Nicolas Guérard, 1648-1719, France, 1695, Musée de l'Armée, Paris)

King Charles XII at Narva – supposedly he had embarked on ships with 8,000 troops in Gdansk. This alarmed Menshikov, and he advised the Tsar to lift the siege of Dorpat, in order at the least to take Narva with their combined forces. Simultaneously the Ingrian governor dispatched a party of 300 men on reconnaissance towards Reval. On this same day, the Tsar from Dorpat sent Menshikov a request to send him 15–20 of the best cannoneers.[70]

8 July

Menshikov sent 15 cannoneers to the Tsar at Dorpat.[71] That night the Russians strengthened their sentries on the road to Lillienbacka and reinforced their trenches with a multitude of gabions.[72]

What Were Gabions?

The gabions were large, woven cylindrical baskets without a bottom, which were put into position and filled with earth or stones. With their help it was possible to raise a breastwork more simply and rapidly than with excavated earth. Large gabions up to 1.8 metres tall and around 1.2 metres in diameter served as cover against enemy fire at batteries, where the cannons were set up between them. More compact gabions with a height and diameter of around 0.75 of a metre ("which made them easier to handle") were used for quickly throwing up a parapet in a trench or sap. In order to make a gabion, 8, 9 or 10 sharpened stakes were embedded in the ground in a circle, and green twigs were woven around them. This work was considered a more qualified

---

70   Ustrialov, Vol. 4, Part 2, pp. 314–315; PiB, Vol. 3, pp. 98, 640–641.
71   PiB, Vol. 3, p. 642.
72   Adlerfeld, Vol. 2, p. 14.

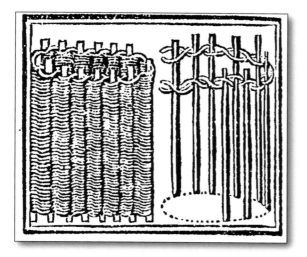

Gabions or Schantz-korben (in German) in the manuals of the 18th century. (Le Blond, *The Military Engineer* (London, 1759); Feuquieres, *Memoirs historical and military* (London, 1735); D. Grundell, *Nödig underrättelse om artilleriet till lands och siös* Stockholm, 1705).

labour than preparing simple fascine bundles; the weaving of one gabion required no less than three hours of work and no less than two men.[73]

9 July

Major General von Rönne wrote Menshikov about the course of work on the fortified line along the Pühajõgi River: the dragoons were occupying dams and binding fascines. The Swedes remained in Reval and were sending out small patrols from there no further than 10 km.[74]

On this day De Prou's squadron approached Kotlin, as well as an English merchant ship loaded with tobacco, fabric, beer, cider, cheese, olives and capers. The ship was inspected and allowed passage to Petersburg.[75]

10 July

In the morning Menshikov ordered to summon volunteers from among the Novgorod select noble horse and dragoons – in return for capturing a prisoner willing to talk, they would each be awarded 30 gold *chervonets* coins. At midday the volunteer noblemen from Novgorod attacked a herd,

---

73   Vauban, p. 16; *A military dictionary. Explaining all difficult terms in martial discipline, fortification, and gunnery* (London, 1704), p. [G].

74   Volynsky, Book 3, p. 253.

75   Bazarova, T.A., *Sozdaniie "Paradiza": Sankt-Petersburg and Ingermanlandia v epokhu Petra Velikogo: Ocherki* [*The creation of "Paradise": Saint Petersburg and Ingermanland in the epoch of Peter the Great: Essays*] (Saint Petersburg, 2014), p. 89; NIA SPbII RAN, F. 83, Op. 1, D. 337, l. 1 obr.

Russian soldiers preparing fascines. Detail of the etching "Delineation der Stadt und Vestung Narva …". The most routine material in siege works were bundles of branches or sticks, bound at the ends and in the middle with withe. For throwing up earthworks or filling ditches, the fascines were made with a length of around 1.2 meters; with such dimensions, a single man could easily carry a fascine. For more monumental works, very lengthy fascines called saucissons were made. When doing trench work, the fascines were staked to the ground. (Artist unknown; 1700s Krigsarkivet)

which was grazing next to the moat under the cover of mounted men; they captured one man, three horses and several head of cattle.

That evening the Russians approaches neared the moat and the western face of the Honour Bastion and the moat of the Victoria Bastion "so closely that it was freely possible to fire accurately with small arms across the moat at the bulwark." All through the night the besieged men conducted cannon and musket fire at the new trenches, where of the siege troops they killed the adjutant Gordon, who was attached to General Schönbeck, and three soldiers.[76] According to Swedish sources, the Russians had a superiority in the exchange of fire thanks to their hand mortars. Each day the besieged garrison had several men killed and wounded. The siege works continued, despite the unceasing fire, and by the next morning the trenches in the new sector had a ready breastwork made from gabions.

On this same day, artillery and supplies arrived by water from Petersburg and Jamburg. The majority of the cannons arrived by land, while the gunpowder and shells arrived on small watercraft from Petersburg.[77]

11 July

The besiegers approached even closer to the Victoria Bastion, having lost six men wounded during the work in the trenches from Swedish fire. Commandant Horn daily headed out to the walls with many officers in order to direct the fire, and on this day while visiting the Victoria Bastion, he lost a finger on his hand due to a shot from a flintlock musket.[78]

---

76 The source does not mention the name of the adjutant; the Scotsmen Gordon served in a multitude of armies in Europe. Oleg Nozdrin suggests that this might be a certain Francis Gordon, who served as a lieutenant in Poland from 1696 and in Russia from 1700.

77 NIA SPbII RAN, F. 270, Op. 1, D. 41, l. 59; *Pokhodnyi zhurnal 1704 goda*, pp. 58–59; Adlerfeld, Vol. 2, pp. 14–15.

78 *Pokhodnyi zhurnal 1704 goda*, p. 59; Adlerfeld, Vol. 2, p. 15; Archiv., p. 261.

Menshikov wrote the Tsar that a group of Colonel Gorbov's dragoons which had been sent out to Reval had captured two prisoners. According to their testimony, Schlippenbach was still encamped five kilometres from the city with 3,000 cavalrymen in his unit; 3,000 infantry soldiers had arrived on ships, as well as one more dragoon regiment from Riga. They also reported the names of the commanders and the strength of the regiments. It was known about the King that he was located in Krakow.[79]

12 July
That morning, Menshikov rode off to Petersburg since it had become known about an attack on the city by the troops of Swedish Lieutenant General Georg Johan Maidel and the appearance of a hostile fleet in the Gulf of Finland that was approaching Fort Kronschlot and the mouth of the Neva River. Around midday, a drunken dragoon of the Narva garrison ran across into the Russian trenches.[80]

At the proposal of King Augustus' general-adjutant Colonel Arnstedt in the camp near Narva, a manifest was proclaimed about taking the residents of Livonia under defence. Sources mention it was signed at Narva on 3 or 12 July, and in Dorpat on 30 August. The document maintained that the Livonian principality had been conquered by Tsar Peter on behalf of the Polish king; all of Livonia's social classes were guaranteed security from the Tsarist troops under the condition that the residents would not rise up against the Russians or spy in favour of the Swedes. It was announced that the generals had been ordered to spare the city, not to destroy it with bombardment, and "to avert any other destruction from the aforesaid, unless the aforementioned people offer stubborn resistance" – in that case, they would be "considered as enemies and no home or person would be shown mercy." To distribute the manifest, all of the generals were directed to issue the residents safety passes, or *salvoguardia*, and the text of the manifest should be read out in every company each week and be circulated among the population in printed form in the French, German and Latin languages.[81]

Meanwhile: the Election of the New Polish King

News was reporting: "The Confederates of Great Poland have elected the Poznan *wojewoda* as Polish king."[82] The Saxon Elector Friedrich Augustus was elected by the Polish Senate to the post of the King of Poland and Grand Duke of Lithuania with the support of Vienna and Moscow in 1697. It was Saxony that had become an ally of Russia against Sweden. With the start of the Northern War, Saxon troops twice unsuccessfully approached Riga in

79   Volynsky, Book 3, p. 87.
80   *Pokhodnyi zhurnal 1704 goda*, pp. 59-60.
81   "Universalia, So Ihre Czaarische Majestät in dem Hertzogthum Lieff-Land publiciren lassen. Gegeben in Unserem Feld-Lager vor Narva, den 3. Julii 1704"; PiB, Vol. 3, pp. 149–152, 681–682; *Leben und Thaten des Czaars Petri Alexiewicz*, Vol. 2, pp. 326–334.
82   *Vedomosti – Moskva (Pechatnyi dvor)*, 22 August 1704.

Election of a King of Poland in 1697 at an election field in the village of Woła outside of Warsaw.
The Russian courtier Petr Tolstoi, who travelled across Poland in 1697, characterized the custom of electing a king that was unusual for Russia in the following way: "For the election, a bridge was laid across boats on the Vistula River, and a guard detail was standing on that same bridge, because during the election many arguments and quarrels and scuffles take place among the Poles, as well as among the Lithuanians, and many fights and killings occur between the Poles and Lithuanians; most often they fight on the bridge because of the quarrels and drunkenness; and they always have little agreement between them, which is why they are losing much of their state. However, when they get drunk they do not grieve or mourn about it, even if they all might die". Other countries were using available means in order to influence the outcome of the elections. In 1697 France used money, Russia – with money and by bringing forces up to the border. In 1704, Sweden used troops directly on Polish territory. (Unknown artist, 1700, Anne S.K. Brown Military Collection)

1700 and 1701 and were defeated by the Swedes in the battles of Düna in 1701, at Kliszów in 1702, and at Pultusk in 1703. Simultaneously a portion of the Saxon regiments as part of the Imperialist forces took part in the War of Spanish Succession. In the Polish–Lithuanian Commonwealth, opposition to King Augustus began to increase – in the Grand Duchy of Lithuania, the Sapiehas, an influential line of magnates, was heading it, while in Poland, the Cardinal-Primate Radzievsky became its leader. Having entered into relations with Charles XII, this group of nobles in February 1704 formed the so-called Warsaw Confederation that was aligned with Sweden and announced the overthrow of King Augustus II. With Swedish military and financial help, on 10 July it declared the least influential candidate, the military governor of Poznan Stanisław Leszczyński, as the new king. Supported by Russia, Augustus' supporters at the Sejm in Sandomir declared their opponents' decision illegal, and two rival kings appeared in Poland. As a result, simultaneously with the Northern War between the Swedes, Russians and Saxons that raged on the territory of the Reczpospolita, a devastating and wasteful civil war went on between the opposing noble parties. In addition to this, there was still the threat of the Crimean Khanate's and Turkey's entry into the war against Russia, and the pro-Swedish Poles were inciting them to join it.[83]

13 July

The besiegers continued to work persistently on the Ivangorod side of the Narova River. They set up a battery with 12 embrasures to the right of the road to Lillienbacka, across the river opposite the Victoria and Sandwall bastions. Several Swedish cavalrymen on the Ivangorod side managed to drive away six head of sheep and nine horses from the enemy.[84]

Ogilvy at the request of Menshikov sent to him a select company of Novgorod nobles and Gorbov's dragoons for the defence of Petersburg and ordered them to hurry while leaving the supply train in Jamburg; he added that he could not send more men, since he had to keep watch over Schlippenbach. The day before, Ogilvy had personally ridden out to inspect the work on Rönne's fortified line, and now reported to Menshikov that the line would have been half-ready now if he had possessed the necessary quantity of "pioneers" for the earthworks. The field marshal as well complained that "on Apraxin's side everything was going very lethargically, because General Bruce has told me that he has an order not to unload his goods from the ships", about which neither Menshikov, nor Golovin, nor the Tsar himself had informed him.[85]

Meanwhile: the Capture of Dorpat

The siege of Dorpat by Sheremetev's forces was continuing in the presence of Tsar Peter himself. Artillery positioned in three places began to make breaches and was placing a heavy bombardment on the city, and on the evening of 12 July it was decided to take the counterscarp and to dig in on the palisades. This limited objective did not presume a general assault; from the occupied positions it would be convenient in the future to break through the walls and go on the assault. Having arrived at Dorpat, the Tsar ordered the dispatch of three companies to the point of attack, and after launching it, to send groups of 100 men to support the attack as reinforcements; a battery salvo would serve as the signal for each new batch of 100 men to move up to the point of combat. The forces for the attack were concentrated on both sides of the Emajõgi River, and they were to lay a pontoon bridge after the action started

83   See Koroliuk, V.D., "Vstuplenie Rechi Pospolita v Severnoi voiny" ["Entry of the Reczpospolita in the Northern War"], from *Uchenye zapiski Instituta slavianovedeniia* [Academic papers of the Institute of Slavic Studies], Vol. 10 (1954), pp. 239–347; Vozgrin, V.E., *Rossiia i evropeiskie strany v gody Severnoi voiny: Istoriia diplomaticheskikh otnoshenii v 1697-1710* [*Russian and the European countries in the years of the Northern War: A history of diplomatic relations in 1697–1710*] (Leningrad, 1986), pp. 118–136.

84   Adlerfeld, Vol. 2, p. 15.

85   Volynsky, Book 3, p. 303; NIA SPbII RAN, F. 83, Op. 1, D. 305, l. 2; extract from Ogilvy's letter dated 13 July 1704 as published in Volynsky, Book 3, p. 100.

Depiction of the bombardment and capture of Dorpat by the Muscovites. A fragment. A schematic image, likely done by a participant and eyewitness of the events, is very clear in such details as the density and direction of the artillery fire, the configuration of the town's fortifications, and the crowding of the troops in the assault sector. (Artist unknown; Sweden, 1705, Krigsarkivet, Sveriges Krig)

in order to get the men across from the opposite bank. Every regiment was to detach two hundred men for the attack and every man was to carry a fascine in front of him.[86]

Around 7:00 in the evening, the three composite companies comprised of the soldiers of various regiments, led by a lieutenant colonel, were the first to enter combat; under the fire of the defenders, they were able to make one passage in the palisade. The Swedish soldiers that were defending the counterscarp were returning fire from behind the palisade; they exhausted their ammunition, but received reinforcements from the fortress and threw back the forward Russian troops. Then at the signals of the battery salvoes, the new commands set out in addition to the attackers; both sides were successively augmenting their forces; in the second hour after nightfall under the cover of a battery on the left bank, the Russians laid down the pontoon bridge, and several more regiments arrived from the opposite bank to aid the attack.[87] Fierce combat continued all night with musket fire, grenades and the fire of the artillery of the fortress; due to the prolonged fire, the defenders had to cool their overheated musket barrels with wet sludge from the canals. The units and reinforcements were massing in a relatively narrow sector, which possibly resulted in a genuine logjam of men: "His Majesty the Tsar himself approached the breach with such a cramped passage that was not

---

86   Sheremetev's military campaign journal 1701–1705, p. 157; *Book of Mars*, p. 26; PiB, Vol. 3, p. 167; Von Huyssen, p. 420.

87   Sheremetev's campaign journal 1701–1705, pp. 157–158.

Russian troops storming the gates of Dorpat.
The etching depicts the moment on the morning of 13 July, when after the struggle that lasted throughout the night for the palisade and ravelin, the Russian units approached the gates. Once again, the Russian infantry is depicted wearing the fur boyar hats; this stereotypical image of the "Muscovites" remained typical for Europeans, even though it no longer conformed to reality. (Artist unknown; Germany, 1710 [Neu-eröffneter Historischer Bilder-Saal, Vol. 6 1700-1704, Nuremberg, 1710)

only congested from the fire, but also difficult to make one's way through all the corpses."[88] By sunrise, the defenders' resistance on the counterscarp was broken. Even though according to the original plan the men should dig in on the captured position, the extended night-time combat at the palisade did not allow the Russians to dig in before daybreak; near sunrise, in the very heat of battle, the decision was made to develop the attack. Soon the Russian troops assaulted and took the ravelin that protected the tower at the Russian Gates. The pursuers caught up with the fleeing Swedish defenders of the palisade and ravelin and slaughtered them in front of the gates, which the commandant had ordered to be bolted shut. Five cast iron cannons on the ravelin were captured, turned around, and began to fire at the gates. Having smashed the outer gates in this fashion, the Russian soldiers and *streltsy* broke into the gate's tower; the inner gates remained the final obstacle on the path into the city, and axes and grenades went into action.

The Swedes in desperation hauled up a large cannon along the streets and began firing case shot, which did not so much kill the assaulting Russians as it did smash the gates themselves. Quickly it became clear to the commandant that this final obstacle would soon fall and the enemy soldiers, inflamed by the assault, would break into the city. Not wishing to bring matters to the point of an inevitable massacre, Skytte entered into surrender negotiations. The fighting subsided, though it cost the Russian and Swedish officers a lot of effort to calm down their enraged soldiers. Thus, the fighting for the palisade that started at 7:00 in the evening spontaneously snowballed into a general assault and concluded by 1:00 in the afternoon the next day with the capture of the fortress. Tsar Peter I reported to his close associates that the "ancestral city" had fallen. He meant that Iuriev Livonsky (the old

---

88   Volynsky, Book 3, p. 385.

Combat for a palisade. The etching is devoted to the French attack against a fortified line of the Allies in 1703, but this image of concentrated fire over the sharpened timbers of the palisade completely resembles the events at Dorpat as well. (Artist unknown; Germany, 1710, *Neu-eröffneter Historischer Bilder-Saal*, Vol. 6, 1700-1704, Nuremberg, 1710)

Russian name for Dorpat) had been founded on the land of the Estonians by the Russian Prince Iaroslav Mudryi back in the 1030s.[89]

14 July

That night the Russians linked up their two trenches before the glacis of the King's Gates' ravelin. Neither the fierce artillery fire from the ramparts nor the musket fire from the counterscarp could prevent them from making a lodgment at the counterscarp. From the direction of Katterumpan, they extended the trench and strengthened it with gabions. On this day, they observed from the fortress a lot of Russian troops in various places.[90]

Ogilvy wrote to Menshikov, who had returned from Petersburg, about the needs of his siege corps at Narva and asked that he gather everything necessary while en route. There were not enough wool sacks (just 300 were found with the artillery, while 4,000 were necessary), "pioneers" and ship anchors for building a pontoon bridge. The field marshal was concerned that Maidel might possibly withdraw from Petersburg in order to link up with Schlippenbach and send a relief force to Narva. Therefore Ogilvy was troubled about the readiness of the troops for battle; in particular, he wanted to attach regimental artillery to the infantry, two cannons for each battalion – "in a similar fashion as the Swedes".[91] In a different letter the commander demanded another 10 24-pound cannons with 8,000 cannonballs, 10,000 woolsacks and 100,000 sandbags, 4,000 picks, 8,000 axes, and two wagons for each battalion in order to transport fascines and gabions; without these supplies, it would be senseless to start making a breach and to approach it without cover. He also required 900 or 1,000 "light cavalry", in order to carry

---

89   PiB, Vol. 3, pp. 167–168; Adlerfeld, Vol. 1, p. 335; Sheremetev's military campaign journal of 1701–1705, pp. 157–159, 166; Von Huyssen, pp. 420-422; Laidre, pp. 144–147.
90   Adlerfeld, Vol. 2, p. 15.
91   Volynsky, Book 3, p. 474.

out distant reconnaissance and in the process "preserve the dragoons until the main battle".[92]

Why the Woolsacks?

Canvas sacks filled with wool were considered a comparatively light and reliable protection against bullets and were used in those same intentions as sandbags. Despite the fact that the classic military engineer of the period Vauban does not mention them, woolsacks enjoyed popularity among German engineers. In the Russian army sacks of two types were manufactured. The most common sacks had a size of 0.9 to 1.5 metres in length and 0.3 to 0.6 metres in width ("… of such size that a soldier could carry them in front and, closing on a fortress, protect themselves against the effects of enemy shots"). Large sacks that were 8 metres long and 2 metres in diameter and weighed 50 kilograms "… a besieger rolled along in front of himself; in case there was not enough soil, they could protect themselves with them on the counterscarp and in the ditch"; it was also possible to erect a battery's breastwork from them. In order to make the sacks they used sheep's wool, or even cheaper cow's hair. Judging from illustrations, the large sacks were corded for convenience, while the small sacks could be attached to a wooden framework.[93]

A soldier behind a wool sack. (Artist unknown, the Netherlands, 1926 – a copy of a picture from 1702 Collection Legermuseum, Soesterberg)

15 July

Menshikov returned to Narva since the Swedish attack against Petersburg had been driven back. That night the besiegers continued to build a battery of large gabions on the Ivangorod side and added another eight embrasures to the previous 12. That night they brought a large number of fascines to Katterumpan, where they began to build another grand battery. On this same day the Russians began to harass the Swedes that were working on the Victoria Bastion, giving musket volleys across the river. With each passing day they brought their approaches ever

The breastwork of an artillery battery made out of large wool sacks. (Wilhelm Dilich 1571-1650, 17th century, W. Dilichii, *Kriegsbuch*, Frankfurt am Main, 1689)

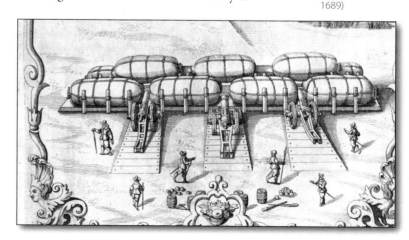

---

92   NIA SPbII RAN, F. 83, Op. 1, D. 291, ll. 1–2 obr.
93   Arkhiv VIMAIViVS, F. 2, Op. 1, D. 1, l. 297; Fäsch, J.R., *Kriegs- Igenieur- und Artillerie Lexikon* (Nürnberg, 1726), p. 270; PiB, Vol. 1, p. 877; Vol. 8, Part 1, p. 382; Vol. 9, p. 119; Laskovsky, p. 98.

closer to the sector of the counterscarp between the Gloria, Honour and Victoria bastions.[94]

Meanwhile: the Attack Against Saint Petersburg and Kronschlot

While the Tsar's main forces were busy at Narva and Dorpat, the Swedish command decided to conduct a diversionary operation towards the new city at the mouth of the Neva River; Lieutenant General Maidel's corps attacked from the direction of Vyborg, while Vice Admiral De Prou's naval squadron was supposed to enter the Neva. However, already by May 1704 the Russians had constructed three batteries and two forts on the Kotlin (Retusaari) Island for the defence of the Neva estuary from the sea, and on a nearby sandbar with a navigational channel – the wooden, two-level Kronschlot Fort. In June De Prou first discovered the Russian fortifications on the island but could do nothing because of the heavy fire from the coastal batteries and Russian ships. The following month the attempt was repeated in cooperation with a land army.

Having embarked up to 800 soldiers from Maidel's corps, De Prou arrived at Kotlin from the Berezovye (Björko) Islands on 7 July. There he ascertained that his ships could not bypass the island from the north because of the shallow depths. On the morning of 10 July his squadron approached the southern navigation channel and detected the Russians' strongly fortified positions on the island, Fort Kronschlot and a multitude of galleys standing under its protection. De Prou opted not to try to break through such a defence and in the course of 11 and 12 July he unsuccessfully bombarded the Russians and withdrew to Vammelsuu (contemporary Serovo), where they disembarked Maidel's troops and sailed on further to Björko. Such is the picture of the events gleaned from the letters of the Vice Admiral himself. Adlerfeld talks about a successful landing made by Lieutenant Colonel Rose and Major Lejon, who put everyone on the island to the sword; the Russian campaign journal of 1704 on its part reports about the repulse of a Swedish landing by Colonel Timofei Treiden's infantry. Other sources are silent about the Swedes' attempted landing.[95]

At the same time Lieutenant General Maidel was attacking Saint Petersburg from the north, out of Vyborg. Crossing the Sestra River and having stopped at Valkeasaari (contemporary Beloostrov), the Swedes were attacked by a Russian reconnaissance. The Obercommandant of Saint Petersburg Colonel Roman Vilimirovich Bruce had sent out along the Vyborg road Colonels Bakhmetev, Zazharsky and Temnik with 2,000 irregular horse (Astrakhan horse *streltsy*, Tatars, and the Urals and Zaporozhian Cossacks) as well as Major Peter Bolkhovsky's 200 infantrymen mounted on Cossack horses (the Swedes referred to them as mounted grenadiers, so possibly

---

94   Pokhodnyi zhurnal 1704 goda, p. 60; Adlerfeld, Vol. 2, p. 15; Archiv., p. 261.
95   *Pokhodnyi zhurnal 1704 goda*, pp. 62-63, 144-145; Adlerfeld, Vol. 1, p. 330; Tatarnikov (ed.), *Ofitserskie skazki*, Vol. 1, p. 1032, 1282; Vol. 2, p. 1906, 1916, 2023, 2025, 2138; *Illustrerad Svensk sjokrigshistoria intill 1814*, Vol. 2 (1923), p. 42; Rosen, pp. 198–201.

The fort of Kronschlot.
The Swedish Vice Admiral de Prou made a sketch of the just built Russian fort (which literally rose from the water over one winter) from aboard a ship of his squadron on 20 July 1704. The pilings embedded in the water, the red flag with the Cross of St. Andrew in a crest (the flag of the galley fleet, or the Third Admiral), and the little figures of the garrison's soldiers are noteworthy and demonstrate the scale of the construction. Thus, this drawing on the margins of a letter is the very first depiction of Kronschlot, preceding even that of Picart's well-known etching, where a tent roof rises above the tower, and on it a flagstaff and flag. The author expresses his gratitude to the archivist Håkan Henriksson, who discovered this letter and kindly offered it for publication. A copy of this drawing was sent by Maidel to Stockholm on 21 July 1704, and it was published in 2014 by Tatiana Bazarova in her book *Sozdaniie "Paradiza" (Creation of Paradise)* on page 82. (Jacob de Prou 1651-1711, 1704 Krigsarkivet, Amiralitetskollegium, kansliet, E IIc: 28)

these were grenadier companies of the regiments of the Petersburg garrison). On 10 July, the scouting party ran into the Swedish vanguard about eight kilometres from the Sestra River and took prisoners; however, later they unexpectedly stumbled upon Maidel's main forces. The Swedes, attacked in their camp during morning prayers, repulsed the attack and set out in pursuit with cavalry, infantry and artillery. The Russian mounted troops fell back to Saint-Petersburg, suffering losses, and in part scattered through the woods; during the flight, the 12 Swedish prisoners captured earlier were slaughtered. In the course of the pursuit Maidel's troops seized "fine horses, a dragoon banner, pistols, lances, sabres and bows" and reached the Neva River on the Vyborg side. Here the Lieutenant General had a relatively harmless exchange of fire across the Bolshaia Nevka River with Bruce's batteries on Berezovy Island (modern day Petersburg side of the city), shelled a wharf on the southern bank of the Neva (at the contemporary Liteinyi Bridge) and set fire to several buildings. Maidel did not have enough strength and floating crafts for an attack against Nyenschantz or the Saint-Petersburg fortress – the absence of De Prou's ships, which had not been able to break through past Kronschlot and enter the Neva, was telling. The diversion was unsuccessful, and the Swedes fell back across the Sestra River.[96]

---

96 *Pokhodnyi zhurnal 1704 goda*, pp. 60–63; Nordberg, Vol. 1, p. 528; Adlerfeld, Vol. 1, pp. 329–330; Rosen, pp. 198–201.

The attack of Maidel's corps at Valkesaari on 10 July 1704. (Aleksei Vladimirovich Temnikov, Vladimir, 2016)

16 July

The Russians continued to work on the batteries and set up one of their mortars on the Segelberg hill. On this same day, a great body of horse arrived at the siege camp from the direction of Livonia. It was Tsar Peter returning after the capture of Dorpat with trophies – 23 Swedish flags.[97]

17 July

A Swedish reiter ran across from Narva into an approach trench. Under interrogation, he said that he had left because of hunger – instead of bread, malt was being given out to the garrison per month.[98]

18 July

That night the Swedes heard two distinct musket discharges, followed by brisk musket and cannon fire from the Livonian side. At midday the besiegers opened a salute of a triple discharge from all the artillery (the Swedes counted 103 guns of various calibres), and all the infantry regiments line up and fired a volley – with this display, the Russian troops were celebrating the capture of Dorpat. In the camp, they conducted a worship service with the singing of the prayer *Te Deum*, while in the forward approach trenches that were just 60 metres short of the Narva moat, they put captured Dorpat flags on display – in this way, they were demonstrating the success of the Russian arms to the besieged garrison.

Several pieces of ordnance were brought to the camp, and the Russians placed a large quantity of gabions on their two lines, which they had drawn around the Ivangorod castle. They also worked on their new batteries. On this same time, they fired at the Swedish fortifications on the Ivangorod bank

---

97   *Pokhodnyi zhurnal 1704 goda*, p. 63; Adlerfeld, Vol. 2, pp. 15–16.
98   *Pokhodnyi zhurnal 1704 goda*, p. 71.

The northern side of the Town Hall square. The Old Town of Narva was famous for its stone carved portals in the style of Barocco on the homes of the wealthy citizens. (Otto Kletzl, 1897-1945 and Richard Hamman-MacLean 1908-2000, Estonia, 1940-1941, Bildarchiv Foto Marbug)

for the last time (subsequently, all the fire was concentrated on Narva).[99]

The Tsar sent a letter off to the commandant of Pskov, Kirill Naryshkin, with an endorsement of Menshikov's request to send 2,000 workers to Narva (those very same "pioneers" that Ogilvy had previously requested). Naryshkin sent the needed number of people off to Narva in several parties between 23 July and 8 August. En route, 105 ran away, but new men were sent to replace them.[100]

19 July

Tsar Peter ordered Sheremetev to dispatch all of his infantry (except for two regiments of *streltsy*) from Dorpat to Narva, as well as mortars, the 18-pound cannons and their ammunition, the regimental cannons and their crews. Sheremetev himself with all of his horse regiments were directed to head towards Rakvere and to link up with von Rönne.[101]

The peasants gathered for digging earthworks were called in the French "pioniere". (Romeyn de Hooghe 1645-1708, France, 1672. A. Mallet Manesson, *Les Travaux De Mars Ou L'art De La Guerre*, Vol. 3 La Haye, 1696)

99   *Pokhodnyi zhurnal 1704 goda*, p. 71; Adlerfeld, Vol. 2, p. 16.
100 PiB, Vol. 3, pp. 102, 646–647.
101 *Ibid.*, pp. 102-103, 646–647.

20 July

The besiegers began work on a new trench towards the hill of Garafemsberg (or Garasemsberg), so that they could command the whole valley around the Ivangorod castle.[102] That evening (at 8:00 according to the Swedish journal and at 6:00 according to the Russian campaign diary), a bright meteor (bolide) appeared in the sky and streaked from the south-east to the north-west. Its appearance was accompanied by unusual sound and visual effects, which lasted for several hours. In the camp talk went around about what sort of events this portent was presaging.[103]

A celestial spectacle from the album *Kometenbuch* (*Book of comets*).
(Artist unknown, Flanders, 1587 Universitätsbibliothek Kassel)

Ogilvy during his time of command at Narva repeatedly observed how certain officers and men in the field, in the trenches, at work and on assignments did not show their superiors the proper obedience and did not fully complete the jobs they had been given. Now an order went out through the army with a demand to obey seniors in rank under the threat of death. It was read out aloud throughout the entire camp accompanied by a drumroll, so that no one could any longer offer excuses due to ignorance.[104]

Sheremetev reported to F.A. Golovin that Colonel Rodion Bauer with his dragoons had raided towards Pernau and Reval and had captured talking prisoners, who had heard nothing about a Swedish relief force for Narva.[105] Tsar Peter repeated the order to Sheremetev to dispatch the 18-pound cannons, mortars, ammunition and infantry, which were in "great need" around Narva.[106]

21 July

In his next letter to Sheremetev, the Tsar ordered a third of the surrendered Dorpat garrison to be released to Riga, and with the remaining Swedes to head to Narva as soon as possible.[107]

22 July

At the Honour Bastion, the Swedish Captain Heinrich Johan Drentel was killed on the rampart by a bullet to the head.[108] The Russians were now carrying on their works in open daylight, paying no regard to the losses.[109]

---

102 Garafemsberg, as mentioned by Adlerfeld, is apparently the nearest sector of the elevated bank of the Narova River to the north of Ivangorod.
103 *Pokhodnyi zhurnal 1704 goda*, p. 72; Adlerfeld, Vol. 2, p. 16; Von Huyssen, p. 433.
104 Volynsky, Book 3, pp. 100-101; Ustrialov, Vol. 4, Part 2, p. 315.
105 PiB, Vol. 3, p. 648.
106 *Ibid.*, pp. 102, 646–647.
107 *Ibid.*, p. 111.
108 Materialen zu einer liefländischen Adelsgeschichte (Riga, 1788), p. 699.
109 Adlerfeld, Vol. 2, p. 16; Archiv., p. 264.

What was Trench Guard Duty?

In order to defend the men labouring in the trenches against sorties of the garrison, soldiers were called upon, who were posted in the already prepared sector of the approaches. By an order of 20 July, 47 soldiers from each of the 36 battalions were designated for guard duty; on 22 July, 50 soldiers from each of 30 battalions were assigned to guard duty. Frequently, nothing at all is said about the guards in the orders, and the personnel duty rosters of the preceding days were used. According to Vauban, an infantry guard detail located in the trenches should be equivalent in number to three quarters of the fortress garrison and should be rotated so that each man was free from guard duty for five or six days. The watch duty was round the clock; according to the order from 11 July, the guards in the camp of the besieging army were to be replaced at 12:00, whereas the trench guards were to rotate at 6:00 in the evening – it was around this time that Dmitry Karpov was killed. Before a shift change, it was recommended to send guides to the assembly point, so that they could lead the fresh detail along the lengthy and often maze-like approach trenches. As soon as the old guard shift left, the soldiers of the new shift would take a seat on the banquette with their back to the breastwork and place their musket between their knees; sentries often remained standing on the banquette and kept watch on the city – they were supposed to give the alarm about any attempts by the enemy to interfere with the works.[110]

23 July

That evening during a shift of the guard details, Lieutenant Colonel Dmitrii Kuzmich Karpov of the Preobrazhensky Life Guards was killed by a musket shot from the Victoria Bastion in the outermost approach. An officer of "superb qualities" and a hero of the storming of Nöteborg, Karpov's death was met by great regret in the entire army. At the order of the Tsar, his body was transported to Saint Petersburg and buried with deserving honours.[111]

Tsar Peter was again prodding Sheremetev day and night to move out of Dorpat together with his cavalry and infantry to link up with von Rönne; the Field Marshal was to reach the indicated point of contact by Wednesday, 26 July, or else he could face the consequences.[112]

Meanwhile: the Capture of Gibraltar

News was reporting: "An allied fleet has taken the fortress and suitable harbour of Gibraltar, where there is an exit from the Atlantic Ocean into the Mediterranean Sea."[113] In the course of the War of the Spanish Succession,

110 RGVIA, F. 2584, Op. 1, D. 6, ll., 1, 2, 4, 7; Vauban, pp. 28, 34, 119; Bland, pp. 269, 270.
111 *Pokhodnyi zhurnal 1704 goda*, p. 72; Von Huyssen, p. 434; Bazarov, *Sozdaniie "Paradiza"*, Appendix 11, p. 362.
112 PiB, Vol. 3, p. 112.
113 *Vedomosti – Moskva (Pechatnyi dvor)*, 5 October 1704.

A shot from a fusil and a military burial ceremony. See page 131. (Etcher unknown; Saxony, 1726, Hans Friedrich von Fleming, *Der Vollkommene Teutsche Soldat*, Leipzig, 1726)

the allies captured a key point on the northern shore of the strait between the Mediterranean Sea and the Atlantic Ocean. A total of 147 soldiers, 250 militia men and 150 cannons were defending the powerful fortifications of the Spanish town on the rock. Admiral George Rooke had 45 English and 10 Dutch ships of the line under his command. After a bombardment on 23 July, in the course of which more than 1,400 shells were fired on the town in a period of six hours, a force made a landing. The allied infantry took one bastion and the monastery, where women of the town were taking cover. They demanded the fortress commandant to surrender, threatening to kill all the residents, beginning with those they had captured in the cloister. The behaviour of the Englishmen during the attack against Cadiz in 1702 made this threat plausible. The Spanish governor Diego de Salinas (Diego Esteban Gómez de Salins y Rodríguez de Villarroel) was compelled to surrender, and the garrison received the right of an honourable withdrawal with their colours and drumming. The attempts by the Spanish and the French that followed later to regain control of the fortress failed. With the Utrecht Treaty of 1713, Gibraltar was enshrined for Great Britain, and has remained its overseas territory to the present day.

The French fleet tried to win back Gibraltar, and the two naval squadrons met on 13 August 1704 not far from Málaga. In this largest naval battle of the entire War of the Spanish Succession, more than 100 ships took part on both sides and the fighting lasted for the entire day. However, neither side obtained a decisive advantage, and on the next day the antagonists parted ways.[114]

---

114 Makhov, S.P. and Sozaev, E.B., *Borba za ispanskoe nasledstvo* [*War of the Spanish Succession*] (Moscow, 2010), pp. 46–63.

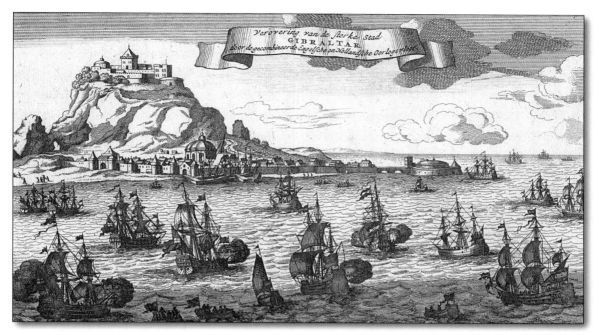

The capture of the strong fortress of Gibraltar by the combined Anglo-Dutch fleet. See page 133. (Pieter Sluyter 1675-1733, the Netherlands, 1704-1713 Collection Rijksmuseum, Amsterdam)

24 July
The Russians began to raise a new battery on the road to Lillienbacka, between the two previous batteries. They were heavily firing over the bastions with small arms and hand grenades.[115]

Who Was Lambert de Guerin?

The French engineer Joseph Gaspard Lamber de Guerin appeared in Russian service in 1701, and in 1702 together with the Tsarist court and guards, he went down the *Osudareva* road to Lake Onega. At the very start of this journey on the shores of the White Sea he killed a ship captain Peter Pamburch in a duel, but suffered no punishment for this, even though duels in Russia were banned under the penalty of death. As General-Engineer, he took part in reconnaissance missions, and then in the siege of Nöteborg. At Nyenschantz on 26 April 1703, "at night General-Engineer Lambert with infantry under his command began to do work on approach trenches in immediate proximity to the town, more precisely 30 *sazhen*[116], which the enemy was continuously harassing with cannon fire, however without any great harm". In the same year of 1703, Lambert de Guerin became a cavalier of the Order of St. Andrew the Apostle; according to one version, he is considered to be the author of the project of the Saint Petersburg fortress.[117]

---

115   Adlerfeld, Vol. 2, p. 17; Archiv., p. 265.

116   Sazhen – an old Russian unit of measure equivalent to 7 feet, 84 inches or 2.1336 metres.

117   *Gistoriia Sveiskoi voiny (Podennaia zapiska Petra Velikogo)* [*History of the Swedish War (Daily notes of Peter the Great)*] (Moscow, 2004), 1st edn., p. 230; 2nd edn., p. 318;

"Monsieur Lambert, the Muscovite general-engineer". See previous page. (Artist unknown; the Netherlands, 1711, *Neu-eröffneter Welt- und Staats-Spiegel, Vol. 24*, The Haag, 1711)

25 July

The besiegers at Narva did little work. Meanwhile Sheremetev's freed-up regiments after the capture of Dorpat set out from there. Eight regiments were sent over land to Narva, while four regiments set out by boat. The Swedes of the Dorpat garrison – Commandant Skytte, two colonels, 50 officers and 1,269 men of other ranks – moved with the Russian troops.[118]

Meanwhile: the Siege of Selburg and the Battle of Jakobstadt

The news was passing word from Warsaw: "The Selburg Castle [modern day Sēlpils] on the Duna River has been besieged by the Muscovites, who had been in Birzai."[119] The Swedes that had marched into Lithuania were supporting the noble Sapieha family clan, with which the majority of Lithuanian nobles were enemies. Therefore, the Grand Duchy of Lithuania, although in fact a constituent part of the Reczpospolita, from 1702 held independent negotiations with Russia regarding military and financial assistance against Charles XII. In March 1703, a combined Lithuanian-Russian force was defeated by a Swedish-Lithuanian corps at Salaty (contemporary Saločiai, Lithuania). In July 1704, the forces of the Lithuanian Great Hetman Michał Serwacy Wiśniowiecki arrived at Selburg on the frontier with Courland. This castle was being held by a Swedish garrison; the Lithuanians besieged it and were intending to storm it. However, Major General Adam Ludwig Lewenhaupt and the Lithuanian magnate and Vilnius potentate Kazimir

The siege of Selburg. (Johann Lithen, 1663-1725)

A. Seelburg. B. Das Ruſſiſche Lager. C. Ihre Approſchen. D. Ihre Batterie. E. Ihre Minen. F. Dünaſtrom.

Prospect und Attaque vō Seelburg

Sharymov, A.M., *Predystoriia Sankt-Peterburga. 1703. Kniga issledovanii [Pre-history of Saint Petersburg. 1703. Book of research]* (Saint Petersburg, 2004), pp. 544–545; Dankov, M.Iu., Lapshov, S.P., "Dueliant Osudarevskoi dorogi, ili vzlet I padeniie general-inzhenera i kavalera Lambera de Gerdena" ["Duelist of the Osudareva road, or the rise and fall of General-Engineer Lambert de Guerin"], *Reiter*, No. 33 (September 2006), pp. 17–27.

118   Sheremetev's field campaign diary, pp. 327–328; Volynsky, Book 3, pp. 77–78; *Severnaia voina 1700–1721*, Vol. 1, pp. 211–213.

119   *Vedomosti–Moskva* [Pechatnyi dvor], 5 September 1704.

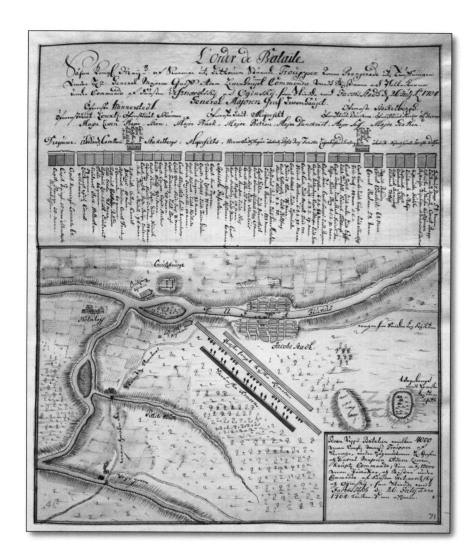

The order of battle of Lewenhaupt's corps and the plan for the battle at Jakobstadt. (Artist unknown, Library of the Russian Academy of Sciences, Department of Manuscripts)

Sapieha hastened to the relief of the besieged garrison; having learned of the threat of the relief force, Wiśniowiecki lifted the siege, abandoned the supplies (including the prepared assault ladders) and hastily retreated, linking up with a Lithuanian unit under Grigory Ogiński and a Russian corps under Major General Bogdan Semenovich Korsak. Lewenhaupt and Sapieha pursued the allies and defeated them on 25 July at the Battle of Jakobstadt (Polish Kryżbork or modern-day Latvian Jēkabpils).[120]

26 July
The besiegers began to raise yet another battery on the Ivangorod bank, a little downriver from the preceding batteries.[121]

---

120 Adlerfeld, Vol. 1, pp. 327–328; Volynsky, Book 3, pp. 77-78; *Severnaia voina 1700–1721*, Vol. 1, pp. 211–213.
121 Adlerfeld, Vol. 2, p. 17.

A battery on the Ivangorod bank. Fragment of the etching "Delineation der Stadt und Vestung Narva, samt des Schlosses Ivangorod". In the rear of the battery, Russian soldiers are dragging a log, obviously for the construction of a platform beneath the cannon. (Artist unknown, Krigsarkivet)

27 July

The Russians laid planks on platforms and armed batteries with cannons and mortars.[122]

Sheremetev meanwhile arrived at the Jõhvi church[123], eight kilometres from the line where von Rönne was standing. However, Sheremetev's dragoons and infantry were being slowed down on the way by swampy roads and poor bridges; Peter in response ordered the infantry and Swedish prisoners, when they caught up, to be sent to Narva as soon as possible.[124]

What Were Batteries and Kessels?

The placement of the siege guns and the equipping of the position for them were critically important for a successful siege. Vauban exhorted not to hurry

---

122 *Ibid.*

123 The Church of St. Michael from the 14th century in the modern-day Estonian town of Jõhvi. This is the largest single-vault Lutheran Church in Estonia.

124 PiB, Vol. 3, p. 114 (in the publication the date of 23 July is mistakenly given); Volynsky, Book 3, p. 374.

and to position the batteries at a later time than the opening of a trench, having closed to a range of effective fire (600–300 metres from the target), and having deployed them in such a way that it would not be necessary to reposition them in the course of the entire siege.[125] Vauban also mentions the possibility of setting up the cannons across a river from the fortress – the presence of an impassable obstacle ensured the security of the battery from garrison sorties.[126] If in 1700 the batteries at Narva were positioned on the Narva side of the river and were lost in the battle with the relief force, then in following years the Russian command often separated the batteries from a city or fortress with a water obstacle. In the cases of Marienburg and Nöteborg there was simply no other option – these fortresses stood on islands, encircled by water from every direction; in other cases, when the fortress also had a ground front, such a disposition of the batteries was a conscious choice: Nyenschantz was bombarded from beyond the Okhta River, Dorpat from beyond the Emajõgi River, and Narva from across the Narova River.

It was necessary to protect the guns from fire coming from the besieged, so therefore a parapet of a battery had to be able to withstand a hit. In the 17th century it was believed that four metres of well-packed earth could stop the strike of a cannon ball, while 0.3 metres of the same could stop a musket ball.[127] Vauban recommended to make a parapet that was six metres thick and at least two metres high, and to fill it with soil that was tramped down and strengthened with several lines of connected fascines that were anchored to the ground with stakes. The battery itself should present a field fortification, unassailable by an assault launched by the enemy garrison. Therefore, a ditch was dug in front of the parapet, and the excavated earth became the material for the breastwork; for this, the workers had to labour in the ditch without cover against fire from the fortress, but a battery thus turned out to be more sturdy.[128] At Narva the batteries were made from large gabions, but the other details about them are unknown; that same summer one of the batteries constructed at Dorpat was 80 metres in length, a thickness of three metres, and its breastwork had been raised to two metres; it was "pierced" with 13 embrasures, which meant one gun occupied six metres of frontage.[129]

The embrasures for the cannons were expanded upwards and to the exterior of the battery, and their walls were strengthened with fascines so that the dirt would not crumble from the discharges. When the cannon was not firing, the embrasures were blocked off from the enemy with thick fascines, gabions or special wooden doors (*portieres*). In order to protect the gunners when aiming

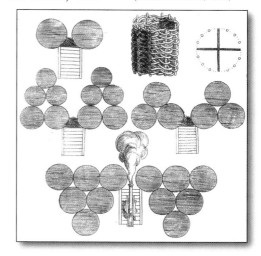

The breastwork of an artillery battery made from gabions. (Pietro Paolo Floriani, 1585-1638, *Diffesa et offesa delle piazza* Macerata, 1630)

125   Vauban, p. 58, 59.
126   Vauban, S., *Kniga o atake i oborone krepostnei* [*Book about the attack and defence of fortresses*] (Saint Petersburg, 1744), p. 64, 66, 125.
127   Montecúccoli, p. 124.
128   San Rémy, Vol. 2, p. 257.
129   Sheremetev's military campaign journal 1701–1705, p. 157.

the gun, a thick wood cover that withstood a musket ball would be placed on the barrel.[130]

A platform would be placed below each cannon no lower than ground level, so that under its own weight it would not dig itself into the ground from the discharge and recoil. The platform also made aiming easier, when the cannon stood on a level surface. According to Vauban, in order to construct the platform behind the parapet, five to six thick wooden joists would be laid out and fastened to the ground with stakes, and the space between them would be filled with densely packed earth. Then a flooring of boards that were six centimetres thick would be laid across the joists. The platform would have the shape of a trapezoid, narrowing from the rear to the front, and would have a length of up to six metres, a width of four metres at the rear, and of two metres in front. So that the cannon would roll back to the embrasure after loading, they made sure the platform had a slight slope towards the parapet.[131] It is hard to say how closely they followed these recommendations at Narva; according to an order from 21 July, each two battalions were to prepare one wooden platform with a length of 4.2 metres.

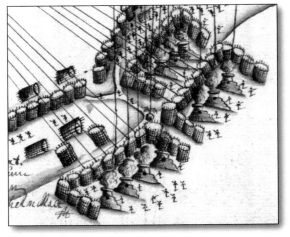

Russian batteries at Dorpat. Fragment of the drawing "Image of the bombardment and capture of Dorpat by the Muscovites". (Artist unknown, Sweden, 1705, Krigsarkivet, Sveriges Krig)

The mortar batteries in the documents of the Petrine era are most often called "kettles", "kessels" or "cauldrons" – which is the meaning of the German word "Kessel". A position for a mortar actually resembled a cavity in the ground. While the number of cannons on a battery could be determined from the outside from the number of embrasures, then it was impossible to count mortars in that way – they conducted plunging fire and the kessels did not have embrasures. According to Vauban, the distance between the mortars at a battery should be 4.5 metres. The platform beneath the mortars should be sunk 0.6 to 0.9 of a metre into the ground; in distinction from the cannon platform, it presented a quadrangle, with each side measuring 3 to 3.5 metres. They built the mortar decks in the same way – from thick wooden joists, packed earth, and boards. Around the perimeter of the mortar carriage resting on the platform was a cradle made from nailed timber, which prevented the mortar from leaping out of the kessel when discharging. Vauban advised to make pits some distance from the battery in order to store gunpowder and live bombs.[132] Since the mortar batteries did not have embrasures and the bombardiers had no direct sight of the target, an observer would head out beyond the boundaries of the battery and take up a good vantage point, while a series of aiming stakes would be set up on the crest of the parapet in order to aim the mortars at a target.[133]

---

130 Vauban, pp. 60–61.

131 *Ibid.*

132 Vauban, pp. 67–68.

133 Duffy, C. *Fire and Stone: The Science of Fortress Warfare 1660–1860* (Edison: Castle Books, 2006), p. 118.

28 July

After a lengthy break, Commandant Horn wrote King Charles XII. It is unknown how this letter reached the addressee, but it plainly described the desperate situation in the city:

> The provisions are so few, that ever since I'have impounded all the stockpiles from the burghers and all of the other classes, I have hardly been able to provide provisions, primarily oats, for the month of July. Up to now I have been able to prop up the soldiers with difficulty, but the majority of the poor people are dying from hunger, and the wealthy people now also have a shortage of food; the foe is aware of all this due to the poor people that are frequently running away, and because of this it seems that he is rather confident in his plan that he will be able to take this place only thanks to the hunger; since he for the more than three months that he has been standing here, has not fired a single shot from a heavy cannon in the direction of the city; or that he has been waiting and inactive for a long time, along with the fact that there is no news or hope for salvation, which leads to the fact that many are losing heart, so I am now doing my best to support their spirits with all my efforts."[134]

Sheremetev's infantry still had not had time to reach Narva, so the Tsar ordered the sending ahead of at least the Dorpat commandant and officers under the escort of a horse squad. On the next day Peter was intending to use these high-ranking Swedes for negotiations with Narva.[135]

Meanwhile: the Naval Battle at Orford-Ness

News was reporting: "The British have captured a Swedish escort ship, which was intending to sail to France with banned goods."[136] Off the coast of England, a curious battle occurred between two friendly forces. The Swedish captain Gustav von Psilander aboard the 50-gun ship *Öland* was escorting a convoy of cargo ships to France. On the Orford-Ness roads when encountering a British squadron of nine ships, Psilander refused to lower his flag as a gesture of greeting; the *Öland* was fired upon and returned fire. At the end of the unequal four-hour battle, the Swede had damaged three British ships, but in return had lost the majority of its crew. The *Öland* was captured and escorted to London. The two countries had friendly relations, and each had been drawn into its own war, so this incident had no serious diplomatic consequences. This incident occurred while the French were conducting a bitter privateer war in the North Atlantic against British and Dutch convoys.[137]

---

134 Rosen, p. 187.
135 PiB, Vol. 3, p. 115.
136 *Vedomosti–Moskva* (Pechatnyi dvor), 2 October 1704.
137 Anderson, R.C., *Naval wars in the Baltic during the sailing-ship epoch, 1522–1850* (London: Francis Edwards, 1910), p. 141; Illusterad Svensk sjokrigshistoria intill 1814 (1923), p. 311; Nilsson, B., "Gustaf von Psilander (1669-1738) <http://members.tripod.com/Bengt_Nilsson/

The combat between Dutch and Spanish ships. (Pierre Drevet, 1663-1738, Collection Rijksmuseum)

29 July

The besieged garrison observed as the Russians were wrapping up the construction of the batteries, but Commandant Horn under the threat of penalty forbid the opening of fire from the fortress cannons, and the Russians were continuing to work without hindrance. It had become hot; Sheremetev wrote Menshikov from the road that he had to drink water with vinegar – the potables had spoiled from the heat.[138] In general, the elderly field marshal, who was plainly irritating Tsar Peter with his sloth-like pace, often complained to the Tsar's favourite: "My health is poor, but they're transporting me in a wagon even if I am dead", as he wrote on 18 July, and on 24 July before departing from Dorpat, he reported "I will stay for a day longer because of my extreme illness, but then I will force myself to drag along. My illness is constantly nagging me badly. You will learn, my highness, that I am very ill, brother, and don't know how to pull myself together, I would be pleased to get at least a little rest."[139]

Marinhistoria/konvojer.htm> (accessed 6 August 2018); Makhov, S.P. and Sozaev, E.B., *Borba za ispanskoe nasledstvo*, pp. 104–108.

138   Archiv., p. 266; Volynsky, Book 3, p. 375.
139   NIA SPbII RAN, F. 36, Op. 1, D. 693, l. 34, 35.

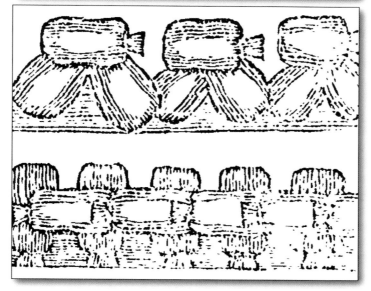

Sand bags, a breastwork and firing embrasures made from them.
Bags filled with dirt were used for a rapid construction or patching a knocked down parapet. The bags held approximately one cubic foot of soil – as much as one person could carry. Since the bags could be carried up from a distance, they were particularly useful in works on rocky ground; given the need, a fortification made with sand bags could be quickly disassembled. (Le Blond, *The military engineer* (London, 1759); Pietro Paolo Floriani, *Diffesa et offesa delle piazza* (Macerata, 1630); Feuquieres, *Memoirs historical and military* (London, 1735)

3

The Artillery Attack on the Fortress

30 July

On Sunday, a church service was held in the Russian camp, and at noon, when in the city people were leaving churches after the Sunday service, the batteries on the Ivangorod side began to bombard the city and to pound a breach in the revetment. At first, they gave a signal from three cannons, before firing a salvo from every cannon and mortar, at which point the guns continued to fire one after the other. From this moment on, the cannons fired each day during daylight hours, while the mortars fired both day and night. According to Adlerfeld:

> … the besiegers began for the first time to batter the bastion *Victoria*, with forty-six heavy cannons, which they fired all at once. At the same time, they bombarded the town with fifteen mortars which they had placed on the *Bleeksberg*. They had three heavy Cannon near *Garasemberg* hill; fourteen guns on a battery adjoining to the bridge of communication between the town and the castle; nine on the battery at *Onnekulla*;[1] twenty on the hill called *Postmeisterberg*,[2] behind which they placed two mortars, two others behind that of Garasim [evidently the Garasemberg hill], and two others near Onnekylla; besides which there were two other batteries with four mortars each, and four mortars near the bridge of boats.[3]

---

1   Onnekyla is a village on the Ivangorod bank to the north-east of the Honour Bastion.

2   Postmeisterberg is not marked on the maps; judging from the context of mentions, this was an elevated sector of the Ivangorod bank of the Narova River. According to the siege map of 1704, the batteries were positioned on the edge of a precipice, approximately along contemporary Nadezhdinskaia Street in Ivangorod.

3   Adlerfeld, Vol. 2, p. 17.

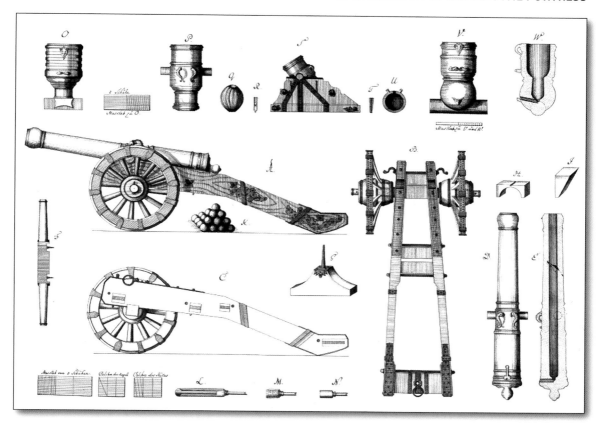

Mortars and an 18-pound cannon with a gun carriage. (Captain Bödicker; Germany, 1791 Hessisches Staatsarchiv Marburg)

In the city a fire began, and from the approach trenches the besiegers watched as people were being thrown into the air from the bomb explosions, and "similar discomfiture" was noticeable.[4]

At the same time the Russians began to lay a gallery to a face of Honour Bastion in order to make a breach by attaching a mine. They created a covered corridor across the dry moat to the wall, through which the miners could lay powder charges at the base of the revetment and blow it up; over the years of the war, this was the first attempt of such a type. Judging from etchings of the siege, the Honour Bastion was fired at by breaching cannons too, but apparently, this came later.[5]

In the afternoon, infantry regiments under the command of Major General Nikolai Grigorievich von Verden arrived aboard ships from Dorpat to join the besiegers; they set up a separate camp above and along the river at the so-called Pskov jetty and conducted "blind entrenchments", which is to say, a false attack. Sheremetev and his cavalry took position on the Pühajõgi River, 40 km from Narva, in order to block the way to a probable relief force.

4   Von Huyssen, p. 434.
5   *Pokhodnyi zhurnal 1704 goda*, pp. 117–118.

What Was Siege Artillery?

The delivery of siege artillery to the location of the siege was one of the most complex and lengthy logistical tasks for the armies of that period. In 1704 the matter was complicated by the fact that initially a campaign towards Kexholm was planned and the artillery was loaded upon ships for shipment to Lake Ladoga; the Russians started their transfer to the siege camp at Narva only after the siege began.

According to the Artillery Administration, a total of 100 guns were assembled at Narva, including 66 cannons, 33 mortars and one howitzer.[6] See Table 1:

Table 1: The quantity, type of gun, caliber, weight of the gun and carriage, rounds supplied and rounds fired by the Russians at Narva

Number	Type or gun; caliber; weight of gun and carriage	Rounds supplied	Rounds fired
19	24-pound gun; 153 mm; 6880-7153 kg	7,748 cannonballs	6,098
22	18-pound gun; 136 mm; 5569 kg	7,634 cannonballs	5,514
13	12-pound gun; 124 mm; 3276 kg	4,300 cannonballs	376
12	3-pound gun, regimental; 76.2 mm	1,560 cannonballs 569 case shot	370 275
1	1-pood howitzer; 214 mm; 2621 kg	120 bombs	15
2	9-pood mortar; 386 mm; 6,749 kg	900 bombs	648
24	3-pood mortar; 327 mm; 2,261 kg	6,440 bombs	5,051
7	6-pound light mortar; 95 mm	1,569 grenades	169

This list of the artillery supplies likely does not include the regimental 3-pound cannons of the infantry units (for example, in Sheremetev's troops there were two 3-pounders for each regiment), or the cannons taken by Apraxin from Jamburg in order to blockade from the sea at the beginning of the campaign. In addition, the document from the Artillery Administration also most likely does not show the seven 12-pound and five 8-pound cannons that were delivered from Pskov, judging from Shchepotev's letter to the Tsar on 20 June.[7]

---

6   The composition and quantity of guns, supplies and the expenditure of rounds are given according to: Arkhiv VIMIAIViVS, F. 2, Op. 1, D. 4, ll. 133-137 obr. (The list as of 10 August 1704 of the artillery that brought along on the campaign, and that of the artillery shells available and expended after the capture of Narva). The gun calibres were taken from OR BAN. PIB No. 160, l. 50 [The album of sketches of the cannons and mortars]. The weight of the guns and carriages taken as they were loaded onto the ships is taken from Arkhiv VIMIAIViVS, F. 2, Op. 1, D. 1, ll. 295–303 (11 to 18 May 1704: List of artillery supplies that were issued and the artillery supplies that were loaded on each separate ship).
7   NIA SPbII RAN, F. 270, Op. 1, D. 41, l. 58; the passage about the arriving cannons was published by Azanchevky in Istoriia Preobrazhenskogo polka [History of the Preobrazhensky Regiment] (Moscow, 1859), Appendix, p. 45 and erroneously included Shchepotev's letter from 10 May in the text.

1 The battle between Petr Matveevich Apraxin's battery and the Swedish ships in the Narova estuary on 28 April 1704. Andrei Anatol'evich Tron'; Saint Petersburg, 2016.

i

2 The defeat of the Swedish flotilla by von Werden's regiments in the mouth of the Emajõgi River, 3 May 1704. Andrei Anatol'evich Tron'; Saint Petersburg, 2016.

3 The capture of Lieutenant Colonel Marquard. Valentin Vadimovich Taratorin; Smolensk, 2015.

4 Battle of Narva 19 November 1700 Alexander von Kotzebue (1815–1889); Russia, 1846, Artillery Museum (VIMAIViVS), Saint-Petersburg.

5 The defense of the moat and covered way of the Narva fortress. Valentin Vadimovich Taratorin; Smolensk, 2015.

6 The Battle of Narva 19 November 1700. Nikolai Valentinovich
Zubkov; Saint Petersburg, 2014-2016.

7 The Russian trench works at Narva. Andrei Karashchuk; Moscow, 2015

8 The fighting in the dark for the Dorpat palisade. Maksim Vladimirovich Borisov; Moscow, 2015.

9 The breaching battery on the Ivangorod bank of the Narova River. Maksim Vladimirovich Borisov; Moscow, 2016.

10 The Swedish artillery Colonel Johann Kinnert at the Honor Bastion a moment before Russian bullet will hit his head. Sergei Igorevich Shamenkov; Odessa, 2015.

11 The storming of the Honor Bastion. Oleg Konstantinovich Parkhaev; Moscow, 2015.

12 The victory – troops mounting Viktoria Bastion.
Nikolai Valentinovich Zubkov; Saint-Petersburg, 2016.

13 Mounting bastion Victoria. By Oleg Fedorov; Moscow 2015.

14 Peter I pacifies his enraged troops after taking Narva in 1704. Nikolai Aleksandrovich Zauerveid (1836-1866); Russia, 1858, The State Tret'iakov Gallery.

15 The Swedish garrison's departure from Ivangorod. Oleg Konstantinovich Parkhaev; Moscow, 2015.

A cannon and its accessories
The breach end of the barrel was boosted with wedges for vertical aiming. The traversing handspike was a lever for rolling the gun carriage. The ladle was made from copper or tin-plate and used for pouring gunpowder into the cannon barrel. The rammer served for packing the gunpowder, wadding and ball, and the sponge for cleaning the barrel after a shot. The gunpowder was stored in a *kapiarmus* – a barrel with a leather sleeve. (Artist unknown; in Timofei Brink, *Opisanie artilerii, Description of artillery*, Moscow, 1710)

In the field and siege artillery, the lighter bronze barrels were used; cast iron barrels were heavier, more fragile and far less expensive – they were intended for fortress and ship cannons. According to the existing data about the number of bronze cannons cast in Moscow from 1700 and sent to the troops, were arguably that the large 9-pood mortars that were at Narva were rare models; from the start of the war (in 1701), only six such pieces were cast and only two were sent to the army in 1703 – they in fact took part in the siege. The sole howitzer was sent to the troops in 1703 from the eight that were cast in 1701. The most common weapon of plunging fire was the 3-pood mortars; in 1700 to 1702, 120 of them were produced, and in 1703 and 1704 28 of them were delivered to the army. Among the siege cannons, the 18-pound cannons were most common: 69 pieces had been cast, and 57 of them were issued. Forty-seven of the 24-pound cannons were cast by 1704, and 32 of them were delivered to the troops. Fifty-two of the 12-pound cannons were manufactured, and 30 were turned over to the acting army. The 3-pound cannons had the smallest calibre and were intended for the field and regimental artillery; 179 of them were produced in 1701 to 1704, and 144 were issued.[8]

According to an experiment that was conducted in 1705, the average lifetime of a bronze gun barrel was around 300 discharges, after which during intensive fire the priming vent hole would expand and knock the gun out of service. For example, at the siege of Nöteborg in 1702, the vents heated up so much that the cannons became inoperable for conducting fire and the breaches in the ramparts were not completed. Cannons that were thus ruined from the firing during a siege could be re-cast; for example, in 1704 after the fall of Dorpat and Narva, the Tsar ordered the re-casting of cannons on the spot – brick stoves were built for this purpose.[9] However, there was also the possibility of repairing the barrels. The Danish envoy Just Juel saw a siege train that had been gathered near Narva in September 1709 and observed:

8   Brandenburg, N.E., *Materialy dlia istorii artilleriiskogo upravleniia v Rossii. Prikaz artillerii (1701–1720)* [*Materials for the history of the artillery command in Russia. The Artillery Administration (1701–1720)*] (Saint Petersburg, 1876), p. 159, 161.
9   PiB, Vol. 3, pp. 154–155.

Artillery guns. Massive iron-bound wooden gun carriages were produced to transport the heavy cannon and mortar barrels – these constructions weighed tons, and their movement and service required considerable efforts. (Nicolas Ulrich Cranach, Germany, 1636, Anne S.K. Brown Military Collection)

Of the number of these guns, twenty had burned-out touch holes due to extended firing and were thus unsuitable for use; they would pour metal down the barrel that would coat the breech of the gun with a layer that was as thick as a cannon ball's diameter. Then they would drill a new priming vent into the new breech. The Russian artillery officers assured me that the majority of their guns were susceptible to such a rapid burning out of the priming vent, and this was because they were cast from metal that was commonly used for bells and contained too much tin; the clergy in the present war had been forced to turn over to the government a certain number of church bells in all of the Tsar's domain for recasting them into cannons.[10]

In addition to the barrels, the wooden carriages also broke down – during the first Narva campaign, wheels and carriages of the siege guns broke due to decay or the poor quality of the wood when mounting them on a battery.[11] They broke as well from the stress when firing and from counter-battery fire. Therefore, in the second campaign they brought along nine spare "mounts" for the 24-pound cannons, eight for the 18-pounders, and three for the 12-pounders.

The English envoy Charles Whitworth in 1705 wrote: "The artillery is at present extremely well served; and general Ogilvy tells me that he never saw any nation go better to work with their cannons and mortars than the Russians did last year at Narva."[12]

---

10   J. von Juel, *Zapiski datskogo poslannika v Rossii pri Petre Velikogo*, p. 60.
11   Allart, No. 1, p. 11.
12   "Doneseniia i drugie bumagi chrezvychainogo poslannika angliiskogo pri russkogo dvore Charl'za Vitvorta s 1704 po 1706," [Reports and other papers of the English special envoy

Nighttime fire from a mortar.
(Charles-Nicolas Cochin II
1715-1790, France, 1741,
J. Dulacq, *Theorie nouvelle
sur le Mecanisme de l'Artillerie*,
Paris, 1741)

31 July

That day the besieged garrison saw a large mass of cavalry and infantry that were moving along the Livonian road towards Joala. That evening at 10:00 one of the bombs dropped on the Narva arsenal – a laboratory at the New Gates. There, despite all safety rules, a large number of prepared grenades, *pech-krantze* (incendiary wreaths) and *licht-kugel* (illumination shells) had been stockpiled under the open sky. All of this was reduced to ashes; the besiegers saw in the city "a large conflagration and cracklings of bombs and grenades." The citizens, who had seen what damage the Russian batteries were doing while the fortress cannons remained silent, gave the burgomeister a petition to be passed on to the commandant with a request to open fire at the besiegers. Over the first 24 hours of the bombardment, 905 bombs fell on the city. In an order issued to the Russian army, each company was to build an assault ladder.[13]

What Were Assault Ladders?

Three soldiers and a sergeant from each company were assigned to build them. The ladders were to consist of three lengthwise beams with a length no shorter than 17 metres and rungs that were 1.4 metres wide. Wheels with a diameter of 35 centimetres should be affixed to the upper section for "rolling" this heavy construction up to the wall. General Allart had demanded ladders with wheels for the first siege back in 1700, and James Bruce had them prepared for the 1702 campaign. The generals were charged with ensuring the preparation of the ladders in their brigades; if the construction of the ladders, like many other duties, rested on 30 battalions, then a total of no less than 120–150 assault ladders should have been ready.[14]

with the Russian court Charles Whitworth from 1704 to 1706"] *Sbornik imperatorskogo Russkogo istoricheskogo obshchestva* (Saint Petersburg, 1884), Vol. 39, p. 56.

13   Adlerfeld, Vol. 2, p. 17; Archiv., p. 267, 269; Von Huyssen, pp. 449–450.

14   RGVIA, F. 2584, Op. 1, D. 6, l. 6, 7; Kurakin, B.I., *Russko-shvedskaia voina: Zapiski, 1700–1710*, p. 297; Kelch, p. 416; PiB, Vol. 1, p. 877.

Assault ladders.
Sectional ladders were easier to carry disassembled to the designated point of the assault; they also allowed the assembly of a ladder of the necessary length on the spot. Rope ladders were even lighter and more compact, but apparently, these devices weren't used at Narva. (*Les fortifications du chevalier Antoine de Ville, contenans la maniere de fortifier toute sorte de places*, Lyon, 1640)

An escalade, or an assault with the help of ladders. A structure using three 17-meter logs was bulky and heavy, but it permitted several soldiers in a row to climb the ladder simultaneously. In the circumstances of a general assault it was necessary to ensure the maximal possible flow of troops, in order to overcome the defenders' resistance as quickly as possible on the walls. (Artist unknown, Italy, 17th century, Library of Congress)

1 August

Commandant Horn dispatched a letter that he had written back on 28 July. Peasants carried it to Reval, having received seven riksdaler in Narva and just as much in Reval for handing the letter to De La Gardie. Judging from the text of the letter, over the time of the siege Horn had sent several letters, including with Lieutenant De La Vallée; the commandant did not know whether they had reached the addressee and asked to be informed how many letters and on what date they had been received in Reval. In order to get information to Narva, Horn proposed to use cannon signals from the ships on the Narova Roads, as well as flags raised in various combinations on the ships' masts.[15]

The besiegers drew their approaches quite close to the Victoria Bastion, to the place where their cannonballs had begun to create a breach. Over the second 24 hours, another 568 bombs were lobbed into the city.[16]

---

15   Rosen, pp. 188–189.
16   Adlerfeld, Vol. 2, p. 18; Archiv., p. 269.

What Was a Breach?

The walls of major fortresses presented a stone revetment that was filled with earth or rubble. In order to bring down this facing as quickly as possible, Vauban advised to pound the bottom of the wall with cannonballs.[17] One can find similar recommendations held by a contemporary artilleryman Ernest Braun.[18] The most detailed explanation of such an approach was given by a British author of the mid-18th Century, John Muller: "The manner of making a breach is to fire at first as low as possible, and to direct the pieces so as to hit in a horizontal line near each other. ... If the wall is cut low in a horizontal line, the part above falls down all at once; whereas if the wall above is beat down at first, the rubbish covers the lower part in such a manner, as not to be destroyed afterwards, and without which the breach becomes impracticable."[19]

The Russian breaching artillery could not boast of successful actions in the initial stage of the Great Northern War. In the first Narva campaign, they were unable to breach the walls of Ivangorod before the siege was lifted, and when taking Marienburg in August 1702, emphasis was placed on bombarding it with mortars, and not on creating a breach with the help of cannon fire. The walls of Nöteborg proved too tough for the artillery, and the breaches were created so high that subsequently they proved useless for an assault. In the following year, the fortresses of Nyenschantz, Jamburg and Koporie were compelled to surrender with a bombardment and no breaches were made in the walls. During the siege of Dorpat, the artillery did pound breaches in the wall, but for some reason they were not utilised in the assault – the attack against the palisade evolved into the storming of a gate. Now at Narva the Petrine gunners had to make a passable corridor through the powerful stone ramparts.

The servicing of a siege cannon.
The lower picture shows the necessary procedure of cooling a gun after a shot. For this purpose, the barrel would be covered by a wet woolen fabric, of which the gunners at Narva expended 254 *arshins*, or 182 meters. (Romeyn de Hooghe, 1645-1708, France, 1672, A. Manesson Malet, *Les Travaux De Mars Ou L'Art De La Guerre*, Vol. 3 La Haye, 1695)

---

17   Vauban, p. 64.
18   Braun, pp. 44–45.
19   Muller, p. 164.

The making of a breach by cannon fire.
(Johann Melchior Füssli, 1677-1736, Zürich,
1714 Zentralbibliothek Zürich)

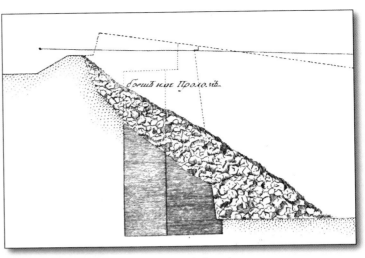

Cross section of a breach.
Artist unknown; Russian, 1744 (S. Vauban, *Kniga o atake i oborone krepostei*, Saint
Petersburg, 1744)

2 August

The besiegers lobbed many bombs onto the Ivangorod castle, but without any particular success. They then shifted the fire to Narva, where they set several houses in the New Town on fire. That night Russian soldiers from the approaches on the Ivangorod side infiltrated past the palisade into the dry moat of Ivangorod itself and captured two dragoons and a corporal, who were inspecting their sentries on the counterscarp.

The Swedish Captain Sperreiter at his own initiative conducted counter-battery fire. The commandant for this action initially placed the captain under arrest, then allowed him all the same to position guns on the hornwork, but it was now too late – the batteries that had been started there had been destroyed by the massive fire of the Russian mortars, so Horn cancelled the order. One of the bombs fell on the Herman Tower, but the fire that started there was quickly smothered. The besiegers were working in the approaches right next to the Victoria Bastion, taking advantage of the silence of the fortress guns. Incidentally, the Swedes from time to time fired mortars, and four bombs successfully struck Russian positions. Another 558 bombs were hurled at the city.[20]

Meanwhile: the Battle of Blenheim

The news was reporting: "The victory that the Allies under the Duke of Marlborough and Prince Eugene gained over French and Bavarians near the Swabian city of Hochstädt has generated indescribable fear in all of Bavaria."[21] It had previously reported, "All of Bavarian land has been pillaged to the end,

---

20   *Pokhodnyi zhurnal 1704 goda*, pp. 73–74; Adlerfeld, Vol. 2, p. 18; Archiv., pp. 269–270.
21   Vedomosti–Moskva [Pechatnyi dvor], 20 September 1704.

THE ARTILLERY ATTACK ON THE FORTRESS

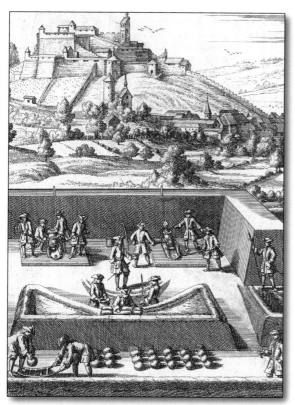

A mortar battery.
The *ketel'* had a ditch and parapet without embrasures – on it, pegs for aiming are visible; in the rear there is a powder magazine and a place for filling the bombs. The bombardiers are firing from the right-hand mortar with a double ignition; when loading, the bomb would be placed in the muzzle on top of wadding of wooden sabots and packed with turf and sand, and a fuse of the bomb would extend outwards; for a shot they would light the fuse with a one linstock, and with another – the mortar's touchhole. In the process, there was the risk of a mistake or misfire when the primer of the gun failed, and the bomb would explode directly within the barrel. There was also a technique of "single fire", when no wadding was used, and the lighting of the bomb fuse resulted from the blast of the powder in the mortar chamber; with the passage of time this approach began to gain favor, but in the Northern War the artillerymen, apparently, preferred the former technique. (Johann Melchior Füssli, 1677-1736, Zürich, 1719, Zentralbibliothek Zürich)v

The bombardment of Arras by the allies in 1712.
(Pieter Schenck, the Netherlands, 1712, Rijksmuseum, Amsterdam)

The major victory of the Imperial and allied troops at Höchstädt (Blenheim) over the French and Bavarians. (Joseph de Montalgre; Nuremberg, 1705, Anne S.K. Brown Military Collection)

and the Allies have obtained a countless multitude of horses, cattle and other things as loot."[22] On the Danube River in the War of Spanish Succession, one of the largest battles between the Imperial, British and Dutch forces on one side, and the French and Bavarians on the other, took place in and around the small villages of Hochstädt and Blindheim (from which the English "Blenheim" is derived). The combat operations of the war since 1701 had been unfolding in Flanders, on the Rhine, in Italy and in Spain. The Allies invaded Bavaria in 1704 with the aim of lifting the threat to Vienna and knocking Bavaria out of the war. The bloody battle at the Schellenberg Heights near Donauwörth on 21 June enabled the Allies to cross the Danube River and to begin to pillage the countryside, in order to force the Bavarian Elector Maximillian Emanuel to break the alliance with King Louis XIV of France. With the arrival of the French forces under Tallard, the Bavarian chances improved, and on 2 August there occurred the Battle of Blenheim, which ended in the full defeat of the French-Bavarian army; one portion of the army fled, while the rest was encircled and surrendered. The victory on the Danube lifted the threat to Vienna and allowed the Emperor to shift his forces to Hungary for the struggle there. Bavaria was occupied by Austria until the end of the war.

The Allied armies were commanded by the most famous and prominent commanders of that time – the British Duke of Marlborough and the Imperial Prince Eugene of Savoy; this duo would have many more successful campaigns. For the vanquished side, the disunity of command between Marshals Tallard and Marsin proved fatal. The lack of coordination and clumsy

---

22   *Ibid.*, 5 September 1704.

leadership over the French armies became the reason for an entire series of defeats, which marked the setting of the "Sun King" of France. The scale of the struggle in Western Europe far exceeded that of everything that happened in the Great Northern War by its geographical size, the number of participating countries, the size of the armies, and the number and strength of the fortresses. For example, at Blenheim the armies' strength on each side exceeded 50,000 men. Certain participants in the War of Spanish Succession happened to appear as well on the fronts of the Northern War: the French soldiers taken prisoner ended up in Saxony's service, and after the defeat at Fraustadt in 1706, transferred to serve in the Swedish army and subsequently fought against the Russians.

3 August

Soldiers of the Narva garrison from Captain Fock's company refused to go out on a patrol to the counterscarp with their commander. Colonel Lode threatened to shoot them, but the soldiers replied that it was better to die in that manner than from hunger. Some Narva dragoons and a woman went over to the Russian trenches and said that in the city there was "great destruction and many casualties" from the bombardment, but mostly the people were suffering from hunger; they were weakened and getting meagre sustenance from Kissel, since the final bread for the week had been allocated to the soldiers. That night Lieutenant Hescho took men out on a sally in order to destroy the Russian gabions that had been put up, but he had to return with losses.

What Was a Bombardment?

In the city they kept count of the falling bombs, and according to the information of the Narva diaries, between 31 July and 8 August 4,567 bombs had been lobbed; according to the information of the Russian artillery administration, over the course of the entire siege, 5,714 bombs of various calibres were expended. The fire from the mortars with their plunging trajectories allowed the destruction of targets that was concealed from eyesight by the walls: the interior of bastions, artillery positions, stockpiles, residential quarters, as well as to inflict casualties on the city's garrison and residents. The bombs that fell on the city crashed through roofing, exploded, and demolished and set fire to structures; people were killed and maimed not only by bomb fragments, but also by flying tiles,

A bomb.
A hollow spherical iron shell with gunpowder inside, it was fired from mortars and howitzers. For the sake of convenience of carrying and loading, the bombs had lugholes. The explosion of the charge of gunpowder was initiated by a fuse (a wooden tube filled with a slow burning composition) that was inserted into a bomb's fuse-hole. The length of the fuse determined the amount of time that would elapse prior to the explosion; for example, the fuse would be shortened so that the bomb would explode in the air (in order to give a signal). (Artist unknown; in Feuquieres, *Memoirs historical and military*, London, 1735)

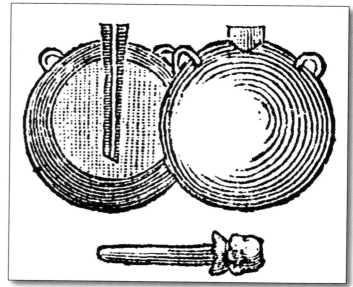

The bombardment of a city. (Charles-Nicolas Cochin II, 1715-1790, France, 1741, J. Dulacq, *Theorie nouvelle sur le Mecanisme de l'Artillerie*, Paris, 1741)

building debris and pieces of pavement. In other sieges, the besieging army resorted to barraging the city with red-hot cannon balls and "carcasses", an early form of incendiary bomb or shell, but at Narva, these apparently were not employed.

Marshal Vauban advised to hurl bombs only at fortifications, and not at residential quarters, but he was a little ahead of his times with such a humane approach, and the European military commanders at the turn of the 17th and 18th centuries considered a bombardment of a city a justified means of forcing a garrison to surrender or to inflict maximum damage. For example, in 1704 the Allies bombarded French-held Namur and Brugge in Flanders. In 1703 Swedes caused fires in the Polish city of Thorn with a bombardment, which included the deliberate firing of red-hot cannonballs at the town hall. In the Ingermanland theatre of the Russian–Swedish war, the fortresses of Nyenschantz, Jam, and Koporie surrendered without breaching and an assault, and Sheremetev emphasised the significance of the bombardment as the main reason for the fall of the fortresses: "Thank God! Your music, Sire, the mortars are playing well with the bombs; the Swedes are already dancing well and are giving up their fortresses; if not for the bombs, God knows what could have been done …"[23] However, bombardments alone were insufficient for taking such powerful fortresses as Nöteborg, Dorpat and Narva.

4 August

A Russian resident of Narva, the fisherman Ivan Petrov[24], left the city and went over to the besiegers. While his boat floated past the fortress in view of everyone, no one fired a shot at him, because the ban on firing without orders was still in effect, and the Russians were shouting to the Swedish sentries: "Don't shoot, or else you will receive 10 strokes with a rod!" In the opinion of the Swedes, Ivan showed the Russian artillerymen where the commandant's

---

23   *Pis'ma k gosudariu imperatoru Petru Velikomu ot generala-fel'dmarshala … Borisa Petrovicha Sheremeteva* [*Letters* to Peter the Great from Field Marshal General … Boris Petrovich Sheremetev], Part 1 (Moscow, 1778), pp. 178–179.

24   Among the citizens of Narva in February 1705 there were 18 fishermen, 13 of whom had Russian surnames. See Smolokurov, A., *Narodonaselenie Narvy* [*Population of Narva*], p. 31.

Bombardment of Brussels by
the French in 1695.
(Simon Fokke, 1712-1784, the
Netherlands, 18th century,
Rijksmuseum, Amsterdam)

home was located, since soon the area was struck by a lot of bombs; they did
some harm to the building, but none of Horn's family was injured. That same
night a grenadier from Captain Frolich's company deserted and escaped into
the Russian trenches. The commandant sent Captain Speerreiter several
times in a row to fix the damage on the fortress batteries and each time called
him back. A fire occurred in the Russian trenches (possibly this was the
result of a spontaneous combustion of gunpowder), but since there was no
fire coming from the fortress, the besiegers were able to repair the damage
quickly and without hindrance. The Russians launched another 256 bombs
at Narva, one of which struck the castle's guardhouse, where an imprisoned
Russian dragoon was killed.[25]

Sheremetev wrote Menshikov from Pühajõgi that he had five dragoon
regiments with him, and that he intended detail three companies from each
regiment to work. They were to build a two-kilometre rampart and two levees
of 200 metres each; prepare 3,000 logs for a palisade and 500 gabions; clear a
forest and build a bastion on a hill. However, they did not have enough tools
for the job – pickaxes, hoes, shovels and axes.[26]

5 August

A Swedish soldier and reiter went over to the Russians from the garrison.
The besiegers shot nine arrows into the town with letters attached to them
"to inform the garrison and citizens that his majesty the Tsar would grant
them proper conditions in return for their surrender." The idea was that the
military men and residents would force the commandant to surrender the

---

25   Adlerfeld, Vol. 2, p. 18; *Pokhodnyi zhurnal 1704 goda*, p. 74; Archiv., pp. 270–271.
26   Volynsky, Book 3, p. 375.

fortress, but Horn ordered for the letters to be gathered and forbade any from opening them at the pain of death.

Lieutenant Blomann's unit was holding the defence of the counterscarp on this day. The Russians were now pushing their approach trenches against the breaches of the Victoria Bastion, but suddenly 50 of their soldiers charged with the intention of cutting the Swedes off. The lieutenant narrowly managed to escape to the King's Ravelin and saved himself, after which he informed the commandant about the new threat. Horn resolved not to expose his men in the ditch any longer, and from that point on conducted only small sallies from time to time to bring off the Russian gabions and to set fire to their works.

That evening at 7:00 there was a sudden downpour; water filled the trenches and flooded the guns. Therefore, the fire from the Russian batteries weakened that evening and night; over the previous 24 hours, just 189 bombs were fired. One when striking split apart into three pieces in such a way that the majority of it remained undamaged, so the Swedes were able to assess the calibre of the bomb at 300 pounds. This super-heavy shell had been fired from a Russian 9-pood mortar.[27]

Meanwhile: the Swedes are Again in Nyenschantz

Maidel made a second attempt to attack the Neva estuary. On 5 August part of his force laid a bridge across the Okhta River and re-occupied Nyenschantz, which had been abandoned and partially demolished after its capture in 1703. The Russians observed that the Swedes brought some sort of materials into the fortress aboard 40 wagons, and judging from the sound of axes, had begun to make repairs there. The troops of the Petersburg garrison gathered around Nyenschantz and just like a year before, prepared batteries. Maidel sent Roman Bruce a letter with a demand to surrender the Petersburg fortress and to abandon the domain of the Swedish King. Bruce replied with a letter with a suggestion that Maidel return to his own land and in the future write no similar letters to him. The Swedish corps stood in place for several more days, but as their provisions were running low, departed again to the north. De Prou again approached Kotlin Island but once more was unable to do anything.[28]

6 August

The foundation of the Honour Bastion at 9:00 a.m. that morning collapsed all at once, and one entire face with the parapet and the artillery were overthrown into the ditch; in the words of a Russian source, the stone revetment and earthen rampart collapsed into a gently sloping pile of rubble, so that the Russians, with the help of their ladders, might have mounted 100 men abreast. Such a result could be expected from a mine, but at this time a mine still was not ready. It seemed that this happened spontaneously

---

27   Adlerfeld, Vol. 2, p. 18; Von Huyssen, p. 450; Archiv., pp. 271–272.
28   Ustrialov, Vol. 4, Part 2, pp. 317–318.

because of the poor quality of the masonry and an unstable foundation, but the besiegers connected the collapse with the consequences of the bombardment. The commandant ordered all peasants, servants and women to work on repairing the bastion, but only a few obeyed. Meanwhile, a considerable breach in the Victoria Bastion was created by the cannon fire. Both bastions had powerful, double flanks (with guns on two levels), which covered the approach to the breaches with their fire. Therefore, the besiegers set up five mortars on the counterscarp and "demolished" their flanks, so that of the 70 cannons that had occupied them, only one remained intact. Since morning, 237 bombs were discharged.

In the afternoon a Russian drummer brought an "exhortative letter about surrender" to the commandant from Ogilvy. The letter said that Dorpat had surrendered to an accord, as well as Nöteborg and Nyenschantz, that the defenders had been given leave with honour, which averted the unnecessary bloodshed during an assault. He informed Horn that the besiegers knew about the difficult situation in the city with provisions and the lack of men and advised him not to count upon a relief force. A breach had been created in the Victoria Bastion by Russian cannons, and "God himself had deigned" to destroy the Honour Bastion, so now everything was ready for a general assault. Thus, if the commandant in such a hopeless situation did not accept the proposed terms and "dare" to wait for an assault, then he could no longer count on any sort of honourable surrender or mercy of the victor.

While the commandant considered an answer to this letter, both sides ceased fire, and the adversaries could socialise with each other. The Dorpat commandant Skytte came into the Russian trenches beneath the Honour Bastion, where he engaged in conversations with officers of the garrison who had come out onto the rampart (the commandant himself had no wish to speak with those who were in the enemy's hands). Skytte informed them how Dorpat had been defended, but how it had been forced to surrender under honourable terms and on the following day he was supposed to have been released to Swedish Reval under these conditions. A captured dragoon from his corps, Diedrich Eriksson, was sent to talk about the fate of the defeated von Schlippenbach. Lieutenant Colonel Marquard, who had been taken prisoner on 8 June, took part in the meeting in the forward trench together with Skytte. He questioned Major Funk about Kinnert, about how Colonel Apoloff was doing, and whether or not Lieutenant Colonel von Schlippenbach from Nöteborg was still under arrest. According to the Russian version, he asked the Swedish officers to summon his acquaintances to the wall, but they

The explosion of a mine, and a retrenchment behind the breach.
It was possible to blow up a rampart by "attaching a miner", and such a mine gallery began to be dug toward the face of the Honor Bastion; however, the bastion crumbled beforehand. The commandant had to build a retrenchment behind the breach, in order to stop the attackers. (Johannes Meyer, 1655-1712, Switzerland, 1711, Zentralbibliothek Zürich)

refused his request, pointing to the fact that these persons were on duty; later it became clear that in fact one of them had been killed by that time, and the others were sick, but the commandant did not want to reveal the weakness of his garrison. The "sad and gloomy" appearance of the Swedish officers informed their conversation partners that the defenders had already lost spirit.

Almost four hours had passed since the Russian drummer had been sent with the letter, but Horn tarried with a response. At first, he offered the pretext of holding a military council, but later he finally announced that he would have a reply on the next day. By keeping the Russian drummer in the city, the commandant was counting upon playing for time and to use the ceasefire for repairing the fortifications, which got underway in front of the Russians' eyes. The besiegers declared that such behaviour was contradictory to the rules of war and demanded the return of their drummer; the soldiers and officers on both sides stood to their posts. Since Tsar Peter was most interested in continuing the negotiations, infantry Colonel Benedikt Ottovich Povisch was sent to the fortress with another letter, which repeated the proposal of surrender. The Swedes did not release the drummer, so at midnight bombs and red-hot cannon balls were again hurled at the city. In order to prevent the repair of the bastions, they hurled bombs from large mortars and grenades from the new-style, small 6-pound hand mortars incessantly at the Honour Bastion.

That evening the garrison in the fortress heard at a great distance from the Livonian direction the signal of two cannon shots, to which Horn replied with two large cannons in Ivangorod. It was not known who fired, but possibly this signalled the next hope of relief to the commandant: because of this he decided to reject the Russian terms in this already hopeless situation. Around midnight a false alarm went up in the garrison. It seemed to the defenders that the Russians had drawn up into assault columns between the Honour and Victoria bastions, and had opened fire at this sector. Possibly, the defenders took the Russian work on the counterscarp as a storming attempt – there a line had been drawn up for musketeers, who were to provide supporting fire during an assault.[29]

Sheremetev received from Menshikov a request to send his "hand mortarmen" to him; immediately dragoons were gathered from all the dragoon regiments, armed with the hand mortars, and together with a supply of grenades they were sent off to Narva.[30]

What Were Hand Mortars?

The Swedes particularly emphasised the effectiveness of the hand mortars, which hurled grenades at the walls of Narva. At the turn of the century, hand

29   *Pokhodnyi zhurnal 1704 goda*, pp. 74–76; Adlerfeld, Vol. 2, pp. 18-20; Archiv., pp. 273-276; PiB, Vol. 3, p. 174; *Zhurnal ili Podennaia zapiska Petra Velikogo*, Part 1, p. 86; von Huyssen, pp. 450–452.
30   Volynsky, Book 3, p. 375.

Dragoon-mortarmen and infantry grenadiers in the trenches outside of Narva. (Maksim Vladimirovich Borisov, Moscow, 2014)

mortars, which were carried by just two bombardiers (so-called "Coehorn mortars") became popular. Vauban acknowledged that these hand mortars could discharge a "great multitude of grenades" but believed that the effect of these weapons was small, while it required too many men and too much material for their service. Instead of the hand mortars of his Dutch rival, the engineer Menno von Coehoorn, Vauban preferred heavy mortars that fired bombs and stones.[31]

In the Russian artillery at Narva there were seven light 6-pound mortars, which throughout the entire siege fired just 169 grenades, approximately 10 percent of their supply. At the same time, 12,547 2-pound hand grenades were expended. They were fired from the hand mortars, which in quantities of eight to 15 armed many of the dragoon regiments (we know about their presence in Bauer's, Kropotov's, Ignat'ev's, Volkonsky's, Inflante's, Grigorov's and von Rönne's regiments). Later, in 1715, Sheremetev recalled, "Before now in the mounted regiments there were small hand mortars, which in their actions were harmful to the enemy … each regiment had a corporalship of them."[32] Among the gear of the dragoon regiments, there are mentions of "mortars with covers", "mortar saddles", "mortar bags" and "mortar rounds".[33]

---

31   Vauban, p. 69.
32   Tatarnikov, *Russkaia polevaia armiia 1700–1730* [*Russian field army 1700–1730*] (Moscow, 2008), p. 67.
33   Sheremetev's field campaign journal 1701–1705, p. 180.

Hand mortars.
Etchings from the Zürich artillery almanac *Neujahrsblatt der Constaffler und Feuerwerker im Zeughaus* presents a unique collection of images of the various types of this weapon – on a bipod, on a woodblock, on a horse saddle, and mounted on a musket muzzle; today, they are all found in museum collections. The image of the cavalryman's hand mortar is especially valuable; apparently, it was this type of weapon that the mortarmen of the dragoon regiments had at Dorpat and Narva. The combat use of the Coehorn mortars – those on a woodblock – is also shown in a form of massed fire from the forward trenches on the covered way and palisade. (Johannes Meyer, 1655-1712, Switzerland, 1711, Zentralbibliothek Zürich)

Possibly, the saddle was of special design, so that the butt of the hand mortar could be propped against it when firing from a horse. They also propped them against the ground, but hand-held firing was hazardous for the men, as tests showed in 1755.[34]

Hand mortars were a rather exotic, but characteristic weapon of that epoch – there are a lot of them in various museum collections. However, the details of their use have so far received little study. Judging from the available information, Petrine soldiers had fully mastered this weapon and executed challenging, intricate missions with their help. For example, descriptions have been preserved about the successful use of the grenades against floating targets! In early 1703 on the way to Jamburg from the recently taken Koporie, Sheremetev's troops captured a Swedish sailing ship on the Luga River; under Russian fire its crew landed on the western bank and headed off into the woods; "meanwhile our men were firing at them from their horse mortars, and they, the Swedes, were fleeing and yelping, 'The Devil trained you, and not humans!'". Sheremetev remembered, "They were operating very well and catching them even at a distance."[35] Von Huyssen described another case, which took place on 12 July 1703, in his journal:

> The dragoon regiments headed to the Narova estuary by the sea, and saw two Swedish ships heading towards Rugodev, and they had an opportunity to fire at them from their hand mortars; one of the ships passed by unharmed, but the other ship had some cargo on deck that caught fire from the hand mortars, when suddenly it lowered its sails, and out of fright the men who had been on it jumped into the water and the ship beached on shore. We burned it after carrying away whatever cargo we could. This is worthy of astonishment that the dragoons captured the ship and then returned in good shape with little loss of men.

Two days later, the men of Major General Nikolai von Werden "went down the Narova River, and seeing three enemy ships approaching that were a kilometre from the city, started firing at it with firearms and to lob grenades fired by the hand mortars at it, from which one of the ships with all of enemy's supplies that were on it were set ablaze."[36] Peter the Great praised these episodes in a letter to Sheremetev: "… It is rather amazing that the dragoons took a ship and burned it."[37] In August of that same year 1703, the Tsar wrote the field marshal: "If you please, take with you the hand mortars as well." Obviously, Peter considered the hand mortars useful in the forthcoming cavalry raid towards the towns of Rakvere, Päide and Viljandi.[38]

The practice of the massed use of the hand mortars, gathered from various regiments, had been tested at Dorpat not long before the storming of Narva. Andrei Andreevich Polozov, who in 1704 had been a wachtmeister

34 Brandenburg, N.E, *Istoricheskii katalog S.-Peterburgskovo Artilleriiskogo muzeia: Ch.P. XVIII vek* [*Historical catalogue of the St. Petersburg Artillery Museum: Accidents of the XVIII century*] (Moscow, 1883), p. 63.
35 Volynsky, Book 3, p. 364.
36 Von Huyssen, pp. 346–347.
37 PiB, Vol. 3, p. 225.
38 PiB, Vol. 2, p. 234.

in Prince Volkonsky's dragoon regiment, in 1720 wrote: "In 1704, when taking the city of Dorpat, dragoons with hand mortars were assigned from the regiments to positions near the city, and I served as the commander of those dragoons from my regiment."[39] The dragoon details with the hand mortars, possibly, were combined into a composite unit under the leadership of Sergeant Shchepotev of the Preobrazhensky Regiment; accordingly, Boris Ivanovich Savin in his story recalled that as a private in Bauer's Dragoons, "I was sent on the assault together with the hand mortarmen and Mikhail Ivanovich Shchepotev at Dorpat on the 13th of July."[40] Another member of the same regiment, Ivan Grigorievich Lopotov, in his story from March 1721 recalled that he had a hand mortar on the attacks at Dorpat and Narva.[41] Sheremetev's dragoon regiments took no part in the siege and storming of Narva, but their hand mortarmen were sent to Narva and took part in the attack under the commands of Captain Kropotov and Captain Veliaminov.[42] The grenadiers of the infantry regiments were sent into the trenches in order to conduct fire together with the dragoon's hand mortarmen, since the infantry was not equipped with hand mortars.

The experience of using hand mortars when taking Dorpat and Narva was deemed as successful, and in subsequent sieges Tsar Peter intended to repeat this tactic. During the siege of Vyborg in 1710, the Tsar instructed to position three batteries of iron and copper hand mortars (of 70, 50 and 50 pieces each) opposite the attacked sectors, "which at night would hinder work [to restore the fortress' destroyed fortifications], and otherwise during an assault to drive men from the ramparts."[43]

7 August

The Russian bombardment continued, and the Russian drummer was not released until around midday. The besiegers conducted dreadful fire at the people working to make repairs to the Honour and Victoria bastions. According to one of the diaries, from the start of the bombardment not a day went by when no fewer than 30 people were killed, and that does not include those who lost an arm or leg. At the Victoria Bastion, 300 Swedish grenades were blown up by the Russian fire, killing two cavalry corporals. That evening, there was another false alarm at the Fortune Bastion. At 9:00 in the evening, Lieutenant Colonel Johann Kinnert of the artillery arrived at the Honour Bastion and ordered fire with illumination rounds at the Russian trenches; in order to get a better look over the parapet, he took a step onto a gun carriage and was immediately killed by a bullet. Over the day, 496 more bombs fell on Narva.[44]

---

39 Volynsky, Book 4, p. 124.
40 *Ibid.*, p. 25.
41 *Ibid.*, p. 18.
42 Volynsky, N.P., *Postepennoe razvitie russkoi reguliarnoi konnitsy v epokhu Velikogo Petra, Kniga 1* [*Gradual development of the Russian regular cavalry in the era of Peter the Great, Book 1*], p. 297; Tatarnikov (ed.), *Ofitserskie skazki pervoi chetverti XVIII veka*, Vol. 1, p. 254, 1281.
43 Pib, Vol. 10, pp. 127–129; Laskovsky, pp. 178–180.
44 Adlerfeld, Vol. 2, p. 20; Archiv., pp. 276–277.

Commandant Horn finally sent a letter of reply to Ogilvy. In it the Swedish commander acknowledged that the observation of the conditions of an accord when taking a fortress honoured the Tsar and "spared innocent blood"; at the same time, he asserted that the condition of the fortifications, the supplies and the garrison remained satisfactory, and therefore the fortress entrusted to him could not be surrendered. Horn wrote about the "unflagging trust" in God, which would support the right cause, and in the King, who this time, as he did before, would come to Narva's relief. The hint at the Russian debacle of 1700 was considered in the Russian camp to be "very rude words", or perhaps Horn had given the messenger something even more humiliating in words. With the receipt of the rejection letter, the besiegers held a military council, which settled on taking the fortress by storm, and for Field Marshal Ogilvy to determine the composition of the assault columns.[45]

Tsar Peter ordered Sheremetev to release five dragoon regiments from von Rönne "to us for Narva". They were needed in order to cover the army during the assault.[46]

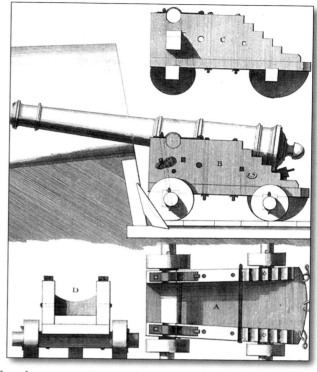

The carriage of a fortress cannon.
(Artist unknown, in Surirey de Saint Rémy, *Memoires d'artillerie*, Paris, 1697)

What Was the Assault Column?

The duty "to determine and assign combatants from all the regiments to the assault" rested on the commander, Field Marshal-General Ogilvy.[47] The contents of Ogilvy's order regarding the composition and arrangement of the assault columns is known from notes of Boris Kurakin. One column consisted of two attacking groups of 1,000 men each and a reserve of 500–700 men. There were two colonels in each attacking group, under the command of each of them the troops went on the attack in the following formation: leading off was a lieutenant with 25 grenadiers; next in order was a lieutenant with 25 musketeers, followed by a captain with 35 grenadiers; next in the attack formation was a captain leading 30 men with axes, followed by a lieutenant with 25 musketeers, another lieutenant with 25 musketeers with axes, and then a lieutenant colonel with 150 musketeers and the colonel himself leading 170 musketeers. The reserve under the command of a general and the chief of the attack column consisted of groups led by majors (each with 100 musketeers),

45   *Pokhodnyi zhurnal 1704 goda*, pp. 76–78.
46   PiB, Vol. 3, p. 117.
47   *Ibid.*, p. 175.

Cross-section of a third parallel, from which the grenadiers emerge for an assault, and behind them – the laborers.
(Vauban, *Kniga o atake i oborone krepostei*, Saint Petersburg, 1744)

and other units of grenadiers and musketeers.[48] Such a principle of arranging the assault column was consistent with the western European practice and would be used by the Russians for assaults in the future.

According to reports, they stormed Narva in three assault columns. Lieutenant General Schönbeck's column of 2,500 "select soldiers" and four colonels (Iurii Ivanovich Bush, Daniil Ivanovich Kuper, Benedikt Ottovich Povisch, and Denis Petrovich Ridder), four lieutenant colonels and five majors stormed the Victoria Bastion. Major General Chambers' column of 2,700 "select soldiers" and four colonels (Pavel Pavlovich Berner, Aleksei Stepanovich Kellin, Ivan Ivanovich Ridder and Nikolai Andreevich Gerink), four lieutenant colonels and five majors assaulted the Honour Bastion. Major General Alexander Vilimovich Scharf's column attacked the ravelin of the Gloria Bastion. Kurakin writes about a fourth column under Major General von Werden which is not mentioned in the reports. It was assigned to attack the Triumph Bastion with 300 *streltsy,* 500 Cossacks and soldiers of Werden's regiments; it is possible that this was feigned attack. Ensign Ivan Semenovich Roslavlev, of Balk's infantry regiment, recalled that he was "on the attack towards a castle [*Vyshgorodok*]" with von Werden; nevertheless, the bulk of von Werden's troops were distributed among the three other assault columns – "They were assigned to other divisions," as Major Avraam Korret, who had arrived from Dorpat, recalled.[49]

If willing volunteers were called upon for the storming of Nöteborg, then at Narva, apparently, there were both those who stepped forward and those assigned to the assault from all the regiments. According to the European practice, the duty of going out to siege work and to guard the trenches was rotated among the companies of each unit in turn each day, then if the day of the assault marked the next company's turn to head out to the trenches, it was designated for the attack.[50] The soldier of the Ingermanlandsky Regiment Vasilii Zuev "went on the attack at his own volition", while at the same time Andreian Maksimovich Sokolov and Fedor Parfentievich Stromyntsev of the Lefortovsky Regiment took part in the assault because "they had been ordered

48   Kurakin, *Russko-shvedskaia voina; zapiski, 1700–1710*, p. 297.

49   Tatarnikov (ed.), *Ofitserskie skazki pervoi chetverti XVIII veka*, Vol. 2, p. 1867.

50   *Voennyi Ustav s Artikulom Voennym* [*Military Manual and Articles of War*] (Saint Petersburg, 1748), p. 120.

to go on the assault."[51] Assault participant Pavel Iakovlevich Spesivtsev, who at that moment was a private in Kellin's regiment, later recalled in his story that 10 men from each company were delegated for the assault.[52]

Many soldiers were participants of the 1700 Narva campaign and were ready to settle accounts with the fortress for this failure. Many were eyewitnesses of how Nyenschantz, Jama and Koporie back in the spring of 1703 surrendered without waiting for the assault. Many others were participants in the bloody storming of Nöteborg in 1702, and the very recent night-time attack against the Dorpat counterscarp. Both battles had lasted for more than 10 hours, and were accompanied by heavy casualties, and in both cases the ramparts remained inaccessible – the Russian soldiers were unable to fight their way into the interior of the fortress, but the defenders themselves had surrendered once they realised the hopelessness of their position. For example, when taking Nöteborg, Captain Miakinin's detachment from Kashpar Andreevich Gulitz's regiment was assigned to raise and emplace the assault ladders; however, half of the 200 men had been killed, and the ladders were in fact never employed.[53] Therefore the soldiers assigned to the assault could plainly see that which lay ahead for them. Like the people of that time, they kept in mind that they were in the hands of the Almighty. As the Articles of War briefly stated: "In the approaches, sieges and assaults, just as in the skirmishes and battles, each man should remember that not a hair on his head can fall out without God's will."[54]

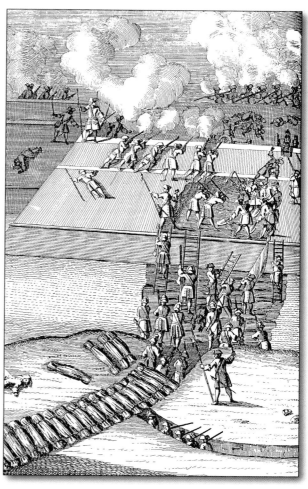

The storming of a bastion. Soldiers are setting ladders in place and engaging in combat, while laborers are demolishing the rampart and reserves are emerging from trenches. (Unknown etcher, Saxony, 1726, Hans Friedrich von Fleming, *Der Vollkommene Teutsche Soldat*, Leipzig, 1726)

8 August

The barrage this day reached its peak; of the 1,027 bombs that were discharged, one fell into a case that was holding 600 grenades – they all burned to ashes but did not cause any other damage. The remaining bombs fell on the city and fortifications, destroying homes and buildings and killing or maiming residents and members of the garrison. Captain Sperreiter was released from

51   Tatarnikov (ed.), *Ofitserskie skazki pervoi chetverti XVIII veka*, Vol. 2, pp. 1631, 1774, 1795.
52   *Ibid.*, p. 1867.
53   Popov, N.N., *Istoriia 2-go grenaderskogo Rostovskogo polka* [*History of the 2nd Rostov Grenadier Regiment*], Vol. 1, Appendix, p. 28.
54   Rosenheim, M.P., "Ocherk istorii voenno-sudnykh uchrezhdenii v Rossii do konchiny Petra Velikogo" ["Essay on the history of military justice offices in Russia until the end of Peter the Great's reign"] (Saint Petersburg, 1878), p. 306.

arrest for conducting the counter-battery fire, but he was now unable to change anything: he began to place six mortars on the Honour battery, but under the bombardment succeeded in putting only two into position, and those in the end were not ready to fire.

The garrison could see that the Russians were ready for an assault, and that night there was once again a false alarm at the Honour and Victoria bastions. Meanwhile, that evening the Russian troops moved into position for the assault in three places: 1) opposite the extreme bastion by the river (Victoria) facing the breach made by the cannons; 2) opposite the collapsed face of the Honour Bastion; and 3) opposite the second ravelin from the river with a small ditch and dual palisade. Ladders, fascines, wool sacks and everything else necessary for a general assault was brought into the approaches. Grenadiers of the infantry and dragoon regiments were also sent into the approach trenches; they were to lob grenades at the bastions from the hand mortars. Four cannons were positioned on the counterscarp opposite the flank of the Victoria Bastion in order to provide supporting fire during the assault. According to eyewitness testimony, the Russian soldiers that were assigned to the assault were expressing "joy, happiness, urgency and eagerness"; those who remained in reserve were envious of them and complaining.[55]

What Was the Time Set For an Assault?

The selection of the time of day or night to launch the assault was determined by a number of considerations. For example, an author of the third quarter of the 17th century Raimondo Montecúccoli believed that the attack should begin a half hour before sunrise, when the enemy would have to fire by guess.[56] Since an assault differed in its objectives – overcoming a fortress' main defences with a general assault or its outer fortifications with a particular assault, Borgsdorf wrote: "As for a general attack I will say that it should begin on a clear day in order to prevent things that might happen in darkness and at a time when any man can best demonstrate his courage, but it is always better to commit to a particular attack at night."[57] The British Colonel Humphrey Bland gave a detailed explanation of this point of view based on the experience of the War of Spanish Succession:

> The most favourable time for the making of an Attack is in the Day. For as the Actions of every Man will appear in full View, the Brave, thro' a laudable Emulation, will endeavour at the Expense of their Lives, to out-do one another; and even the Fearful will exert themselves, by performing their Duty, rather than bear the infamous Name of Coward, the Fear of Shame being generally more powerful than the Fear of Death. The Batteries will be likewise of greater Service, by their Firing with more Certainty on the Defences of the Town, and the Top of the Breach,

55 *Pokhodnyi zhurnal 1704 goda*, pp. 78–79; Adlerfeld, Vol. 2, p. 20; Archiv., p. 278; von Huyssen, p. 453.
56 Montecúccoli, p. 149.
57 Borgsdorf, *Pravila*, pp. 35–36.

to keep the Enemy from opposing the Grenadiers in Mounting it. Besides, in the Night, those who go on first will run great Danger from the Fire of those who sustain them; therefore an Attack on an Out-work, or the Covert-way, is generally a little after Sunset, that Night may come on by the time the Attack is finished, to favour them in making the necessary Lodgments: But this Rule will not hold good in an Attack on the Body of the Place, for if Night should come on before the Town is entirely reduced to our Obedience, great Inconvenience would attend both your own Troops, and the poor Inhabitants, to avoid which, it is generally made in the Forenoon.[58]

Under the concepts of "things that might happen at night" and "great Inconvenience", the authors had in mind the disorder on the streets of the city, the abuse of inhabitants on the part of the soldiers inflamed by the attack, the loss of control by the commanders over their troops in the darkness, and as a consequence, their vulnerability to a possible sudden attack by enemy reserves.

Such an approach, it seems, was not always followed in the Russian army: the storming of Marienburg began "in the night, three hours before sunrise," and the assault on Nöteborg began "at half past three in the early morning").[59] In contrast, the attack against the counterscarp and outer fortifications of Dorpat, in full accordance with Borgsdorf and Bland, was undertaken in the evening. The defenders of Narva in 1704 were in fact expecting a night-time assault; three nights in a row, they had been raised in response to a false alarm, taking movements in the approaches as the start of an assault. However, among Tsar's generals there was no single opinion regarding the choice of time. According to the testimony of Alexander Gordon, who was serving in the Tsarist army, the Russians were accustomed to night-time assaults, and Menshikov "and the others as ignorant as himself were for carrying on the attacks in the night-time, which Marshal Ogilvie strenuously opposed". Ogilvy pointed to the danger and inconvenience of night attacks, when the men in the darkness could not discern an enemy from a friend, and believed that all such actions should be conducted in daylight hours, leaving nothing to chance. The Tsar ordered Ogilvy to act as he saw best, and in response Ogilvy told the Tsar that he would answer for the success and promised his majesty that the town should be his within a few days.[60]

Vauban recommended raising a flag above the trenches to give the signal for the start of the assault; however, the Russians gave artillery salvoes, which were visible and audible from various sectors of the positions, even ones distant from each other. At Marienburg the attack began when three bombs were lobbed at the city; the attack against Nöteborg began after three salvoes from five mortars; the signal for the general assault at Narva was a salvo from five mortars at the Victoria Bastion.

---

58 Bland, p. 280.
59 Sheremetev's military campaign journal 1701–1705, p. 112; *Book of Mars*, p. 6.
60 Gordon, A., *The History of Peter the Great, Emperor of Russia: To which is Prefixed a Short General History of the Country from the Rise of that Monarchy and an Account of the Author's Life*, Vol. 1 (Aberdeen, 1755), pp. 184, 188.

4

The Fall of the City

9 August

Before sunrise, the troops designated for the assault, for the reserve and those who were supposed to provide supporting fire moved out of camp and into the forward approach trenches.

It was necessary to scout a path for the assault columns, and one of the scouts ("a surveyor for measuring the ditch and ladders") was the soldier Fedor Tokarev of Berner's regiment. With the start of the assault, the heavy and cumbersome ladders had to be hauled out of the trenches as quickly as possible and set against the walls and breaches. At the Honour Bastion deserters ("guilty soldiers who had fled their regiments back to their homes") that had been caught were supposed to carry out this task, according to the *Journal or daily notes of Peter the Great*; however, in other points of attack this task was done, apparently, by normal assigned soldiers, like, for example,

Prince Boris Ivanovich Kurakin.
Born in 1676, from 1683 Kurakin became part of the Tsar's inner circle as a chamber servant. He passed through both Azov campaigns as an ensign, and then as a lieutenant of the Semenovsky Guards Regiment. In 1696-1697, under the pseudonym of "Boris Ivanov" he studied mathematics, navigation and fortification in Venice. A participant of the first Narva campaign, and the capture of Nöteborg and Nyenschantz. (Pieter Gunst, 1649-1731, the Netherlands, 1717, Rijksmuseum, Amsterdam)

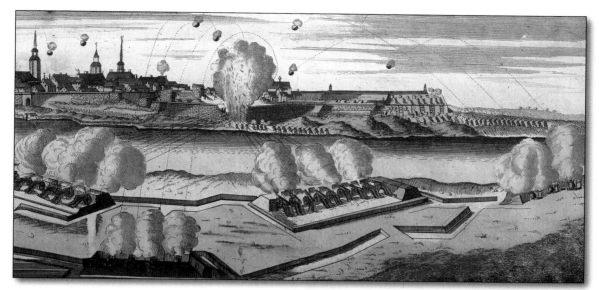

A panoramic view of the siege of Narva. Fragment of an illuminated etching. (Workshop of the Saint Petersburg printshop; Russia, 1715, Library of the Russian Academy of Sciences, Department of Cartography)

the Preobrazhensky soldiers Tikhon Kirillovich Volchkov and Bogdan Petrovich Neliubov, who had entered service that same year. The remaining infantry moved out of camp and took position near the river not far from the approaches, in order to support the attack columns.[1]

It was the Day of Saint Matthew the Apostle, and in the morning they held a prayer in the Tsar's campaign chapel.[2] Prince Boris Kurakin, Major in Semenovsky Life Guards recalled: "before the attack I had confessed and received Sacrament, these are the behests of my spiritual father that I should always have remembered and to which I adhered."[3] He obviously realised the perils of the coming combat for he had already been under enemy fire in the trenches at Nyenschantz and recollected it as a "grand and frightful occasion".

In the second hour of the afternoon, the artillery preparation began – "a very tremendous fire from all of the batteries of our cannons and mortars at the breach and at other places (so thereby to drive the enemy from the guns of the bastions)". According to the testimony from the Swedish side, in addition several musket volleys were fired at the bastions, but particularly awful was the effect of the grenades that the besiegers were lobbing at the defenders.

The assault began at the signal from five mortars. Simultaneously in all three sectors of attack, the forward teams of grenadiers moved out of the trenches, and under their cover the soldiers carried out and began to place the ladders, towards which assault groups were already approaching: 25 grenadiers, followed by 25 musketeers, 35 grenadiers, and so on. Among those who were in the first wave ("at the front of the attack with the ladders") was a sergeant of Titov's regiment, Petr Vasilievich Griaznoi and a major of

1   *Pokhodnyi zhurnal 1704 goda*, pp. 78–79; Tatarnikov (ed.), *Ofitserskie skazki pervoi chetverti XVIII veka*, Vol. 2, pp. 1550, 1859, 1950; *Zhurnal ili podennaia zapiska*, pp. 88–89.
2   Von Huyssen, pp. 453–458.
3   *Arkhiv kniazia F.A. Kurakina* [Archive of Prince F.A. Kurakin]. T. 1. (SPb, 1890), p. 267.

Attack against a bastion of Barcelona..
The defenders detonate a mine, while the besiegers are mounting a breach. Fragment. (Jacques Rigaud, 1681-1754, France, 1732, Anne S.K. Brown Military Collection)

Repnin's regiment Grigorii Petrovich Chernyshev, who was "wounded in the head by a stone and stabbed with a sword in the right arm."[4]

At the breach of the Victoria Bastion, the defenders had previously placed a mine, and now as the Russians were climbing the ramparts, they detonated it. The Swedes were rolling down *Sturm-Fasser* [incendiary barrels] and other incendiary devices, which were igniting or exploding in the midst of the soldiers, setting fire to the ladders and uniforms. The fortress artillery, despite the preliminary barrage on the bastions, still had a certain number of guns intact and operational, and now they were firing at point-blank range at the soldiers who had moved out of cover. The captain-of-arms of the Semenovsky Life Guards, Stepan Andreevich Iuriev, later recalled that "during the attack, when on the ladder below the rampart I was wounded by case shot fired from a cannon, and they shattered the left leg, so it was amputated below the knee with a saw." The canister shot was cutting down men and mangling their weapons – the list of gear lost during the assault includes among others the broken barrels of flintlock muskets. The ground was blanketed with corpses, but the units of the assault columns continued to advance one after the other; soldiers in rows of four were climbing up the wooden rungs of the ladders.

The Swedes saw that the Russian columns went on the attack under green banners: obviously, these were the company colours of certain regiments. The testimony of two participants in the assault have been preserved, each of them recorded that they were flag bearers in the assault; this was Petr Ivanovich Naumov, Ensign of Dennis Ridder regiment, and Efrem Semenovich Likharev, Ensign of Mevs' regiment.[5] One more ensign, Danil Borisovich Sikorsky from von Deldin's regiment, recorded that his flag was perforated by a cannonball ("the flag was wounded from a cannon") in the assault under the command of Major General von Werden.[6]

Chambers' column was the first to climb the rampart of the Honour Bastion. The soldiers of the Preobrazhensky and other regiments ascended and with their fire forced the defenders to retreat. The chronicler Kelch wrote that just several soldiers and burghers were on the Honour Bastion at that moment, thanks to which the Russians were able to overcome the resistance quickly. However, Chambers' column that led the way had suffered serious casualties. Colonel Berner was killed and Colonel Kellin was wounded. That means the attack had required the immediate leadership of senior officers, and even the collapsed fortification with a small number of defenders and knocked-out artillery represented a serious obstacle for the attackers.

---

4   Adamovich, p. 97; Chernyshev, G.P., "Zapiski G.P. Chernysheva", *RS*, No. 6 (1872), p. 793.
5   Tatarnikov (ed.), *Ofitserskie skazki pervoi chetverti XVIII veka*, Vol. 2, pp. 1938, 2048;
6   *Ibid.*, p. 1901.

Sturm-Fass and Pech-Kranz..
Barrels filled with gunpowder or incendiary agents were lit and rolled down among the attackers, where they would explode or break apart and cover everything with a burning mixture. Wreaths woven from straw and branches saturated with tar were used to set homes ablaze in settlements or construction materials in an adversaries' positions. (Wilhelm Dilich, 1571-1650, 17th century, W. Dilich, *Kriegsbuch*, Frankfurt am Main, 1689)

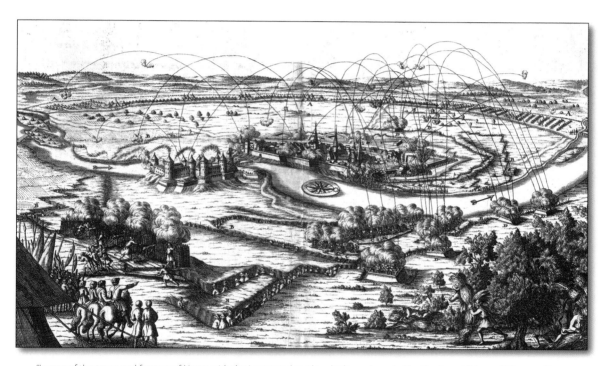

"Image of the town and fortress of Narva with the Ivangorod castle, which was invested by the Grand Prince of Moscow Peter Alekseevich on 27 April 1704; formally attacked on 29 May, then bombarded and encircled by approach trenches, which led to a passable breach that had been made; on August 10 of the same year, the town was stormed and taken, while the castle was surrendered according to an accord on the 18th". ("Delineation der Stadt und Vestung Narva, samt des Schlosses Ivangorod"). (Artist unknown, Krigsarkivet)
Apparently, this is the only contemporary battle scene representing the fall of Narva. The authorship of the etching and its dating haven't been determined; judging from the text of the legend and the calendar dates, the etching was made "from the Swedish side", while according to the style of the drawing, one can assume that the author of this etching was Dahlberg's assistant Johann Lithen. Many images of the sieges and battles of the Great Northern War belong to his engraving tool; some were made by him as an eyewitness, others (including this etching) on the basis of information available to him. The disposition of the approach trenches and camp, apparently, was based on the map "A provisional plan …" from the Library of the Russian Academy of Sciences, Department of Manuscripts, which has been published above on page xviii. The explanations of the legend are as follows: A. Enemy camp; B. Approach trenches; C. Batteries; D. Mortars; E. Attack against the breach and the collapsed face. (Artist unknown, Krigsarkivet)

Commandant Horn sent reinforcements to the attacked sectors, however the help arrived late at the Honour Bastion, and soon the defenders became disorganised. Lieutenant Colonel von Treyden,[7] Major Funk, Captains Aminoff and Gyllenspang, two lieutenants and two ensigns were directing the defence. They were all, with the exception of von Treyden and Aminoff, stabbed in the battle together with their soldiers.

In the wake of the capture of the Honour Bastion, the Victoria Bastion fell – after the explosion of the mine, Schönbeck's soldiers once again put the ladders in place and charged into the breach. In the campaign journal it is stated that the triggering of the mine did not do any harm, but the powerful charge of gunpowder with the force of its explosion and the blown apart fragments of the wall could not fail to find victims in the dense mass of attacking men; according to Alexander Gordon, up to 100 men were killed or injured by the mine explosion. A private of Schönbeck's regiment, Fedor Timofeevich Panov, and a sergeant of Cooper's regiment, Pavel Petrovich Gorbunov, ended up among the wounded; they were fortunate to survive and to make a career. In their autobiographies they both noted that they had been "wounded and buried by the rubble caused by the explosion."[8] Nevertheless, in the words of von Huyssen, "the brave Russian soldiers under the command of fine officers did not know what it meant to fall back, and with exceptional valour and a militant glint in their eyes, disdaining death, but trusting the Lord and loving their Tsar" pressed forward. Soon the third attacking column, Scharf's, took the ravelin and then the Gloria Bastion. Thus, over 45 minutes, the assault columns had seized the ramparts of the New Town.

According to military theory of that time, the task of the assaulting units was to climb the walls of the fortress and before doing anything else, establish a lodgment there, which meant to consolidate on the newly occupied line in the event of a counter-attack by the garrison. In order to erect this temporary fortification, gabions, fascines and woolsacks had been stockpiled in the approaches. Now the engineers, the Italian Andre de Brilli and the Mecklenburger Mark Heinson, together with Russian soldiers clambered up in order to "re-entrench" on the bastions. However, events were developing rapidly. An observer saw from a distance that the Swedes on the ramparts were "completely slow and did not have time to fire at the Russians"; then they fled under the protection of the stone walls of the Old Town, and the commandant ordered the gates be bolted. Invigorated by the success and enraged by the losses, the Russian soldiers without a pause rushed in pursuit. The lodgment, which had started to be built on the Honour Bastion, was completely forgotten.[9] Led by their officers, the Russians hauled several assault ladders up through the breaches, dragged them through all of the New Town, and used them to climb the ramparts of the Old Town; others at the same time were barging into the gates. Having seen that the cause was lost, Horn ordered a drummer to beat the chamade and for a white flag to be raised above the rampart; however, these late signals of surrender

---

7   Adlerfeld and the manuscript in the Annex spell the name as Freiden.

8   *Ibid.*, pp. 2064, 2067.

9   Von Huyssen, p. 455.

and appeals for mercy did not help. To "the sound of victorious weaponry and yelps of martial joy", the besiegers overcame the second line of defence and with waving swords chased the defenders back to the castle, into which they broke in on their bootsteps. During this fierce pursuit, several of the drummers who were beating the drums for parley were killed; the victors could not and did not want to listen to it. Many of the fleeing Swedes were run down and slaughtered, and in the heat of the moment this included civilians and women with children. Ultimately, deprived of his musicians, Horn was forced to beat on a drum for parley with his own hands. Von Huyssen writes that Colonel Rebinder was defending the castle, and he decided to open the gates to the Russians in exchange for mercy for the soldiers and residents that had taken shelter in the castle. A participant of the events, Major Chernyshev, recalled that after the assault he entered the castle "with fierce fighting", where he deployed sentries and took prisoners; among the latter was even Commandant Horn, who was sent to Ogilvy under the guard of Lieutenant Iakovlev of the Semenovsky Regiment.[10] Horn himself, recalling these events in 1722, recorded that when Chambers' column broke into the Old Town through the Karriporten Gate,[11] he threatened to blow up the gunpowder magazine and thereby halt the Russians' advance. Then Horn asked who was commanding the Russian column and asked for a security guarantee for himself and the entire city. Chambers stepped forward, and having struck his chest with his fist, promised complete immunity to Horn, then sent him back to his home under the guard of a major and 150 soldiers. However, meanwhile the other assault columns also penetrated into the city, and knowing nothing about the achieved agreement, settled down to looting.[12]

Colonel Fersen was leading the defence of the Waterside Gates with 100 soldiers of his regiment, but later he was taken prisoner, and only few of his men escaped. Some of the defenders and residents managed to run across the bridge in order to take shelter in Ivangorod. The gates of this last Swedish citadel slammed shut literally under the nose of the pursuers, who took all of the outer Ivangorod fortifications without any combat.

The speed and effectiveness of the storming of Narva was even more impressive by the fact that they could only be compared with the attacks against Nöteborg and Dorpat, which both took many hours of time. The laudatory entry in von Huyssen's journal was on the whole not far from the truth:

> Such boldness and discipline have never before been seen as how the men went
> on this attack when exposed in full daylight; dragged along and set the ladders
> in place under the enemy's whiskers; and attacked without fear of musketeers
> and grenades, bombs, cannon case shot, and the explosion of a mine. Even more

---

10   Chernyshev, "Zapiski G.P. Chernysheva", p. 793.
11   The Cattle Drive Gates were located in the vicinity of the intersection of the modern Suur Street and Kraavi Street.
12   Rosen, C. von., *Bidrag till kännedom om de händelser, som närmest föregingo svenska stormaktsväldets fall* (Stockholm, 1936), pp. 190–191.

courageous, however, was how they chased the enemy to the rear with their swords across two towns even as far as the castle, which they also took in an hour of time with few losses.[13]

Now the troops scattered throughout the city, and the swift pursuit turned into plundering. It was that same violence and mayhem, that Peter I, Ogilvy and Horn had foreseen in advance. That was why the proposal to surrender a fortress and spare innocent bloodshed, so typical for its time, was not just a figure of speech or empty threat, and that was why not a single Swedish commandant over the years of the war either before or after Narva waited for a final assault.

The plundering of a town. A fragment. French and Spanish soldiers indulge in looting and violence, while their commanders order the drummers to beat a retreat, in order to halt the chaos in Barcelona, the capital of Catalonia, which had been taken by storming after a year-long siege. (Jacques Rigaud,1681-1754, France, 1732, Anne S.K. Brown Military Collection)

The unenviable fate of the civilian population of a city captured by storming was obvious to the contemporaries, and the Tsar himself in his letters seemingly bragged about the terrible details: "The enemy was treated so well that not even many infants were left." The Swedish diarist of the defence of Ivangorod reported that the slaughter in Narva continued for several hours, and in addition to the 3,000 Russians and the multitude of Swedes killed during the assault, the bodies of unfortunate residents were lying in piles on the streets, blood was flowing in currents, and the enemies were later busy for three days with the removal of the dead, wounded and sick, which they pitilessly threw into the water from the Ivangorod bridge.[14] It remains only to conjecture how much this grim picture corresponded with reality, but at least the number of Russian losses in the storming has been exaggerated approximately tenfold in this source. The Russians really could not flaunt this aspect of their victory, but the Swedes in contrast were free to describe enemy actions in the darkest tones. The testimony of a resident, who survived these terrible minutes, has been preserved. Having caught word from people fleeing down the street that the New Town was now in Russian hands, he hurried to the home of burgomeister Schwartz and holed up in the basement together with other people who were seeking salvation, among which was the former commandant of Nöteborg, von Schlippenbach. They had hardly bolted the doors when Russian grenadiers who had appeared began to knock on them. The German Major Weide (possibly, the major of the Ingermanlandsky Regiment Franz Adamovich Weide, the son of Peter the Great's General Adam Weide, who had become a prisoner in 1700) was

13   *Ibid.*, pp. 457–458.
14   Adlerfeld, Vol. 2, p. 22.

The capture of Narva in 1704. According to the artist's rendering, Peter was observing the fall of the town from the Ivangorod bank of the Narova River; in this case, he would have had to cross the river quickly in order to enter the town and put a stop to the chaos. (Alexander von Kotzebue, 1815-1889, Russia, 1847)

with them. He promised to spare the citizens of the inevitable death that was awaiting them and kept his word.[15]

Even though the massacre immediately following the assault seems to be a circumstance of uncontrollable force, the Russian high command sought to placate the soldiers – two hours later, the Tsar and generals rode into the city. The soldiers were banned from killing residents, as long as they did not offer armed resistance; eyewitnesses of the events von Huyssen and Kurakin directly gave credit to the Russians for the fact that they spared civilians and that they "did not give way to the soldier's fury", as custom allowed. Shafirov reported that the Tsar forbade the bloodshed, having only entered the city, and to the astonishment of the foreigners, the troops promptly obeyed, and no one else was killed, "which in such violent cases it is rare for other regular troops to heed such orders." According to a city legend, which Kelch wrote down and which the Dutchman Just Juel heard, the Tsar himself cut down a soldier who refused to obey the order to halt the violence. Peter then went to the burgomeister Christian Götte's home and tossed his bloody sword on the table with the words, "Don't be afraid: this is Russian blood, not Swedish; saving you, I did not spare my own subjects."[16]

Riding along a street, Peter I and Ogilvy encountered "one of his soldiers carrying a chalice, with some other pieces of plate he had taken out of a church"; he gave orders to return everything to its place, to post sentries at the churches and the best houses of the town, and to restore order in the city by nightfall. Security posters (*salvoguardia*) that guaranteed immunity were

---

15 Ustrialov, N.G., *Istoriia tsarstvovaniia Petra Velikogo*, Vol. 4, Part 1 (Saint Petersburg, 1863), p. 313. See also: Hansen, H.J., *Geschichte der Stadt Narva* (Dorpat, 1858), pp. 219–220.

16 Juhl, J., *Zapiski datskogo poslannika v Rossii pri Petra Velikim*, p. 52; Kelch, p. 417; Petrov, A.V., *Gorod Narva*, p. 295.

hung on the homes of the *Ratsherren* (town council members). The same paper was given to home of Lieutenant Colonel Marquard, where his wife was hiding in the cellar from the slaughter.[17] The lieutenant colonel himself was kept in imprisonment in the Russian camp, and he could observe the preparations for the assault and was likely concerned about his spouse's fate. Clearly, he requested such a protection letter from the Russian command. The homes and warehouses of the Dutch and British merchants were also taken under protection; as a result, many citizens fled to them and brought along their valuables, in order to safeguard them from the Russian soldiers. The order which was re-established in the city relatively quickly confirmed that the choice of the time of the assault was correct – in the light of day, it was easier for the chiefs to regain control over the troops; at night, this might have been impossible.[18]

All the same, the victorious troops were not deprived to right to loot, which was legal in those times – they had access to all the remaining homes, buildings and cellars in the city. The Russian side placed all of the responsibility for the misfortunes that befell Narva as a result of the assault on Horn, whose "stubbornness had led to the unnecessary slaughter and plunder of the garrison and civilians."[19] Later, when Horn was brought in front of the Tsar, Peter treated him harshly, and it is said, even struck him as punishment for his rude response to the latter's offer of surrender. It is said that the Tsar gave him a slap, but Horn himself does not recall this, though he does remember how two of the Russian officers that were escorting him to jail slapped him across the face, and the chests in his commandant's home were opened and plundered.[20] Tsar Peter ordered Horn to be placed in the same jail that had previously held Colonel von Schlippenbach, whom Horn accused of failing to put up proper resistance before surrendering Nöteborg. To be sure, by the day of the storming of Narva, von Schlippenbach had already been freed from arrest, and later the Tsar allowed him to go to Stockholm under his word of honour, so that he could stand trial over the affair of his capitulation of the fortress. When releasing Schlippenbach, Peter supposedly said that he had shown himself to be a better warrior than Horn by withstanding the Russian assault for 13 hours, while the latter did not hold out for even an hour, and then hid out in a cellar together with several officers and did not leave it until everything had quietened down in the city. According to another story, Horn was arrested for his poor treatment of the Russian prisoners, who were liberated after the fall of the city.[21]

17 *Leben und Thaten des Czaars Petr Alexiewicz*, Vol. 2, p. 344.
18 Von Huyssen, p. 458; Kurakin, *Russko-shvedskaia voina*, p. 297; Gordon, A., *The History of Peter the Great, Emperor of Russia*, Vol. 1 (Aberdeen, 1755), p. 189; "British Officer in the Service of the Czar", p. 155.
19 PiB, Vol. 3, p. 177.
20 Grauers, S., "Henning Rudolf Horn" in Svensk biografiskt lexicon <http://sok.riksarkivet.se/sbl/artikel/13821> (accessed 6 August 2018).
21 Adlerfeld, Vol. 2, pp. 20–22; Adlerfeld, *Leben*, Vol. 2, pp. 109–110; Nordberg, Vol. 1, p. 531; Archiv., pp. 278–282; *Leven und Thaten des Czaars Petri Alexiewicz*, Vol. 2, pp. 343-345; Gordon, *The History of Peter the Great, Emperor of Russia*, Vol. 1, p. 190.

While Narva was filling with Russian troops, the Swedes who had taken refuge in Ivangorod were coming to the realisation that while they had avoided the slaughter and murders, they had instead fallen into a different hopeless situation. Several hundred soldiers and a multitude of townsfolk were ensconced in the stone fortress: there were practically no provisions and there was no hope for a relief force, and they could not count upon the notion that the castle would withstand the siege batteries that had now become available after the Narva attack. In the evening of that long day, the Russian Colonel Ridder (according to a Swedish source, or

The musket movement "Lay down your muskets". (Unknown etcher; Saxony, 1726, Hans Friedrich von Fleming, *Der Vollkommene Teutsche Soldat*, Leipzig, 1726)

Petr Pavlovich Shafirov, privy counsellor of the Foreign Chancellery, per Russian sources) arrived at the gates with a truce proposal and a demand for surrender at the mercy of the victors. The truce played into the hands of the garrison, and its commandant Lieutenant Colonel Magnus Stjernstråle sent Lieutenant Blaman out to amuse "the Muscovite" at the ramparts, while he himself hastily ordered the organisation of a defence with his meagre available strength. The Russian colonel was insisting on negotiating with the commandant, so he was told that no one knew where he was, but nothing could be done without his approval. While Ridder returned with this answer to Narva, Arnstedt, the envoy of the Polish King Augustus, appeared before Ivangorod – he handed over a letter from the captured Horn with orders for Stjernstråle to surrender. Lieutenant Colonel Stjernstråle replied that he could not carry out an order from a general being held by the enemy and announced that he had decided to defend to the last drop of blood.[22]

10 August

The Russian troops pulled out of Narva back to the camp, and no one was permitted to enter the city. The regiments had to compile the rosters of the dead and wounded during the assault; the burial of the fallen officers was postponed until a special order came from the Tsar. All of the soldiers and officers, under the threat of the penalty of death, were ordered to bring their "loot and prisoners" taken in Narva to a sentry post in the camp and to turn them in and were also to do the same with the return of the cash they had received from those stolen things that they had already sold.[23]

What Were the Spoils of War and How Were They Handled?

Peter the Great's famous *Articles of War* was put together on the basis of analogous articles of war from Sweden, Denmark, the Holy Roman Empire,

---

22 Adlerfeld, Vol. 2, pp. 22–23.
23 RGVIA, F. 2584, Op. 1, D. 6, l. 8.

The amputation of a limb. The most common medical assistance for the wounded in battle. (Unknown etcher; Saxony, 1726, Hans Friedrich von Fleming, *Der Vollkomene Teutsche Soldat*, Leipzig, 1726)

Brandenburg and Holland, and an entire chapter in it was devoted to "the capture of towns, fortresses, loot and prisoners". However, this document was drawn up and published only in 1716, and for this reason it did not regulate the norms of conduct and measures of punishment in 1704. Other regulations and standards were operational back then, for example the "Code of justice or the rights of the military conduct for generals, mid-ranking and junior officers, and the rank and file".[24] It appeared as a translation of the 1683 Danish Articles of War, made, most likely, for Vasilii Vasilievich Golitsyn's Crimean campaign of 1687. At the start of the Northern War, one copy of this document was signed by Sheremetev and served as the regulations for his troops.[25] A little later, in 1705, Baron von Huyssen compiled the *Brief articles of war selected from ancient Christian laws*, which was operational in Menshikov's regiments.[26] Both of these documents formulated the specifications of troop conduct during combat and assaults, and also determined their rights to the spoils of war, i.e., to booty.

24   Rosenheim, pp. 269–294.
25   Bobrovsky, P.O., *Voennoe pravo v Rossii pri Petre Velikom* [*Martial law in Russia under Peter the Great*] Vol. 2, Part 2 (Saint Petersburg, 1898), p. 21.
26   Rosenheim, pp. 294–313.

A collection of plundered loot.
(Martin Engelbrecht, 1684-1756, Augsburg, 1745, Anne S.K. Brown Military Collection)

The instructions *Stat'i vo vremia voinskogo pokhoda*" ["Articles during a military campaign"], which were published in 1703 and confirmed in 1704, banned being diverted by looting during a battle on pain of death: "No one should turn to even a kopeck worth before orders", which meant no looting before the commander allowed it. Point 47 of the Articles of War, Point 16 in Chapter VIII of the *Brief Articles of War* and Point 106 of the Code of Justice all repeated the same thought: "Should a fortress or some other place be taken by an attack, no one at this time should plunder or get drunk, until the enemy troops lay aside their weapons … and an order has been issued to obtain loot. Those who transgress will be shown no mercy and punished with death."[27] On one hand, these norms point to the substantial problem of loss of control over the troops that have broken through into a city; on the other hand, they infer that "permission to plunder" (as expressed in Point 106 of the Articles of War) from the command was a regular matter. Similar specifications concerned looting during a battle in the field – they were particularly urgent since troops who went after pickings at the height of battle became easy marks for a counter-attacking enemy. This means plunder was permitted as long as it did not break down combat discipline.

Point 98 of the Code of Justice said that stockpiles of gunpowder, artillery and other government storage facilities, as well as public repositories of foodstuffs, ought to be preserved; they should be treated as the sovereign's property "without any contrary misappropriations" (the *Brief Articles* in Point 17 of Chapter VIII added bells to the list of public loot). Point 112 of the *Articles*

---

27   Rosenheim, p. 277.

The plundering of a town. Fragment from a pack of playing cards about the 1st Duke of Monmouth's rebellion in England, 1685. (Artist unknown, England, end of 17th century, British museum)

later clarified that after the inventorying of the compiled loot, all the rest (obviously, private property) belonged to the troops; in so doing, a tenth of it was to be set aside for the sick and injured. It was forbidden to loot buildings and residents who had received mercy. It was also forbidden to destroy without orders a building that had been taken by combat. Higher officers were supposed to settle disputes, "when the allocation of booty caused confusion, arguments or conflicts" (Point 102 of the Code). At the same time commanders did not have the right to deprive their subordinates of the loot if it was taken properly (Point 103).

The Code recognised that "great misfortune comes from unregulated drunkenness" so both officers and soldiers were not only to abstain from drinking, but also not to induce others to drink. Even though an intoxicated condition during the commission of "malicious deeds and idleness" was considered a common excuse, the Code called drunkenness an "aggravating circumstance" (Point 73). According to Point 74, anyone who got drunk before a combat action or attack was punished by death or a severe punishment with stripping of rank and expulsion from a regiment.

Permission to loot a city in official historiography, as a rule, is not mentioned; only in one journal was it directly written: "Our soldiers … amused themselves in Narva with the pillaging of a lot of locals' belongings and possessions worth many millions; this booty was allowed to our soldiers in exchange for their labours."[28] Kelch wrote that the Tsar gave his soldiers two days to plunder the city, but this period of time was extended, and the looting continued as long as the residents still had something left: "At the beginning of this looting, the residents remained in cellars and in their homes, holed up behind heavy doors, and did not open them until the Russians were swearing on a cross that they were no longer killing a single person. When the doors opened, they then took everything valuable that they could find, stripped the people naked; and everyone could now guess what this barbaric mob was going to do next – it was necessary only to recall what even more civilised nations did in such situations."[29] An archive document allows us to correct the emotional description left by the Livonian chronicler. According to an order down to the army on 10 August, the troops had already left the city and all of the loot was supposed to be turned over under signature for the following distribution among the participants. Thus, the sacking of Narva lasted only one day, which is also confirmed by the letter from Reval.

---

28   *Podennaia zapiska ili zhurnal voinskogo i inogo povedeniia // Pokhodnyi zhurnal 1704 goda*, p. 80.
29   Kelch, pp. 418–419.

Later, on 21 August, Tsar Peter wrote to Prince Repnin as to how the plunder taken in Narva should be distributed: "1). Give back all the silver, and also the gold, to those who brought it in; 2) Having collected all the copper, pay three roubles each to the soldiers and two roubles each to the others; 3) Whatever belongs to the King, take with no pay; 4) Everything else, including the money, which happened to be paid for the copper, issue to the officers and soldiers who have been determined to have taken part in the attack, for allocation."[30] As is clear, the sharing of the loot corresponded to the existing laws – practically all of the plunder was returned to the soldiers, or was bought from them; only the Swedish government supplies were allocated unconditionally to the Tsar's treasury. It is interesting that Field Marshal Ogilvy believed that he was deprived of his full share and complained to the Tsar on 21 March 1705: "In return for the glorious conquest of Narva, all of the ranks from the common soldier to the highest-ranking officer received a considerable loot. Only I alone, even though the entire commandant's house belonged to me by military rights, did not receive anything, because when others were seizing homes, cellars and other places, I was subduing Ivangorod."[31]

At the start of the 18th century in Russia, the concept of private imprisonment still existed. It was regulated by law, and according to Point 99 of the Code, all of the prisoners captured in a large battle or during an assault ("a large military event") ended up as the sovereign's property. Those captured in skirmishes or by small parties ("in various small actions or in the country") accrued to those who took them. According to Point 100, it was necessary to present all of the prisoners immediately to the commander to be recorded and questioned by the General Auditor, after which they were to be left under the supervision of General Gewaldiger. No one had the right to kill or release "prisoners that had been promised mercy" (Point 101).[32] In practice this meant that just as in previous centuries, when campaigning across enemy lands, a large number of villagers were seized and led away to Russia or to Ukraine, where they fell into service under new masters or sold to new masters. Just as under Tsar Alexei Mikhailovich, when "captives from other lands" made up a significant share of the servant class, under Peter Alekseevich prisoners continued to fall into personal subservience as "domestics" or "servants"; according to the norms of those times, they could be sold, inherited and so forth. In the social structure of Russian society at the turn of the centuries, this social stratum was one of the most numerous, since not only nobility, but also merchants, townsfolk, bureaucrats, clerics and even wealthy peasants acquired servants in this way.

Kelch, when describing the horror of the fall of the city, reports that all of Narva's children between the ages of six and 14 were separated from their parents and led away to a camp, and held there for five days, where they were to be persuaded to be baptised in the Russian Orthodox religion, and then readied for transportation back to Russia. However, supposedly the Tsar

30 PiB, Vol. 3, p. 140.
31 Ustrialov, N., *Istoriia tsarstvovaniia Petra Velikogo*, Vol. 4, Part 2, p. 330.
32 Rosenheim, pp. 269–294.

himself intervened and under the fear of death ordered them not to seize the children, who as a result were returned to their parents. It is hard to confirm the account of events offered by the Livonian patriot, but certain details regarding the fate of the prisoners can be found in Russian documents.

A lieutenant of the Ivangorod garrison, Hans Adam Hald, after the surrender went over to Russian service and began to search for his family, who had gone missing after the storming of Narva. Tsar Peter himself took part in the matter and through an order to the regiments sent out a demand to find those who had captured the Lieutenant's wife Maria Berkbom and her three children, and ordered the prisoners to be delivered to Major General James Bruce under the fear of punishment.[33] According to the 1710 Russian Census, in one of the noble families in Tobolsk "there were prisoners from Narva who had been purchased in Moscow; a Chude, the 28-year-old Iakov Kuzmin, and the 50-year-old Lavrentii Danilov, also a Chude, and they had both served as soldiers in Swedish regiments."[34] In Saint Petersburg in 1718, servants comprised a little less than half the population, and of them, six percent were captive foreigners.[35] During the invasion of Ukraine by Charles XII's army, the Swedes came upon not a few Finns and Livonians there, who had been previously carried off by Cossacks.[36] The future Empress of Russia Catherine I became the most famous member of this category of captives; she had been taken prisoner in Marienburg in 1702. According to the Treaty of Nystad of 1721 "all people who had been taken away from one or another country during this war" (with the exception of Swedish subjects who had accepted the Russian Orthodox faith) received the right to return to their homes together with the prisoners of war.

11 August

Work began to restore the ramparts of the city that had been destroyed during the siege – the fortress now had to be defended against a possible Swedish attack. In this case, all of the approach trenches had to be refilled and levelled with the ground, so that in the event of an attack, the enemy could not make use of the already prepared siegeworks. It was recommended that the quartermasters begin allocating quarters in the city, and engineers and labourers by this time had cleared the streets and passages of rubble and debris. Now it would be possible to introduce some of the infantry in order to take up the most important posts, then bring in artillery, followed by all of the sick and wounded soldiers for treatment in the city, and not in field conditions.[37]

---

33   RGVIA, F. 2584, Op. 1, D. 6, l. 9.

34   1710 Census Book of the town of Tobolsk; census record of Prince Vasilii Meshchersky. The 1710 Census is available on-line at <http://census1710.narod.ru/perepis/214_1_1317.htm> (accessed 6 August 2018).

35   Kosheleva, O.E., *Liudi Sankt-Peterburgskogo ostrova Petrovskogo vremeni* [*People of the Saint Petersburg island at the time of Peter the Great*] (Moscow, 2004), pp. 195–203.

36   Laidre, p. 90.

37   *Leben und Thaten des Czaars Petri Alexiwiecz*, Vol. 2, p. 347; Mallet, A.M., *Les Travaux de Mars ou L'Art de la Guerre*, Vol. 3 (Paris, 1691), p. 313.

Churches of the Old Town of Narva.
The white belfry on the right belonged to the German Church of St. John the Jerusalemite. It was built in the 15th century as a Roman Catholic church; during the Reformation it became a Lutheran church. In 1708 the building became consecrated as the Russian Orthodox *Spaso-Preobrazhensky* (Transfiguration) Cathedral; at the end of the 18th century, the addition of the Chapel of Nikolai Chodotvorets with the cupola was built. On the left of the photograph is the Swedish cathedral from the mid-17th century. It served as the residence of the general superintendent, the main cleric of Swedish Ingermanland. Charles XII celebrated his victory in it on 1 December 1700. From 1704 to 1708, it was the Russian Orthodox Church of St. Aleksandr Nevsky; it was then closed until 1747, before becoming the Church of St. John of the German Lutheran community. Both buildings were destroyed during the fighting of 1944 and have not been rebuilt. (Otto Kletzl, 1897-1945 and Richard Hamman-MacLean 1908-2000, Estonia, 1940-1941 [Bildarchiv Foto Marburg])

12 August

One of the city's two large stone churches, the Swedish Cathedral, was converted into a place of Russian Orthodox service under the name of the Saint Alexander Nevsky Church, and the army's campaign iconostasis was delivered to it. The German Johann Jerusalem Church, according to von Huyssen, was left to the residents; however, the city chronicle states that it was simply closed.[38]

13 August

The Polish ambassador was given a public audience with the Tsar in Narva, in the house given to Menshikov. Tomasz Dzialinsky in the accompaniment of the Lithuanian hetman Oginsky and the Vilnius canon Mikhail Belozor arrived from the camp in a carriage that was escorted by a half a regiment of dragoons and was met in the city by a battalion of the Preobrazhensky Guards Regiment. During the official ceremony the envoys "most humbly recommended to his Tsarist majesty the keeping and defence of their

---

38   *Leben und Thaten des Czaars Petri Alexiewicz*, Vol. 2, p. 347; Archiv., p. 282; Kelch, p. 422; Hansen, pp. 241, 286.

homeland against a common adversary"; after the audience, the ambassador returned to his camp in his carriage.[39] In addition, yet another order was issued to the troops, which instructed them to inform the command about the prisoners and loot that had been taken.[40]

14 August

The Russians were continuing to put the city back into order – to remove corpses and to clear streets and buildings. In order to avert a possible contagion, it was ordered to throw the dead, the half-dead and the sick over the cliff and into the river.[41] Twenty-four soldiers from each regiment were assembled for this work. The colonels received a directive to provide information about the personnel, and to specify how many soldiers had been wounded and could no longer continue service. Prisoners were allocated to the regiments and supplied with an allowance of rusk.

The Tsar together with generals, ministers and foreign envoys often rode to inspect the fortress and to direct the reparation of the breaches and destruction. During such an excursion, they all "with extreme astonishment saw the height of the bastions, cavaliers, ramparts and other fortifications that the Russian attackers had overcome."[42] Even today, the height of the preserved Victoria Bastion is impressive to tourists. In order to repair the breaches and for the other restoration work, Menshikov ordered Ulian Akimovich Seniavin, the commissar of the Chancellery of the Towns, to come to Narva with stoneworkers and lime burners.[43]

15 August

In the newly dedicated church, the former Swedish cathedral, where in 1700 King Charles XII had commemorated his victory, now the Russians conducted a liturgy and a thanksgiving for their victory. Then they arranged a salute by firing three salvoes from all of the bastions with their captured cannons and from the Russian batteries, and in the camp the arrayed soldiers in formation fired a volley. Tsar Peter announced Menshikov as the governor-general of Narva, while Major General Chambers was honoured with the Order of Saint Andrew the Apostle. The upgrading of the city continued – ruins were being rebuilt, lamps were being installed on the streets, and by evening, a holiday event was organised. The new governor directed for a grand gateway to be constructed in front of his home – an "arc of triumph". Decorative lights with inscriptions and emblems in honour of the Tsar were fixed up for the night in the town hall and other buildings, while Peter himself went around the city singing the *Te Deum* hymn with an a cappella group. The Tsar set up a mortar

39 *Pokhodnyi zhurnal 1704 goda*, p. 80; Von Huyssen, p. 458.
40 RGVIA, F. 2584, Op. 1, D. 6, l. 8.
41 Archiv., p. 283; Kelch, p. 422.
42 Von Huyssen, p. 459.
43 Slavnitsky, N.R., "U.A. Seniavin and his activity to repair and construct fortifications in north-western Russia" from the 2014 conference "Petrovskoe vremia v litsakh" [Personalities of Peter's Time]. Materials of the academic conference (Saint Petersburg, 2014), p. 358.

in front of the governor's home that was filled with wine, and invited people to partake in celebration of the great victory.[44]

16 August

That evening, after much discussion and thought, the Ivangorod commandant decided to surrender his fortress. In order to reach agreement on the terms, the two sides exchanged hostages. Three Swedish officers went from Ivangorod to Narva, and three Russian officers entered the Ivangorod castle. Stjernstråle was ready to open the gates in exchange for the right to march out with colours flying and drums beating, all their arms and baggage, and four cannons, and to have liberty to go to Reval; and that those officers and soldiers whose wives were located in Narva might fetch them along to Reval. Ogilvy agreed on all of Stjernstråle's terms, except regarding the flags and cannons.[45]

The palace of Peter the Great in Narva. (Otto Kletzl, 1897-1945 and Richard Hamann-MacLean 1908-2000, Estonia, 1940-1941, Bildarchiv Foto Marburg)

The home of the silversmith Jakob Lude (second half of the 17th century) on the corner of Ritter Street and the Narova embankment was bought as a Tsarist residence, although Peter during his visits to the town didn't reside only in it. In 1865 it was transferred from the War Department to the Narva society of citizens of the Grand Guild as a building to house the Historical Museum. The building no longer exists. (Otto Kletzl, 1897-1945 and Richard Hamann-MacLean 1908-2000, Estonia, 1940-1941, Bildarchiv Foto Marburg)

What Was the Process of Surrendering to an Accord?

Vauban dedicated his famous book to the description of all theoretically possible means of attack and defence, with the assumption that the fortress commandant would defend "to the last possibility"; at the same time, the great engineer acknowledged that over his career, such had practically never happened. For the besieged it was considered admissible to surrender as soon as the besieger had undertaken significant efforts to take the city (built artillery batteries, led the approach trenches to the ramparts, and create a breach in the walls). The time and effort spent by the adversary on siegeworks justified the commandant in the eyes of his superiors and indicated that every possible effort had been made to defend the city. Given its stubborn defence, the garrison could "earn" more honourable terms of surrender from the enemy.

From the start of the war, the Russians conquered a succession of fortresses. In certain cases the commandants waited until the besiegers

---

44 *Pokhodnyi zhurnal 1704 goda*, pp. 80–81; Von Huyssen, p. 445; Archiv., p. 230; Adlerfeld, Vol. 2, p. 24; Allart, No. 2, p. 141.
45 *Pokhodnyi zhurnal 1704 goda*, p. 81; Adlerfeld, Vol. 2, pp. 25-26; PSZRI, Vol. 4, pp. 264–264.

The symbols for ceasing fire: a white flag or the beating of the chamade by a drum. (Johann Melchior Füssli; Zürich, 1714, Zentralbibliothek Zürich)

had constructed a battery and then yielded the fortress after a short bombardment. In May 1703, the Swedish garrisons of Nyenschantz, Jama and Koporie, "unable to endure our abundant harassing fire and seeing the exhaustion of their own troops", requested mercy and were released under the terms of an accord.[46] Occasionally, the bombardments alone were insufficient, and the two sides agreed upon a capitulation only after the besiegers had created a breach in the ramparts and were beginning to storm the fortress – for example, when taking Marienburg and Nöteborg in 1702, and Dorpat later. There were occasions when a fortress was yielded without resistance prior to the start of an assault or siege. For example, in 1700 during the first Russian campaign towards Narva, the small Swedish garrisons of Jama, Koporie and Syrenets abandoned their fortresses without combat. In the same manner, in 1703 the Polish cities of Elbing and Poznan surrendered under the threat of a Swedish assault.[47] During the entire time of the week-long negotiations with the Ivangorod commandant, not a single shot was fired at the fortress by the Russian side, even though all of the Russian artillery had been freed up after taking Narva.

In the military tradition of the 17th century, the chamade and a white flag served as the symbols for the start of negotiations and the ceasing of fire. The white flag is not often mentioned in the sieges of the Great Northern War, though the chamade (a certain drum beat or sound of a trumpet) were constantly employed. The term "capitulation" meant the conclusion of any sort of agreement about ceasing military operations. This was a transaction favourable for both sides. The besieging force spared their resources (which would have been expended to continue the siege works, bombardments or when storming the fortress), but the main thing was that it won time. The besieged force, by capitulating, at the very least saved lives, and at the most – baggage and reputation. Then there was surrender "at discretion", which is to say an unconditional surrender, when a garrison, captured with all of its baggage and could not dictate any conditions whatsoever, would be totally at the mercy of the victor. All of the remaining options, when a garrison was given a more or less honourable possibility to give up a fortress and avoid imprisonment, were called "surrender to an accord" (which is to say, by

46   Sheremetev's field campaign journal 1701–1705, p. 129; PiB, Vol. 2, p. 160; PiB, Vol. 3, p. 436.

47   Adlerfeld, Vol. 1, pp. 257, 272–275.

agreement), while the specific terms of the surrender were called "articles of an accord". The traditional honourable surrender presumed that the garrison could march out of the fortress "with drum playing, flags flying, with a match [of a matchlock musket] smouldering at both ends and a bullet held in the mouth, and with several cannons, as well as with wagons and a convoy for baggage, wounded and the sick.[48] The unfurled flags and the playing music symbolised the garrison's martial prowess and their preserved regalia (drums and colours, as well as the cannons, were highly regarded as trophies of war). The smouldering match and the musket balls in the mouth meant the full combat readiness of the garrison, which although had indeed surrendered, remained a danger for the adversary. According to the manner of loading a matchlock musket that was prevalent in the 17th century, a musketeer before firing would take a musket ball being held in his mouth and drop it into the musket barrel following the charge of gunpowder.[49] By the start of the 18th century, these attributes were preserved, most likely, only as symbols, since flintlocks had arrived in the infantry to replace the matchlock muskets, and the separate loading had been replaced with the introduction of the unitary paper cartridge. Custom dictated that the garrison march out through a breach in the ramparts; however, passable breaches were a rarity, so as a rule the defenders would simply march out through the gates.

After the fall of Narva, Ivangorod remained under the control of a small Swedish garrison, to where certain soldiers and citizens could flee from the captured city across the bridge. The Russian forces quickly seized the hornworks around the Ivangorod fortress, but afterward combat operations ceased. A truce was offered to the commandant, to which he agreed with readiness (with no hope to resist an entire army with several hundred of his own soldiers), but he refused to surrender. While the victors were putting captured Narva back into order and giving their soldiers rest, Stjernstråle sought to ready the castle for a defence, even though he had virtually exhausted his food supply. According to Adlerfeld, the commandant announced that if an attempt was made to take the castle by assault, he would blow it up with all his garrison. Learning of the commandant's reply, the Tsar became highly incensed and sent back Arnstedt to tell him that if the commandant did not immediately accept the terms that were offered to him, he would offer no quarter, even to the prisoners in Narva, and would deal with the Swedish defenders in the same way, not even sparing nursing infants. The commandant replied that these threats would not induce him and that he considered that it would be dishonourable to cowardly surrender at the discretion of the enemy a castle that the King had entrusted to him, but that if he was given an honourable capitulation, he might then turn over the castle

48   Feuquières, A., *Memoirs historical and military* … (London, 1735–1736), Vol. 2, p. [CAN-CAP]; Mallet, A.M., *Les Travaux de Mars ou L'art de La Guerre*, Vol. 3, p. 308; Vauban, pp. 163-164.
49   Regarding the smouldering match of the musketeers at both ends, see Wallhausen's treatise *Kriegskunst zu Fuss* (1615); regarding the bullet held in the mouth, see: *The exercise of the foot* (Dublin, 1701), p. 23; *Förordning och Reglemente för infanteriet Som den Stormäckstige Konung oche Herre, Herr Carl den XII: Sweriges, Götes och Wändes Konung &c. &c.* (Reval, 1701), p. 28.

The Tsar accepts the surrender of Dorpat. Fragment of a cartouche, the map of Dorpat's capture on 13 July 1704. (Unknown artist; Russia, 1704; the Netherlands, 1710s Russian National Library)

and place it in his Majesty's hands. At this point, Ogilvy agreed to release Stjernstråle and his garrison, but without the colours and cannons.[50]

The commandant bore the responsibility for the decision to surrender a fortress, but he could share it with his subordinates. For example, the commandant of Nöteborg von Schlippenbach according to one source surrendered the fortress under threat of the massacre of his own soldiers, but according to others did so at the persuasion of his own officers.[51] The Dorpat commandant Skytte listened to the persuasion of his deputy Colonel Tiesenhausen, and for the discussion of the articles of capitulation, gathered the garrison's colonels and lieutenant colonels together in one of the towers of the fortress, as well as both of the town's burgomeisters and the pastor of the German church.[52] The Ivangorod commandant also questioned his officers, and they confirmed that he had every possible justification for a legitimate capitulation.[53]

The besieger agreed upon an honourable accord, but only if the garrison had earned it with its courageous defence and was in a condition to put up a defence. When taking Dorpat, the attacking Russian troops literally stopped at the smashed gates of the fortress, and to Skytte's request for honourable conditions Sheremetev replied that it was already too late to ask for favourable terms. However, it was permitted to bring out the garrison together with their family members and a month's worth of provisions; all of the officers and only three of the garrison's companies were permitted to carry their personal arms, while the remaining men had to come out without weapons, powder or bullets.[54] The Russians had every basis to consider Ivangorod's situation to be hopeless and to wait for its surrender due to hunger in the very near future, and therefore they considered surrender at discretion; however, Peter "due to his exceptional Tsarist mercy" allowed the garrison and residents that totalled a number of 3,000 people to come out

50   Adlerfeld, Vol. 2, pp. 24–26.
51   Ustrialov, N.G., *Istoriia tsarstvovaniia Petra Velikogo*, Vol. 4, Part 1, pp. 202–203; Part 2, p. 591; Shaskol'sky, I.P., *Shvedskii istochnik ob osade Noteburga Petrom I: Materialy i soobshchenii po fondam otdela rukopisnoi i redkoi knigi* [*Swedish source about the siege of Nöteborg by Peter I: Materials and reports according to the files of the department of manual and rare books*] (Leningrad, 1987), pp. 222–223.
52   Palli, Ch. E., *Mezhdu dumia boiami za Narvu* [*Between two battles for Narva*], p. 240; Laidre, pp. 147, 148.
53   Adlerfeld, Vol. 2, p. 25.
54   PiB, Vol. 3, pp. 663–664.

freely, "to be escorted to Reval, but without colours, drum beats or drawn swords, and with their arms shouldered upside down."[55]

The carrying of a musket upside down, which is to say with the butt up, was one of the motions in the manual of arms, which in English drills was known as "Club your musket" and in Russian drills was called "turn around off the field".[56] Usually, a musket was carried on the left shoulder with the muzzle pointing upwards, and the having it other way had a particular sense. According to the Petrine Regulations of 1715, soldiers who had been relieved at their sentry posts carried their muskets "off the field". During the triumphal ceremony in Moscow in November 1703 in honour of the return of Ingria, Tsar Peter ordered his soldiers "to march, not with arms presented, but as off the field with the muzzle of the musket pointing downward, and with the buttstock in the air." By this gesture the Tsar was demonstrating to the Swedish resident Thomas Knipper that having won back "all that had belonged to his state since antiquity", he was now ready to conclude a peace.[57] Thus, by carrying their muskets with the butt upwards, they demonstrated a waiver of further resistance, and this was a symbolic departure from the field of battle.

The transfer of the fortress into the hands of the besieger did not mean a simultaneous marching of the garrison out of the fortress and a return of it to "friendly forces". An officer of the Swedish garrison of Ivangorod wrote that "they took possession of the castle with a regiment of foot, where they detained us eight days, before we were suffered to depart."[58] At Peter's direction, several of the garrison's officers were to be held in exchange for the previous violations on the Swedish side regarding the rules of the exchange of prisoners."[59]

17 August

At 8:00 in the morning, Russian infantry crossed the bridge and took up station in front of Ivangorod; several hours later, the gates opened and the new owners entered. Peter's soldiers took up their posts, while the Swedish garrison remained in the city for another eight days, after which they were given boats for transporting their wounded and baggage, while the able soldiers and their families marched overland to Reval.[60]

The musket movement "Club your muskets!" (Unknown etcher; Saxony, Hans Friedrich von Fleming, *Der Volkommene Teutsche Soldat*, Leipzig, 1726)

55 Von Huyssen, pp. 437–438.
56 Tatarnikov, K.V., *Stroevye ustavy, instruktsii i nastavleniia russkoi armii XVIII veka: Sbornik materialy v 2 tomakh* [*Drill regulations, instructions and guidelines of the Russian army of the XVIII century: Collection of materials in 2 volumes*] Vol. 1 (Moscow, 2010), pp. 35, 56, 129, 151.
57 Von Huyssen, p. 375.
58 Adlerfeld, Vol. 2, p. 26.
59 PiB, Vol. 3, pp. 127–128.
60 Adlerfeld, Vol. 2, p. 26.

19 August

The signing of an agreement with the Polish ambassador Dzialinsky took place. This agreement entered diplomatic history as the Treaty of Narva.

The Narva Allied Treaty

The treaty was concluded between His Majesty Tsar Peter Alekseevich on one side and the Polish King Augustus II (jointly with magnates of the Polish crown and of the Grand Duchy of Lithuania) on the other through their authorised representatives – Fedor Golovin and Tomas Dzialyński. The document consisted of eight paragraphs, according to which the sides concluded a defensive and offensive pact until the end of the war with Sweden; the terms obliged the partners to coordinate their actions and not to enter separate negotiations with the enemy. Tsar Peter accepted the obligation of returning to Poland the Ukrainian places that had been conquered by the Cossacks of Semen Paliy, and for his voluntary surrender Paliy was promised amnesty as a Polish subject.

The fifth paragraph dictated that Russia would transfer its conquests in Livonia to Poland, and this gave King Augusust II the hope of acquiring the cities of Narva and Dorpat that had been paid for with Russian blood. However, the formulation as it was proposed by the Russian side (namely, by R. Patkul) referred to the Livonian places "that had previously belonged to the Reczpospolita") and said nothing at all about Estonia. Therefore, there could only be talk about Dorpat and Pernau, which had temporarily belonged to Poland from 1583 up until their conquest by Sweden; Russia was not obliged to give up Narva, which had never belonged to Poland.

The Tsar also promised to dispatch 12,000 Russian infantry, clad in European-style uniforms, and place them under the command of King Augustus. Russia was also supposed pay its ally an annual subsidy of 200,000 roubles for military needs; the transfer of the funds depended on the Poles' ability to field an army of 48,000 men for the war, which was highly improbable and also allowed Peter with the passage of time to cease the payment. The final point of the treaty obliged the Reczpospolita to continue the war even if the Swedes abandoned the Polish-Lithuanian lands.[61]

The military potential of the new, formal ally was low – he required a lot of Russian troops, and even more Russian money. However, the military–political alliance enabled the strengthening of the anti-Swedish position in Poland and prevented the consolidation of the Polish elites around the pro-Swedish king Stanislaw Leczynski. Thanks to this, King Charles XII continued to be "bogged down" in Poland.

---

61   PiB, Vol. 3, pp. 129–135; PSZRI, Vol. 4, pp. 266–269.

20 August

The Polish ambassador "obtained a pass", left Narva and headed towards Pskov. In execution of the treaty that had been concluded the day before, General Repnin was ordered to set out to Polotsk together with six foot and six horse regiments. The Nöteborg commandant Gustav Wilhelm von Schlippenbach was informed that he was being freed under the guarantee of Swedes remaining in Narva. The Tsar set the bail for Lieutenant Colonel von Schlippenbach at two colonels, a burgomaster, and seven more of the townsfolk.[62]

21 August

Tsar Peter wrote instructions to Prince Repnin regarding how to distribute the plunder that had been taken by the troops in Narva.[63]

22 August

The Tsar, together with his close associates, left Narva and headed to Dorpat by water; however, having waited in Syrenets on Lake Peipus for 5 days and never getting a fair wind, they set out by land and arrived in Dorpat on 30 August. Meanwhile, the Tsar directed Repnin to march into Lithuania with his troops – that is how the fulfilment of the promise for Russian troops according to the treaty with Poland began.[64]

24 August

Prince Repnin's troops, which had been designated for the campaign into Lithuania, began to move out of Narva; under the command of Major General Scharf, the six infantry regiments headed to Pskov. Later six dragoon regiments under Major General von Rönne set out for the same place.[65]

Meanwhile: Charles XII's Storming of Lwow

The news was reporting: "The Swedish General Steinbock issued decrees, ordering that provisions (bread stocks) be brought to him, and asking 10,000 barrels of beer and 30,000 measures of flour from the town of Lwow."[66] Later: "The Swedish king took the city of Lwow with an attack and demanded that he be given 300,000 silver tallers within the next six hours."[67] Lwow, the largest city of the Polish region of Ruś Czerwona[68], refused to pay the tribute to the Swedish corps under Count Magnus Stenbock in the hope of quick relief from King Augustus' Saxon troops and Mazepa's Cossacks.

---

62 *Pokhodnyi zhurnal 1704 goda*, p. 81; PiB, Vol. 3, pp. 135–136; Archiv., p. 284.
63 PiB, Vol. 3, p. 140.
64 *Pokhodnyi zhurnal 1704 goda*, pp. 81–82.
65 Volynsky, Book 3, pp. 310–311.
66 *Vedomosti – Moskva (Pechatnyi dvor)*, 5 October 1704.
67 *Ibid.*
68 Red Ruthenia, a region comprising present-day south-eastern Poland and an adjacent portion of Ukraine.

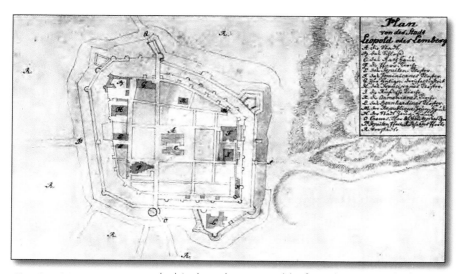

The plan of the city of Lwow. (Unknown cartographer; Sweden, 17th century, Krigsarkivets kartsamlingar)

Not long before this, the Russian corps under Prince Dmitry Mikhailovich Golitsyn had arrived at Lwow from Kiev. He was cordially greeted by the townsfolk and marched on to link up with the Saxons, where Patkul took command of the regiments. Now Charles XII hurried to Lwow, having left his infantry and artillery behind, and appeared before the city with three regiments of dragoons. A small unit of Polish cavalry rode out to meet the Swedes, but refused battles and galloped away, leaving Lwow guarded only by city militia. The attack began early on the morning of 24 August against the fortified Monastery of Carmelites, after the capture of which the Swedes broke into the city, on the boot heels of the fleeing defenders. The King personally, together with his friend, the 15-year-old Prince Maximilian Emanuel Württemberg-Winnental, was the first to mount the ramparts. The dragoons began to plunder the homes and churches, until they were stopped two hours later and fell into formation on the market square. Under the threat of putting the place to torch, the merchants and clergy were ordered to pay the victors a large monetary contribution, which beggared the previously wealthy city.[69]

Dramatic events were unfolding at this time in other parts of Poland as well. On 25 August, King Augustus captured and took prisoner Swedish Lieutenant General Arvid Horn and his troops in Warsaw. After Lwow, Charles XII actively pursued the Saxons and inflicted a defeat on General Schulenburg on the border of Silesia in the Battle of Punitz [Poniec]. After several combat encounters, the Saxons in October besieged the Swedish garrison of Poznań. Patkul's Russian corps took part in this operation; a rampart was breached, and everything was ready for an assault, but on 2 November under the threat of an arriving relief force commanded by King Charles XII himself, at King Augustus II's order, the siege was lifted and the allies retreated. In Lithuania on 14 September, after a month-long siege by the forces under Lewenhaupt and Sapieha, the fortress of Birżai was surrendered under an accord and subsequently demolished. In November, Wiśniowiecki's Russian–Lithuanian corps crushed Sapieha's Lithuanians near Szkuodas. The war in the Polish–Lithuanian Commonwealth continued.

69   Nordberg, J.A., *Histoire de Charles XII* (Naué, 1748), Vol. 1, pp. 478–491; Adlerfeld, Vol. 2, pp. 39–44; *Gistoriia*, Vol. 1, p. 248; *Gistoriia*, Vol. 2, p. 384; Shutoi, V.E., "Oborona L'vova v 1704", *Kratkie soobshcheniia Instituta slavianovedeniia*, Vol. 17 (1955), pp. 14–35.

26 August

A ship left from Narva, aboard which was Schlippenbach who had just been
released to Sweden; the ship passed through the drawn pontoon bridge, then
the coastal Russian batteries and anchored in the estuary of the Narova River.
Having waited for several days in vain for a favourable wind to Finland, the
ship departed to Reval. The victors sent a portion of the defeated garrison –
two officers and 50 soldiers – to Vyborg, in order to carry the news about the
Russian victory to this part of the Swedish kingdom.[70]

On this day, Colonel Bauer was sent out towards Reval with select
companies of eight dragoon regiments and Kalmyks "in search of the
enemy". On 30 August the detachment approached Reval; General von
Schlippenbach and his troops declined battle, Bauer gathered "captives and
loot" in the Reval suburbs and departed to Dorpat.[71]

3 September

The first Narva prisoners – a major general, 92 officers, 19 men of lower
ranks, 19 women and 22 children – reached Moscow. By this time, 117
officers, 82 men of lower ranks, 12 civilian men, 16 women and 28 children
were already located in the capital.[72]

8 September

The Tsar set out from Dorpat by water to Pskov, and from there through
Novgorod to the Olonets shipyard, where he arrived on 20 September. During
this trip, the town of Novaia Ladoga on the River Volkhov was founded.
From Olonets, Tsar Peter arrived in Petersburg on 5 October and on the 9th
of the same month set out for Narva, where he remained until 6 December.[73]

10 September

Peter I's foreign minister Fedor Golovin returned to Narva from Dorpat.[74]
On this same day, an English ship that had set sail from Saint Petersburg
loaded with resin and tar from the Olonets shipyard was intercepted by the
Swedes "for carrying contraband". The Swedish brigantine *Göija* escorted it
back to Karlskrona. This was the second merchant ship that had arrived in
Saint Petersburg over the first year of the city's existence; the next British
trading ship arrived at the Neva only in 1710.[75]

18 September

One hundred soldiers of Fedor Balk's infantry regiment set out from the
Dorpat garrison, "who had enlisted in the Preobrazhensky Regiment."
Meanwhile one of the first floods in the history of the city took place in Saint

70   Adlerfeld, Vol. 2, p. 26; Archiv., pp. 285, 286.
71   *Pokhodnyi zhurnal 1704 goda*, pp. 82–83.
72   Ustrialov, Vol. 4, Part 2, p. 321.
73   *Pokhodnyi zhurnal 1704 goda*, pp. 82–83; *Gistoriia*, 2nd Ed., p. 388.
74   *Pokhodnyi zhurnal 1704 goda*, p. 83.
75   NIA SPbII RAN, F. 36, Op. 1, D. 693, l. 60, 101 obr.; Rosen, p. 204.

The return from a campaign. Charles-Nicolas Cochin I, 1688-1754, after a drawing by Jean-Antione Watteau, 1684-1721, France, 1710, Anne S.K. Brown Military Collection)

Petersburg. The surging water swept away ships, bridges and timber pilings and flooded the barracks in the fortress that was under construction.[76]

24 September

Two divisions, those of Schonbeck and von Werden, set out from the Narva camp to winter quarters in Pskov. Upon parting, all of the cannons in Narva fired a single salvo; the regiments, having fallen into formation, replied with a volley and set off on the march.[77]

The new peaceful life settled down in Narva and vicinities after the troubles of the siege and the storm. The residents of the districts, who had taken shelter in Narva during the summer campaign, began to return to their homes. A number of passes, written out by Narva's city secretary Peter Holstein, have been preserved. According to these documents, the peasants and pastors together with their families "swore by the Almighty" (in other words, took an oath) in the town hall and were released "to free residence" to their own villages – Päite, Kupanitsa [Gubanitsy], Koprina, Novaia Buria and Soikino [Soikkola].[78]

---

76   NIA SPbII RAN, F. 36, Op. 1, D. 693, l. 100, 147 obr.
77   *Pokhodnyi zhurnal 1704 goda*, p. 83.
78   NIA SPbII RAN, F. 83, Op. 1, D. 424–429.

3 October
Menshikov, Golovin and others of Tsar Peter's "close circle" left Narva; they headed out by land to Saint Petersburg in order to meet with Peter there.[79]

5 October
A Swedish party of 30 soldiers led by a lieutenant by the name of Peter arrived from Vyborg at the rapids on the Neva River "at the behest of Chudes from various villages who live near the rapids" and fell on "the Sovereign's workers" who were felling timber on the northern bank of the Neva. Having killed 20 of the workers, wounding five more, and having taken one alive as a prisoner to interrogate, the Swedes disappeared in the woods in the direction of Saint Petersburg. One Vyborg soldier fell ill and remained to have a lengthy rest in the abandoned huts of the woodcutters; there he was captured ("without a weapon and wearing a uniform grey coat and hat") by soldiers of the 8th Company of the Schlisselburg commandant Poroshin's regiment, which on that day was moving by boat along the Neva River and had been alerted by the surviving woodcutters. The captured soldier, a Chude by the name of Fedor Shibi testified that Swedish units from Vyborg had made several raids in order to take prisoners around Schlisselburg and Petersburg.[80]

7 October
The Swedes returned the four Russian ships that were transporting members of the released Ivangorod garrison to Reval, and brought them to Kotlin Island. Commandant Treiden reported to Menshikov that a Swedish constable had arrived from the Swedish fleet aboard a dinghy to inform the Russians that they were to receive the boats and man them with their people.[81]

17 October
Inglis' regiment was assigned to garrison Ivangorod, pursuant to Menshikov's order to James Bruce.[82] Colonel Inglis himself prior to this, on 3 October, had turned over the town of Jamburg to Evstrat Kudaev.[83]

1 November
Field Marshal Ogilvy, who had remained in Narva over all this time, wrote to Menshikov about his project to hire up to 2,000 "German people" into Russian service in the dragoons. At the same time, he requested that as a colonel and captain of the senior company of his regiment he be paid according to foreign and not Russian wages – 50 roubles a month of a commander's salary and 18 roubles a month as a captain's salary, effective 1 August. Ogilvy also proposed to release on bail and on parole the captured Colonel Morath, so that he could facilitate the exchange of General Weide.[84]

---

79 *Pokhodnyi zhurnal 1704 goda*, p. 83.
80 NIA SPbII RAN, F. 36, Op. 1, D. 693, ll. 28–29.
81 *Ibid.*, l. 28.
82 Arkhiv VIMIAIViVS, F.2, Op. 1, D. 1, l. 176 obr.
83 NIA SPbII RAN, F. 36, Op. 1, D. 693, l. 58.
84 *Ibid.*, ll. 29 obr.–31.

The wall of a house in Narva – a witness of the sieges of 1700 and 1704.
The citizens built these bombs, 3-pood in caliber judging from their relative size, in the wall after the war as a remembrance of the siege they had experienced. When conducting plunging fire, the shells would practically be unable to embed themselves in the wall so tidily. Buildings, thus decorated with cannon balls and bombs, can be encountered in many European places. (Otto Kletzl, 1897-1945 and Richard Hamman MacLean, 1908-2000, Estonia, 1940-1941 Bildarchiv Foto Marburg)

Colonel Carl Peresvetoff-Morath, who commanded the Åbo Reiter Regiment, also belonged to the "boyars", Swedish nobles of Russian origin. When in captivity after the fall of Narva, he served as a guarantor for officer Bremsen, who had been released under his word of honour to Sweden for negotiations about the exchange of prisoners; the latter never returned, so the guarantors, including Morath, received harsher conditions of confinement and were freed only with the end of the war.[85]

8 November

Ogilvy sent the Tsar his plan for reorganising the Russian army. The baron proposed obvious and useful things, such as giving all the regiments the same table of organisation; increasing the infantry companies to 150 men each, as in the Swedish army; unifying the calibres of the firearms; rejecting the use of ponderous baggage trains; recruiting skilled officers and discharging incompetent ones; and most importantly, to "entrust the main command to one person" (namely, himself). From the point of view of recruiting, he recommended taking one recruit from every 20–30 households so as to have the possibility of quickly assembling a large army. Up to this point

---

85   Buchholz, F.-V., *Dnevnik kamer-iunkera Friedrich-Wilhelm Buchholz, 1721–1725: Neistovyi refermator* [*The diary of the chamber Junker Friedrich-Wilhelm Burchholz, 1721-1725: The mad reformer*] (Moscow, 2000), p. 292.

the army had been manned by conscripts (from among the serfs owned by landlords and monasteries, but not the farming peasants) and "any free people" (mercenaries and "vagrants" consisting most often of fugitive peasants).[86] In essence, Ogilvy proposed a model of recruiting to which the Russian government first turned in 1705, having selected among the farming peasants one recruit from every 20 households.[87]

In November, half of each of the two Guards regiments were sent to Moscow with the trophies, while the other half headed by Colonel Mikhail Mikhailovich Golitsyn remained for the winter in Narva.

2 December

A Narva magistrate handed over to the new authorities, namely to Governor Count A.D. Menshikov a "memorandum" with a number of requests, which appealed for the correcting of the affairs for the citizens (under the Swedes they were called "burghers" but were now known as "townsmen") after all of the upheavals they had endured.[88] The first of the 21 articles concerned allowing the Narva citizens to trade throughout all of Russia like other Tsarist subjects were able to do – this request was granted. The second request "to allow townsfolk who are completely devastated to brew beer and mead and to distil wine and vodka"; in response, they were allowed to brew only beer or mead (there were a large number of taverns in the city – 146 in 1706).[89] The third article was: "When peace arrives, no overseas trade will be allowed other than by townsfolk"; at the time it was difficult to foretell that Narva's trade would be completely undermined by the neighbouring new Russian city on the Neva, Saint-Petersburg. To the request to establish daily postal connection with Russian and overseas cities, the answer was given that such a postal exchange had been established in Moscow. There was also a request to ban craftsmen from trading goods other than those of their own handiwork; that, apparently, is how the town merchants wanted to protect their own businesses from competitors. Two articles concerned the inflating costs of foodstuffs. One wanted a ban on repurchasing in the districts, so that the peasants themselves brought their produce to market in Narva and sold them without any middlemen. At the same time, they wanted to ban the same peasants from bringing livestock and game into the city, since "customer pick-up" was cheaper for the townsfolk. Finally, the Narva magistrate asked to return to the citizens the use of their suburban gardens and fishing nets.

In several of the memorandum's articles, the citizens were describing the condition of the city after the siege and assault. The municipal buildings, particularly the school, hospice and orphanage were completely devastated.

---

86   See Rabinovich, M.D., "Formirovanie reguliarnoi armii nakanune Severnoi voiy" ["Formation of the regular army on the eve of the Northern War"] in *Voprosy voennoi istorii Rossii XVIII – pervoi poloviny XIX vv.* [*Questions of military history of the history of Russia of the 18th and first half of the 19th centuries*] (Moscow, 1969).

87   Ustrialov, Vol. 4, Part 2, pp. 324, 478–486; Volynsky, Book 3, pp. 103–104.

88   NIA SPbII RAN, F. 83, Op. 2, D. 1, ll. 297–300; F. 36, Op. 1, D. 693, ll. 116 obr.–119 obr.

89   Smolokurov, A., "Narodonaselenie Narvy: Demograficheskii obzor istoriia goroda" ["Population of Narva: Demographic survey of the city's history"] in *Sbornik Narvskogo muzeia* [*Compilation of the Narva museum*] (Narva, 2000), p. 31.

A street of the Old Town. Soldiers and citizens once marched over this pavement, and the fragments of bombs and roof tile knocked loose from the roofs have rattled on it. This photograph allows us to "fill" this snapshot with various scenes of the peaceful, then wartime and then again peaceful life of the town from three centuries ago. (Otto Kletzl, 1897-1945 and Richard Hamman MacLean, 1908-2000, Estonia, 1940-1941 Bildarchiv Foto Marburg)

The governor, who they had proposed to repair and rebuild the ruins, adopted a resolution: "A decree will follow, but build the schools yourselves." Through their own efforts, the water supply system began to be restored – they proceeded to repair the canal, "so as to take up water into the city". Those townsfolk whose homes were occupied under the requirements of the new rulers requested authorisation to have their homes returned to them, or to gather whatever belongings that remained in them that had not been plundered. The looting of graves, about which the Narva residents were complaining, the governor ordered to ban under the penalty of death. Article 13, in which Menshikov was asked to authorise the sewing of uniforms for the "town hall couriers", remained without an answer.

4 December

The punishment of 29 Russian officers, who "after the first Rugodev campaign were unwilling to serve his Majesty and had left their regiments and posts" took place on this day.[90] They were gathered in Narva and beaten with a knout (and three by a rod), after which, according to the Tsar's decree, they

---

90   RGA VMF, F. 177, Op. 1, D. 56, l. 19; NIA SPbII RAN, F. 36, Op. 1, D. 693, l. 131.

A parade with the war trophies in Moscow. (Aleksei Fedorovich Zubov 1682-174? Russia, 1711)

were sent to Moscow and from there exiled for life together with their wives and children to Azov, where at that time the construction of Peter's first naval fortress was continuing.

This punishment, obviously, was the result of a hearing that had taken place in Narva two days earlier. At the hearing, officers who had been marked as being absent without leave from their regiments after the first Narva campaign were checked and questioned. As became clear, the reason for the absence of majority of them were wounds or illness. Others were no longer on a regiment's payroll, which meant they were "outside the regiment", and the hearing board gathered personal testimonies and requested verification letters from the Office of Military Affairs for each of them. It was found after further investigation that certain officers who had gone missing had died or were now serving in a different regiment, so the panel accepted notices about death or about service in other regiments. In particular, as an example there is the case of a certain Mikhail Ivanovich Shchepotev of von Deldin's regiment "who was permitted to leave Novgorod to go to Moscow", and a note had been made about this in the documents which "cleared" him from further service in his former regiment, since he had switched to serving in the Preobrazhensky Regiment."[91] Only those officers who had no legitimate excuse for going absent without leave from their regiments during the campaign were publicly punished by being flogged by a knout or beaten by a rod.

19 December

A triumphal procession took place in Moscow in honour of the victory at Narva. Major General Chambers rode at the head of the column, followed by the Preobrazhensky Guards Regiment. Then came soldiers carrying the captured Swedish colours and a company of bombardiers led by two captains – Peter I and Menshikov. In their wake came 12 horses drawing a large Swedish mortar, with the Imperial jester Prince Iurii Fedorovich Shakhovskoi seated upon it. The Ingermanlandsky Regiment came next, followed by Major General Horn and all of the Swedish prisoners. Behind them marched a grenadier company of the Semenovsky Regiment and the Field Marshal's riding horses. The commander-in-chief Ogilvy rode on a sleigh and closing up the rear of the procession was the Semenovsky Regiment. Eight triumphal arcs were built in the capital in order to greet the victors.[92]

91 NIA SPbII RAN, F. 83, Op. 1, D. 489, D. 498; F. 36, Op. 1, D. 693, ll. 131 obr.–143 obr.
92 Kurakin, B.I., "Russko-shvedskaia voina: Zapiski, 1700–1710", pp. 300–301; Maslovsky, D.F., *Sbornik VIM*, 1st edn., p. 316.

27 December

The work to set up the palisades around the Narva fortress was completed. Under the Swedes, there were no palisades from the Victoria Bastion and along the river, but now they enclosed the entire city. Large *chevaux-de-frise* were emplaced in the ditches. Andrei Shakhovskoi, who apparently was carrying out the duty of city commandant at this time, reported on the completion of this work to Menshikov.[93]

---

93   NIA SPbII RAN, F. 36, Op. 1, D. 693, l. 52 obr.

5

Conclusion

The siege of Narva in 1704 can be considered one of the most complex operations that the Petrine troops had to carry out over all the years of the war. The attempt to take this same fortress back in 1700 demonstrated the shortcomings in organisation and preparations, and following the debacle on 19 November, a much different command staff was now directing the war. The conquest of small fortresses like Marienburg and Nöteborg in 1702, and Nyenshantz, Jama and Koporie in 1703 enabled Peter's army to acquire certain experience in the tactics of bombardment and an open assault, and to learn from all the mistakes, but if you will, the main achievement of the "training sieges" of 1702–1703 was overcoming the syndrome in 1700 and getting the troops accustomed to winning. At Dorpat, which had a fortress comparable to Narva's in both the strength of the fortifications and the size of the garrison, it became obvious that Boris Sheremetev struggled to conduct a "formal" attack, and Tsar Peter personally had to get involved in the situation.

According to the sources, the decision about a full-scale siege of Narva was taken by the Tsar because of the changing situation only at the end of May, when the campaign towards Kexholm that was already underway was cancelled. At the same time the dispatch of Peter Apraxin's corps to the Narova River in April speaks to the existence of some earlier plans regarding Narva; after the fall of Ingermanland, the threat to Narva was obvious even to the Swedes.

The lessons of 1700 were not for naught, and the Russian command took reliable measures to secure itself from a possible relief force. It was necessary, since Maidel's Swedish corps was threatening from Vyborg, von Schlippenbach's corps from Reval, and out at sea, De Prou's Swedish fleet reigned supreme; moreover, recalling the first campaign, the Russian commanders continued to be concerned about the possible appearance from Poland of Charles XII himself. The siegeworks were screened by a blockade of the Narva estuary, the construction of fortified lines at a distance, as well as by cavalry raids against von Schlippenbach; the besieging army itself on this occasion was ready to meet a relief force in a field battle, and was not taking shelter behind a circumvallation line. The timely construction of batteries at the mouth of the Narova River and of Fort Kronschlot near the Neva estuary neutralised the superiority of the Swedish fleet at sea.

The tactics and methods of warfare was in full accordance with the European military traditions of the early 18th century, but the treatment of the local population on enemy territory to a great degree carried the imprint of the old traditions of "Muscovite" troops. The devastation of the land in the style of war of the preceding centuries turned out to be an effective means of isolating the fortress and made operations by major enemy forces on the "stripped" territory impossible. Through the active use of cavalry in all of these stages – with the help of raids, patrols and blocking detachments – the Russian command kept the Swedes under constant pressure and collected relatively reliable reconnaissance information about the enemy.

The foot-dragging of the Swedish administration with the delivery of provisions from Reval had catastrophic effects for Narva – they postponed it from autumn to winter, and then from winter to spring, but by springtime it was already too late. On the whole, the Swedish side by this moment had lost the initiative in this region. The actions of von Schlippenbach's troops in Estonia, of Maidel's in Finland, and of De Prou's squadron in the Gulf of Finland were uncoordinated and were unable to impede the Russian operations. One can assume that with proper planning, energy, and the attacking elan that was characteristic of the Swedish generals under the direct command of their king, the second Narva campaign might at the very least have been significantly more difficult for the Russians.

Commandant Horn's ban on conducting fire from the fortress without special order, as mentioned in the sources, seems strange – this allowed the besiegers to do their work on the approach trenches and batteries with fewer losses and with considerable speed; judging from the descriptions of the captured trophies, the fortress was not experiencing a shortage of ammunition. At the same time, the silence of the fortress artillery and musketeers was only episodic – the garrison's fire, when it did happen, was often effective, which has been reflected in the materials of both sides.

Whereas in 1700 the garrison conducted frequent and successful sorties, in 1704 such forays were few. Initially the commandant was ready to send out major forces, but the shenanigans of 8 July drove out the commandant's desire to venture risks with large detachments. Horn did stand out for the fact that he refused to surrender the fortress even after the ramparts had been breached and was completely vulnerable to an assault. Bearing responsibility for the fortress that had been entrusted to him by the King, Horn consequently bore personal responsibility for the unavoidable devastation of the city that was taken with battle. It is known that he criticised the conduct of his subordinates – the commandants of other fortresses that had surrendered – and it is possible that for this reason he had no desire for his words to diverge from his actions. However, it is possible to assume as well that the enigmatic cannon signal, heard in the fortress on the evening of 6 August, gave Horn his final hope for relief and preordained Narva's fate.

The number of days spent on taking a fortress is just as an important characteristic of a siege as the numerical strength, number of guns of final outcome. Therefore, in conclusion it is worth turning once again to separate stages of the Narva operation and their length in time.

The date of 27 April, when Peter Apraxin's unit reach the Narova estuary and interrupted the city's communication with the sea, can be considered the starting point, the stage of blockading and encircling the fortress. Next, in pace with the arrival of new forces, there followed the gradual isolation of the city from the land side. On the whole, this stage continued for a significant amount of time – 48 days, since the decision regarding a full-blown siege was made on 22 May, and only after this date did events begin to unfold rapidly.

The gradual siege or formal attack began with the opening of trenches on 15 June. This stage lasted for 45 days; by all appearances, the earthworks were conducted in the expectation of the arrival of artillery and the readiness of siege batteries. The configuration of the trenchworks and approaches on the map of the siege speaks to the fact that the besiegers had ample time and manpower for the conducting of extensive, possibly even excessive earthworks.

The opening of fire with the batteries on 30 July marked the next stage of the siege. It was delayed not only because of the tardy delivery of the guns, but also in expectation of the trophies sent from Dorpat – Tsar Peter was willing to postpone the bombardment for the sake of the possibility of inducing Horn to capitulate with a demonstration of the successes of the Russian army. The work of the breaching cannons to pound a breach in the Victoria Bastion lasted for a week and was effective in comparison with Peter's preceding sieges. The barrage with bombs did damage not only to the fortifications and garrison, but also to the city's population; however, it was viewed as a legitimate means to force the fortress to surrender. The project of emplacing mines beneath the Honour Bastion was also underway, but the bastion's face collapsed before this work was completed.

The final assault was undertaken only after all of the possibilities to induce the commandant to surrender had been exhausted. When organising the assault, the latest methods were employed – an assault with several columns in daylight hours with the support of fire from hand mortars. This enabled to break the defenders' resistance quickly and with comparatively few losses. The bloodshed on the streets of the city in the first hours following the assault was unavoidable, however, soon the population received a guarantee of safety, and a certain share of the city's inhabitants were given a guarantee of inviolability of property. The looting of the city that ensued corresponded to the customs of war but did not last more than a day.

A portion of the garrison was isolated in Ivangorod; after a week of negotiations about surrender, the Swedes were allowed to abandon the fortress and go to join their own. Nearly all of the Russian sieges of Swedish fortresses came to an end in this manner, and only Narva became an exception to this pattern. The resistance of Ivangorod after the fall of Narva calls to mind a number of sieges in European history, in the course of which the garrison defended the fortress until the last possibility, and then fell back into a citadel, in order to continue the defence there. However, in fact the combat operations ceased on the day of Narva's capture, and an attack against Ivangorod never took place before its final surrender.

In comparison with the preceding sieges, the Narva siege of 1704 became the longest for Tsar Peter's army. The culminating successful storming made the capture of Narva the single operation of its type in all the years of the Northern War; all of the following lengthy sieges of large cities ended with a surrender to an accord, while Peter's troops took weaker fortresses by storm and without a preliminary formal siege. The various types of siege tactics used in the course of the Narva operation by the Russian army were repeatedly employed in the future Russian sieges.

6

The Further Fate of the City and Some of the Participants

Remembrance of the successful assault was kept alive both in Narva and in Russia. On 9 August, the Day of St. Matthew, the city held a sacred procession along the walls of the fortress around the entire city and also fired a ceremonial cannonade. In Saint Petersburg, prayer services and a cannonade to celebrate the capture of Narva were also conducted until the edict of 18 October 1723 signed by the Tsar. According to it, "each city was supposed to mark its own day, which is to say the day of its capture, with cannon salvoes in that city." In other cities of Imperial Russia, this day of victory was noted by "joint prayer services in all the churches", but with no salutes.[1] In Saint Petersburg, the Narva victory was memorialised by a cathedral. The wooden building of the Church of Saint Peter and Paul was built in 1703 in the Saint Petersburg fortress; this was the first Peter and Paul Cathedral, but after the construction of the stone cathedral, the wooden church was disassembled, moved to the Petersburg side, and was dedicated in January 1720 in the name of Saint Matthew.[2] Today, the Matveevsky Garden on Bolshaia Pushkarskaia Street in Saint Petersburg is a reminder of it.

What happened to Narva after being taken by the Russian forces? The city's new authorities made the residents swear allegiance to Tsar Peter and conducted a census of the population:

> All of the merchants and artisans, other than [Swedish] servicemen, except for those servicemen who desired it, were all brought to an oath of allegiance to his Majesty. The oath was given by a pastor in the town hall. There, those who gave their oath of loyalty, signed their names below it. As was customary at that time,

---

1   PSZRI, Vol. 7, p. 134.
2   Bogdanov, A.I. and Ruban, V.G., *Istoricheskoe, geograficheskoe i topograficheskoe opisanie Sanktpeterburga, ot nachala zavedenia ego, s 1703 to 1751* [*Historical, geographical and topographical description of Saint Petersburg from the day of its founding, from 1703 to 1751*] (Saint Petersburg, 1779), p. 498.

when swearing the oath, they held their right hand up with two fingers extended, with thumbs were pressed to the palm.

Many Swedes from Narva and Ivangorod signed up for Tsarist service in the artillery – nine artisans, 20 corporals and 400 gunners.[3]

In subsequent years, the war's main events shifted to Courland, Lithuania and Poland. The situation in the cities that had been captured in 1704 was relatively calm; they had Tsarist garrisons and had become Russian border fortresses, beyond which stretched Swedish territory with the large Swedish cities of Reval, Pernau and Riga. The residents and peasants who travelled outside the city in search of provisions continued to maintain relations with their recent defenders – the Swedes, and obviously the imaginary and real cases of the passing of espionage information to the enemy and even the intentions to surrender the fortress to the Swedes troubled the Russian administration.[4]

After 1706 the war turned to the east – having finally dealt with King Augustus and having subdued Poland, Charles XII with his main army marched towards Russia, but the direction of his attack was unknown – it might be Saint Petersburg, Moscow or Kiev. General Lewenhaupt's Swedish troops in Livonia was menacing the Russia's north-western regions, including the newly won Dorpat and Narva. Lübecker's Swedish army was looming over Saint Petersburg from the direction of Finland. In the course of 1708 Charles, before reaching Smolensk, pivoted towards Ukraine; Lewenhaupt, who was on the road to link up with the King, was smashed at the Battle of Lesnaya, while Lübecker only bypassed Saint Peterburg, before boarding ships standing off the Soikina peninsula for evacuation. However, it was impossible to foresee such a course of events, so the Tsar took all possible steps to strengthen the western lines of defence. For example, in 1706 construction began of a defensive line stretching from Pskov to Smolensk, Briansk and further to the south – felled trees forming abatis in the woods, earthen ramparts in the fields, and fortifications on the roads were supposed to impede the advance of small enemy units and slow the advance of major forces.

At the beginning of 1708, the threat to the north-western border became real, so it was decided to focus the defence of the Livonian possessions in Narva, while Dorpat was evacuated. The local population, deemed as unreliable given a Swedish offensive, faced eviction. On 3 February Tsar Peter issued an edict: "Send all of the Narva residents away to Vologda, as well as pastors of the Chude and the Amtmann.[5] … In Dorpat, withdraw all of the artillery and similar to Pskov, blow up and devastate the fortress, and send all of the residents together with the Narva citizens to Vologda."[6]

---

3   PiB, Vol. 3, p. 743.

4   Pib, Vol. 4, pp. 100–101; Petrov, p. 315.

5   In Germanic countries from the time of the Middle Ages, the Amtmann was a municipal official, usually a member of the nobility or a cleric, who collected taxes from the district, administered justice and maintained law and order.

6   *Severnaia voina 1700–1721: Sbornik dokumentov*, Vol. 1, p. 329.

Baron von Huyssen cited the official version, explaining the decision made by the Russian authorities regarding deportation, in his journal:

> Around 1706 it became known … that the Germans and Swedes of Narva and Dorpat were unable to forget (as usually happens) their allegiance to their former monarch, and being tempted or bribed by the governors of Reval and Riga and by other Swedes, were keeping secret correspondence with their friends in those cities that were in favour of Sweden and very harmful for the Russian garrisons, and many were discovered and confessed. Because of that his Tsarist Majesty, having considered the likely evil and sad consequences of that, and being the one to carry on the war with Sweden, found it better not to leave his troops exposed to danger in those places and not to allow them to be attacked and captured by the enemy with the help of the locals. Stating that suspicion or distrust is the mother of security, and wanting to keep his troops secure, his Majesty ordered – by rule of the proper state government – that the inhabitants of those towns (who by their conduct had lost the favour that had been kindly offered to them by his Majesty) were to be transported to Kazan and Astrakhan, to Vologda, Ustiug, Riazan and other good Russian towns.
>
> This order was supported by giving the deportees wagons for themselves and their belongings without cost, and by granting them freedom of religion and freedom of trade and craft. It is true that this behest seemed cruel to those who were innocent, but in such cases for the good of the people and for purposes of security, it is allowed to punish the innocent together with the guilty …. Later, when everything had calmed down in those borders, Livonia was captured and the danger was gone, his Majesty allowed all the inhabitants, who had been dispersed across many provinces, to return and to take back freely their homes and property.[7]

The deported residents of Dorpat together with their families (a total of around 460 people) were divided into groups and sent to various cities: representatives of the higher classes, burgomeisters, ratmans, clergy and members of great guilds were sent to Vologda and Kazan'; members of small guilds to Moscow and Velikii Ustiug; families of the military to the Moscow environs; and a small portion of the artisans to Voronezh. Approximately 1,700 people were resettled from Narva, but this was not the entire population; in May 1708, 300 citizens remained in Narva – artisans with their families. In 1710 with the fall of Riga, Reval and Pernau, the question was raised about returning the displaced residents, but the outbreak of war with Turkey delayed its resolution. Only in 1714 were the residents of both cities allowed to return to Narva, since Dorpat was in ruins and needed to be rebuilt from scratch. The returns continued until the 1720s, and in total about 45 percent of the displaced people returned to their homeland. Many chose voluntarily to remain in Russia, since they had acquired houses, profitable businesses and land in a more comfortable climate; others, in contrast, could not leave, because they did not have the means for this.[8]

---

7   Von Huyssen, pp. 314–316.
8   Smolokurov, p. 32; Laidre, pp. 217–221.

By coincidence, the resettled Narva residents in Russia escaped a terrible epidemic of bubonic plague, which enveloped Eastern Europe in the first decade of the 18th century. Brought in to Poland from the Balkan region, in 1708 it began to spread rapidly. Right up until 1713 it spread into Prussia, Denmark, northern Germany, the Baltics, Sweden, Finland, Ukraine and north-western Russia. The disastrous plague, just as it did in the Middle Ages, carried away many thousands of lives, such that the population of major cities was literally dying off. The plague arrived in Narva in August 1710, after which tens of thousands of people died in the cities and counties of Livonia and Estonia; 25 people became victims of the epidemic in Narva.[9]

When the war finally ended, Livonia and Estonia remained parts of the Russian Empire. Whereas the Dorpat fortifications were destroyed in 1708, the Narva fortress continued to develop. Since the Swedes did not manage to complete the fortifications as projected by Dahlberg, it was now the Russian authorities that finished their construction. In the conditions of the continuing war they raised a ravelin between the Honour and Victoria bastions – the only one that has survived to the present day; finished the construction of ravelins of the remaining curtains; and made an earthen embankment in front of the Victoria Bastion so as to prevent the creation of a breach, as had happened in 1704. According to the testimony of the Dane Just Juel, the Tsar ordered to rename the Honour Bastion as the Divine Breach, in remembrance of how the bastion's face had collapsed shortly before the assault. Reconstruction work in the fortress which had fallen into a state of disrepair went on in the 1730s, and in the 1750s projects were compiled to make alterations to the fortifications.

In the Russian–Swedish War of 1808, batteries were established at the mouth of the Narova River against a British fleet, but they never had to act. In 1812 Emperor Alexander I viewed the fortress and river as a reliable line of defence on the approaches to Saint Petersburg in the event of an advance of Napoleon's corps from Riga; however, Frenchmen appeared in Narva at the end of the war only as prisoners of war. During the Crimean War, they were expecting an allied landing in Narva, and on 6 July 1855 in Hungerburg (at the mouth of the Narova River), the coastal batteries of 20 fortress cannons engaged in an artillery duel with two propeller-driven ships and two gunboats. Despite an overwhelming superiority in fire, the ships in the course of the day were unable to suppress the batteries, inflicted no serious damage to them, and sailed away out to sea. Until 1863, the Narva fortress remained an object of military significance with cannons and a garrison, but then it was abolished; the bastions were handed over to the municipality and partially pulled down. In 1853, a monument was established at the Victoria Bastion dedicated to the "Final resting place of brave Russian soldiers, who fell when capturing Narva by assault on 9 August 1704".[10] After the two revolutions of 1917 and subsequent collapse of the Empire in the course of World War One, Narva in 1918 became part of the new independent state

---

9   Juhl, p. 194; Vasil'ev, K.G. and Segal, A.E., *Istoriia epidemii v Rossii* [*History of epidemics in Russia*] (Moscow, 1960), pp. 94–99; Smolokurov, p. 32.

10   Laskovsky, Vol. 2, p. 451; Vol. 3, pp. 198–203; Petrov, pp. 445–454.

Plan of the city and fortifications of Narva after 1704.
A copy of the drawing kept in the Royal Library in Copenhagen. The original was created after 1704 in the 18th Century, since it shows ravelins that were added later. (Author unknown; Denmark, 1938, Krigsarkivets kartsamlingar)

Cross-section of the Tall
Hermann Tower of the
Narva Castle.
The square wooden watch
house that rises above the
tower's roof was built in 1786.
(Aleksandr Il'ich Oprits 1843-?
Russia, 1886, *Atlas of sketches
of the ancient castle with the
Tall Hermann Tower in Narva*,
1886)

– the Republic of Estonia – and was occupied by German troops. By the end of 1919, in the ensuing Russian Civil War, General Yudenich's White North-western Army under pressure from the Red Army fell back to Narva, where the Whites were disarmed by Estonian authorities. According to the 1919 Treaty of Tartu between Estonia and Soviet Russia, both Narva and Ivangorod remained as part of the Republic of Estonia, and the border with Russia ran east of the Narova River, closer to Luga; in 1940, the Republic of Estonia became part of the USSR.

With the start of the Great Patriotic War the casemates of the old bastions were converted into bomb shelters for local residents against German air raids, but on 17 August 1941 the city was abandoned by the Red Army. After the lifting of the Siege of Leningrad in February 1944, a battle for Narva began – Soviet forces made attempts to force a crossing of the Narova River and to break through the powerful Nazi fortified region on its western bank. Among other attacks against the enemy's defensive positions, on 6 March 1944 in the course of an aerial bombing attack, Narva's historic centre was destroyed. The winter and following spring offensives brought no success, and stubborn fighting for the area continued until summer. Ivangorod badly suffered; its towers were blown up by the Germans. The Tall Hermann Tower was used by them as a machine gun position and observation post, from which they had a splendid view far into the Russian positions on the eastern bank of the river and corrected artillery fire. Therefore, in the course of yet

Heinrich von Huyssen.
Yet another participant of the siege of Narva. Von Huyssen, "a native Caesarian from the city of Essen", was a jurisprudence doctor, who published diverse works on history and jurisprudence; in 1702 as a member of the Saxon forces he fought against the Swedes, and Patkuhl invited him to join the Russian service as a general-auditor. From 1703 he served as tutor to the heir to the throne, Prince Aleksei Petrovich; in 1704, he was near Narva together with his pupil and kept records in his diary. Probably, these notes later entered a history of the Northern War that was written by von Huyssen, but not approved by Peter the Great; this work was only published in 1788 by Fedor Tumansky as *Zhurnal barona Gizena* [*Journal of Baron Huyssen*]. Among host of his services to Petrine Russia, one of the most important was his work to spread the Russian view of the war's events in the European press. In the years when the Western public opinion was charmed by Charles XII, von Huyssen himself wrote articles and hired journalists for publication in journals and almanacs about the victories of the Tsarist arms and to discredit Swedish propaganda. He was also instrumental in the publication in 1710 of the first biography of the Tsar, *Des Moscowitischen grossen Czaars Petri Alexiewiz Leben und Thaten* [*Life and deeds of Moscow's Great Tsar Peter Alekseevich*] in Germany. (Artist unknown; Saxony, 1711, *Neuer Bücher-Saal der gelehrten Welt* Leipzig, 1711)

another offensive, on 25 July at 1400 hours, the tower was destroyed by Soviet artillery fire; the enemy abandoned Ivangorod, but not before destroying the remaining structures in the town as they withdrew. On 26 July 1944, Narva was liberated.[11] In that same year of 1944, the boundary between the two entities of the USSR – the Estonian Soviet Socialist Republic and the Russian Soviet Federative Socialist Republic – was shifted to the west to run along the Narova River, so that Ivangorod was now back in Russia.

After the war, the local authorities made a decision not to restore the badly damaged historical buildings of the Old Town, and today only the restored buildings of the Town Hall and two residential houses on Koiduhla Street recall Narva of the 17th century. The Livonian Castle of the Middle Ages on the whole had been rebuilt by 1986, but work on it continued into the 21st century. Of the bastions of the fortress, the Victoria and Gloria bastions have been preserved practically intact; a face, a side, and a portion of another face have been preserved of the Honour and Triumph bastions; the Fama Bastion has been completely razed and in its former place is a city medical clinic. The restoration of the Ivangorod fortress began later, and its towers have not been rebuilt up to their historic heights. Today works to make restorations and improvements continue on both banks of the Narova River. Such is the fate of the stone ramparts, but what became of the people who took part in the Narva events of 1704?

Major General Petr Matveevich Apraxin, who had started the siege, in the winter of 1705 conducted a march across the ice of Lake Ladoga to the environs of Kexholm and laid waste to Serdobol [Sortavala]. After quelling the Astrakhan uprising in 1706, he was appointed as the governor there, and

---

11   Krivosheev, E.P. and Kostin, N.F., *Bitva za Narvu: Fevral' – sentiabr' 1944 goda* [*Battle for Narva: February–September 1944*] (Tallinn, 1984), pp. 97, 98.

in 1708 became the governor of Kazan. Occupying this post, he induced the Kalmyk Khan to submit to Russia, successfully fought against the Crimean Tatars and organised the delivery of the necessary materiel for the needs of the army and fleet. Apraxin served as a senator from 1717 and passed away in 1728.

Sergeant Mikhail Ivanovich Shchepotev continued to carry out the Tsar's special missions – in 1705 he acted as an engineer during the siege and capture of Bausk, and in 1706 he was "keeping an eye on" Field Marshal Boris Sheremetev during the suppression of an uprising in Astrakhan and was even captured by the insurgents. His fondness for the sea also remained; whereas near Narva Mikhail was ready to block the path of the Swedish warships with fishing boats, in 1706 his desire was fulfilled. In October during the siege of Vyborg he gathered a detachment of 45 grenadiers and attacked the enemy ships in the Vyborg harbour in boats and was killed in a savage and glorious boarding fight.

The commandant of Narva, Henning Rudolph Horn, having been captured during the assault, was transported to Russia where he remained until 1709 as the only prisoner with the rank of general and was the senior of all the Swedish prisoners. In 1715 Horn was sent aboard ship from Finland to Sweden in offer of an exchange for the Narva prisoner Avtomon Golovin; the Major General left behind his children in Russia in the role of hostages and gave a guarantee that he would return if the prisoner exchange did not take place. His wife had died shortly before the storming of Narva; his son and four daughters were entrusted to the care of General Chambers (who had been the first to break into Narva together with the grenadiers). However, the Swedish side refused to make the exchange, Horn failed to return, and moreover detained the Russian galley and crew under the pretext that the ship was supposedly spying along the Swedish coast; this generated a protest from the Russian side. It is difficult to call the arrival of the Narva commandant in Sweden a return to his homeland because he had spent his entire life in Germany, Karelia and Ingria. He took no further part in military operations, but in 1715 he received a promotion to General-Feldzeugmeister; he passed away in 1730.[12]

The guide Butynsky, who had shown the Tsar the new path from Saint Petersburg to Narva received as an award the exclusive right to fish on the Luga River near Jamburg, 1.5 km above the bridge.

Captain Georg Staël von Holstein, who in May 1704 had provided such valuable information to Apraxin, in captivity married the daughter of Commandant Horn; in 1711 he was exchanged in return for a Russian officer and took further active part in Charles XII's campaigns. His wife remained in Russia until the end of the war, and her return prevented him from marrying

---

12   Ustrialov, N.G., *Istoriia tsarstvovaniia Petra Velikogo*, Vol. 4, Part 1, pp. 314–315; Shafirov, P.P., *Rassuzhdenie, kakie zakonnye prichiny Petr Pervyi k nachatiiu voiny protiv korolia Karla XII in 1700 imel* [*Consideration of what legal justifications Peter the First had for starting the war against King Charles II in 1700*] (Saint Petersburg, 1717), p. 82; the London Gazette, 20 August 1715; Grauers, S., "Henning Rudolf Horn" in Svensk biografiskt lexicon <http://sok.riksarkivet.se/sbl/artikel/13821> (accessed 6 August 2018).

a second time. He rose in Sweden to the rank of Field Marshal in 1757 and died in 1761. His stone house was demolished along with the Old Town in the Second World War; the stone carved doorway found among from the rubble of his home has been reassembled and now exists on a home built since the war at 11 Pushkin Street in contemporary Narva.

Admiral Jacob De Prou, although unable in fact to render assistance to Narva from the sea, accurately pointed out the danger Kronschlot posed to the Swedish presence in the Gulf of Finland. In 1705 another unsuccessful attempt was made to throw the Russians off of Kotlin Island. De Prou took no part in it, but later operated against the Danish fleet. He died at the Swedish naval base in Karlskrona in 1711 during the bubonic plague epidemic.

Carl Ewald von Rönne, who received the rank of Major General at Narva, became one of the best Russian cavalry commanders; in 1709 he was leading the dragoon regiments in the combat near Krasnyi Kut, where he nearly captured King Charles XII himself. He was wounded at the Battle of Poltava. In 1711 during the unsuccessful Pruth campaign, his detachment of dragoon regiments apart from the main army assaulted and took the fortress of Brăila, which had to be returned to the Turks within a matter of days in connection with the news about the Treaty of the Pruth. He died in 1716.

Major General Wolmar Anton von Schlippenbach, who in fact proved unable to help Narva from the land, in that same year became the Vice-Governor of Estonia and held this post right up until the campaign into Russia. He took part in the Battle of Lesnaya, and was captured at the Battle of Poltava. He switched to Russian service, and in 1714 participated in the Battle of Gangut; he received the rank of Lieutenant General and in 1718 became a member of the Military Collegium and the Supreme Court. He died in 1721. His brother, the Nöteborg commandant Gustav Wilhelm von Schlippenbach, with the Tsar's permission travelled to Stockholm, but then returned to Russia where he in fact died in captivity around 1710.

Georg Benedikt Ogilvy after Narva in 1705 and 1706 commanded the Russian army in the Grodno operation. Over these years, his quarrels with the other Russian field marshals – Menshikov and Sheremetev – kept intensifying, and his conduct at Grodno prompted the Tsar's dissatisfaction. He was released from Tsarist service in 1706 and joined the Saxon Army in the rank of field marshal; he died near Danzig in 1710.

General-Engineer Lambert de Guerin deserted in 1706 after the Grodno operation. In subsequent years he roamed across Europe, continuing to wear his previously granted Order of St. Andrew the Apostle (which kept prompting the indignation of the Russian government) and periodically requested to return to Russian service, but never received a reply.

Major Boris Ivanovich Kurakin led the Semenovsky Regiment in the triumphal procession through Moscow on the occasion of the capture of Narva, and in 1709 commanded a regiment at the Battle of Poltava; on the whole, however, his military service felt like a burden to him. In 1705 he was sent on a trip abroad for treatment, and in 1707 became the Russian emissary in Rome; over time, he rose to become one of the most prominent Russian diplomats in the time of Peter the Great. He died in 1727 in Paris, in the post of Russian ambassador. He left behind his personal notes, which for

Male heads in wigs and hats.
We'll consider this sketch as a group portrait of the anonymous military officers in the year of Narva's capture. (Bernard Picart, 1673-1733, the Netherlands, 1704, Rijksmuseum, Amsterdam)

Russians of that time was a rarity; his papers, even more than the letters of Peter the Great himself, are full of ponderous (at times even improbable) mixture of the Old Russian language with foreign languages.

Lieutenant Colonel Magnus Stjernstråle after the capitulation of Ivangorod served as the commandant of Kexholm. In 1708 he was wounded in General Lübecker's unsuccessful campaign towards Saint Petersburg. In 1710 he became a Colonel and led the defence of Vyborg, which also ended in a surrender to an accord; however, on this occasion the garrison was held by the victors as a measure of satisfaction for the "injustices" of the Swedish side in the matter of the exchange of prisoners. Stjernstråle left captivity with the end of the war in 1721 and was promoted to Major General. He passed away in 1734.

The bas-relief medallion in honor of the fall of Narva. (Carlo Bartolomeo Rastrelli 1675-1744, Andrei Konstantinovich Nartov 1693-1756, Russia, 1720s)

Sergeant Petr Vasilievich Griaznoi in 1706 was transferred into a grenadier company of his regiment and took part in the first campaign towards Vyborg. In 1708 he was wounded when assaulting a Swedish retrenchment on the Soikina peninsula on the southern bank of the Gulf of Finland, where Lübecker was being evacuated on ships. The following year he fought in Ukraine and took part in the Battle of Poltava. Then together with his company he became part of the 2nd Grenadier Regiment. He was part of the capture of Reval in 1710, and in 1711 he received promotion to Second Lieutenant. He fought in Karelia and Finland, and in 1719 was with the fleet of galleys "on the Stockholm side". He ended the war in the rank of a regimental *fiscal*; he had no villages or ancestral lands in his possession.[13]

The fate of the peasant Andrei Nikulaev is unknown to us, but his village of Mattiia still exists in the Kingisepp (which is how Jamburg is called now) District of Leningrad Oblast (Saint Petersburg area) up to our present days.

Melnikovo – Saint Petersburg, 2013–2016

---

13   Adamovich, p. 97.

Appendix I

The Russian Forces

The composition of the Petrine forces, which took part in the second siege of Narva, is found in full or in part in several published sources. The materials published before include rosters of the entire army, which were compiled soon after the operation's conclusion. These are documents, prepared by Ogilvy, and the most complete one is the "Table with the numerical strength in the 30 infantry regiments that turned up on 15 August during their withdrawal from Narva." The given source contains the actual numerical strength of each of the 29 (not 30) regiments and demonstrates how many men they needed in addition to bring them up to the table strength as proposed by Ogilvy; for the two Guard regiments the strength is given for 7 November, and for the remaining regiments 15 August.[1] In Menshikov's Chancellery there was a version of this document that has been previously unpublished; the figures in it completely coincide, but the numerical strength of the Ingermanlandsky Regiment is for 26 November and only 25 regiments have been listed, excluding P.M. Apraxin's regiments.[2]

Another published document is the "Boevoi poriadok za podpis'iu Ogilvi" ["Order of Battle signed by Ogilvy"] from 12 October 1704. In it, 30 regiments of infantry and 16 dragoon regiments have been arranged in a conventional array, in two lines with partitioning by formations. The regiments have been named for their colonels (in somewhat distorted German), but without their numerical strength of the regiments or the names of the major generals and lieutenant generals that were commanding the formations.[3] A more detailed depiction of the combat formation (in the genre of diagrams typical for that era, with coloured and labelled rectangles representing the combat units) has been found in a collection of Peter the Great's maps and plans in the Russian Academy of Science's Department of Manuscripts.[4] Obviously, the document belongs to the end of 1704 or the beginning of 1705 and presents the development of a project started on 12 October. It shows the names of

---

1   *Severnaia voina 1700–1721*, Vol. 1, pp. 226–227.
2   NIA SPbII RAN, F. 83, Op. 1, D. 390, ll. 1–4.
3   Ustrialov, N., *Istoriia tsarstvovaniia Petra Velikogo*, Vol. 4, Part 2, pp. 478–481, 486.
4   OR BAN, F. 266, T. 3, l. 69.

the unit commanders (16 dragoon and 25 infantry regiments, without P.M. Apraxin's regiments) and the formations (cavalry, infantry and artillery of the right and left wings) written in Russian, and the number of battalions and squadrons is indicated. However, the sequence of the arrayed regiments in the lines does not coincide with that of the October project. For us, what is important in the document is the direct indication of the renaming of the one of the regiments (from "Berner's" to "Scharf's"). Russian regiments until 1706–1708 bore names of their colonels and it is sometimes hard to track lineage.

The composition of the Russian army at Narva was also described by the memoirist Boris Kurakin, and although his text is not an official document, it indicates which regiments were subordinate to which generals, and in particular, gives the strength of Apraxin's regiments.[5]

The rosters of separate corps as of dates preceding the siege, during the siege and after it are known, too. For example, strength of P.M. Apraxin's troops which were the first to set out on the campaign are known from his letter on 25 April.[6] Sheremetev's troops have been listed in his campaign journal, which gives their strength before the start of the campaign on 26 April, before the start of the campaign at Dorpat (shortly before 9 June) and for the march from Dorpat to Narva on 25 June, with the indication of the regimental commanders, the number of officers and lower ranks, as well as the casualties from the assault.[7] The troops located under the command of General Repnin on 13 May when sent to Kexholm amounted to five infantry regiments, but after taking Narva, six infantry regiments and six dragoon regiments were made subordinate to General Repnin before they set out from Narva to Pskov, and from there to Lithuania on 15 September.[8] Some of the sources contain only the names of the regiments, other – their numerical strength.

The "Specification of the regiments" from the papers of Robert Harley, the British Secretary of State of the early 1700s, which are preserved in the University of Nottingham's collection of manuscripts in Great Britain, supplements the information from these sources.[9] The document presents two lists. The first lists the higher officers of the Russian Army and the noblemen that were commanders during the siege of Narva in 1704; the individuals' names, as a rule, are accompanied by their ranks and a brief commentary about their backgrounds. The second list gives the infantry regiments that took part in the siege with an indication of their subordination and brief remarks about their numerical strength, organisation and uniforms.

5   Kurakin, B.I., *Russkaia-shvedskaia voina. Zapiski. 1700–1710*, Book 1, pp. 295–296.
6   PiB, Vol. 3, pp. 610–611, 615.
7   *Voenno-pokhodyni zhurnal B.P. Sheremeteva*, Vol. 1, pp. 142, 150–152, 170–171.
8   Zeziulinsky, N.K., *K rodosoviiu 34-kh pekhotnykh polkov Petra I* [*On the lineage of Peter I's 34 infantry regiments*] (Petrograd, 1915), p. 93; Volynsky, Book 3, p. 311.
9   Megorsky, B.V., "Podrobnoe opisanie polkov, zaniatykh v osade Narvy" 1704 goda [Specification of the regiments, engaged in the siege of Narva" 1704] in *Istoriia voennogo dela: issledovaniia i istochniki* [*History of military affairs: research and sources*], Vol. 1 (2012), pp. 391–420; <http://www.milhist.info/2012/06/30/megorskiy_1> (accessed 6 August 2018).

The origins and author of this document are not given; one can only presume that the information came from someone who was present at the siege from the Russian side. The information could have been passed to England through the British trade Consul Charles Goodfellow. Kurakin informs of his presence during the siege; likely, this was only a brief visit, since on 24 July Goodfellow was in Petersburg and handed gifts from a British merchant ship to Roman Bruce for Menshikov.[10] The document is undated, but judging from the mention of von Werden's regiment, which had arrived from Dorpat, the lists were compiled after 30 July. A copy of this same document exists in the German language which is preserved in the Swedish Royal Archive and was published by Rosen in 1936.[11] It should be noted that in Kelch's *History of Livonia*, the Russian generals at Narva are listed, with the very same information about their backgrounds and with similar mistakes in the text (for example, Briss instead of Bruce).[12] Possibly, both lists from the British and Swedish archives had a common source, which Kelch also used and the origin of which is still unknown to us. On the whole this document is of undoubted value, even though it is not free of mistakes; for example, it lists Scharf's regiment, which in reality was not present at Narva, and mentions Generals Sheremetev and Rosen, who were not participants in the siege.

Then finally, an order to the army from 2 July 1704, which has been revealed in the files from Menshikov's Chancellery, describes the army's order of battle with the number of battalions in the regiments, and the assignment of the regiments to the flanks and to formations (there was no long-standing designation, and in other sources they were called "brigades") under the command of one or another general. The order's important details provide the renaming of certain regiments.

All of the above-mentioned documents permit the reconstruction of the army's order of battle at the moment of the completion of the Narva operation. It should be noted that the composition of the formations was not constant throughout the year. For example, General Repnin headed his own command back in May 1704, but during the siege in July and August and until being sent to Lithuania he no longer had a detached command, and almost all of his former regiments ended up under Schönbeck's command. The composition of P.M. Apraxin's force kept changing throughout the year.

The Russian combat units in this period, with rare exceptions, were known after the names of their regimental commanders; however, the twists and turns in changes of command does not always find a reflection in the published documents and are poorly illuminated in the literature. Even the specialised research of N. Zeziulinky's "K rodosloviiu 34-kh pekhotnykh polkov Petra I" ['About the lineage of 34 infantry regiments of Peter I'] and M.D. Rabinovich's fundamental reference book *Polki petrovskoi armii 1698–1725* [*Regiments of Peter's army 1698-1725*] which were dedicated to

10   NIA SPbII RAN, F. 83, Op. 1, D. 337, l. 1.
11   Rosen, C. von, *Bidrag till kännedom om de händelser, som närmest föregingo svenska stormaktsvälets fall* (Stockholm, 1936), pp. 194–195.
12   Kelch, C., *Lieflandische Historia oder Kriegs- und Friedens-Geschichte. Continuation 1690–1706* (Dorpat, 1875), p. 382.

this question in certain cases cannot give a unequivocal answer about the history, combat path and commanders of a regiment.[13] Thanks to the officers' autobiographies published by K.V. Tatarnikov, it has become possible to clarify certain details regarding the forming and renaming of regiments, for example Cooper's, Chambers' and Shkot's regiments.

Von Rönne's dragoon regiments for a certain time were located in the siege camp, blockading the city and fighting with the garrison's troops. Therefore, they can be considered participants in the siege.

Certain regiments took only episodic part in the Narva operation. For example, the "regiment of newly-drafted soldiers", about which we know that it was dispatched to Narva on 22 May 1704 aboard small boats together with two companies of the Preobrazhensky Guards was apparently Hamilton's regiment, which had returned back to Saint Petersburg after the delivery of cargo.[14] Several regiments arrived at Narva only after the end of the siege and therefore also did not become part of the order of battle. One of these was Prince Ivan Lvov's regiment, which numbered 1,013 men, which had been sent from Moscow to Olonets, and from there to Menshikov at Narva, where it joined P.M. Apraxin's command.[15] In addition, the Ingermanlandsky Dragoon Regiment, which had just been formed, arrived at Narva on foot after the town was captured.

On the basis of the sources and reference books examined above, the Russian army's reconstructed order of battle at Narva in August 1704 is offered here. Both the regiments that took direct part in the siege and assault, as well as those units that supported the siege from a distance (for example, Bauer's dragoon regiments) and the nearby major garrisons in Saint Petersburg and Dorpat have been included in this appendix. The footnotes contain reference data on the commanders of the formations and units, and when available, information about the regiments' numerical strength and losses.

The forces that took part in the siege of Narva

Commander-in-Chief Lieutenant Field Marshal Baron Georg Benedikt Ogilvy[16]
General Repnin[17]

13 Zeziulinsky, N.K., *K rodosloviiu 34-kh pekhotnykh polkov Petra I*; Rabinovich, M.D., *Polki petrovskoi armii 1698–1725* (Moscow, 1977).
14 *Pokhodnyi zhurnal 1704 goda*, p. 28.
15 *Severnaia voina 1700-1721*, Vol. 1, p. 208.
16 Baron Georg Benedikt Ogilvy (Iurii Iurievich Ogilvi). See the background information about him in the book's main text under 21 June on page 27.
17 Repnin, Nikita Ivanovich (1668–1726). A prince and general. In the period of the Tsar's absence between 11 and 26 June, he remained the senior general of the Russian siege corps at Narva [Pokhodnyi zhurnal 1704 *goda*, p. 44; PiB, Vol. 3, p. 87]. With Ogilvy's appointment to the post of commander-in-chief, he became the second in seniority. After Narva's capture, in accordance with the agreement with Poland, he was sent to Lithuania with a corps of six infantry regiments (under Major General Scharf) and 6 dragoon regiments (under Major General von Rönne). PiB, Vol. 3, pp. 135–140.

Infantry

Major General Chambers[18]
Preobrazhensky Life-Guard Regiment[19]
Semenovsky Life-Guard Regiment[20]
Ingermanlandsky Regiment[21]
Butyrsky Regiment[22]

18 Chambers, John (Ivan Ivanovich Chambers), a major general. An Englishman, in Russian service since 1689, he was first a colonel of the (future Guards) Semenovsky Regiment and took part in the Azov campaigns, in suppressing the uprising of the Moscow *streltsy* in 1698, and in the Battle of Narva 1700. In 1701 he was promoted to major general, but temporarily departed from the Guards: he was commanding the entire infantry in B.P. Sheremetev's army and took part in the Battle of Erastfer. Obviously, Chambers had developed a warm relationship with Sheremetev, since prior to the start of the 1704 campaign, the Field Marshal requested Chambers' assignment to his corps. He took part in the siege of Nöteborg and Nyen at the head of the Guards. Chambers directed an operation against the Swedish General Kronhjort at the Sestra River on 7 July 1703. On 22 December 1703 he was appointed as commander for the defence of Koporie, Jamburg, Saint Petersburg, Novgorod and Pskov. In 1704 he commanded a brigade consisting of the two Guards regiments plus the Ingermanlandsky and Butyrsky Regiments. On the day of the assault, he led the assault column, which captured the Honour Bastion and was the first to enter Narva.

19 The Preobrazhensky Life Guard Regiment. The senior officers in 1704: Lieutenant Colonel Dmitrii Kuz'mich Karpov, who was killed in the trenches on 23 July; Major Aleksei Borisovich Golitsyn; Major Fedor Nikitich Glebov (see Kurakin, p. 300). Losses during the assault: 21 killed, six mortally wounded and 91 wounded [Bobrovsky, P.O., *Istoriia L-Gv. Preobrazhensky regiment* [*History of the Life Guard Preobrazhensky Regiment*] (Moscow, 2007), p. 371].

20 The Semenovsky Life Guard Regiment. Its senior officers in 1704 were Colonel Prince Mikhail Mikhailovich Golitsyn; Major Efim Vestov, Major Boris Ivanovich Kurakin (Kurakin, p. 300). Losses during the assault: one officer and 32 men killed, and two officers and 63 men wounded [Dirin, P.N., *Istoriia L-Gv. Semenovsky polka* [*History of the L.-Gv. Semenovsky Regiment* (Saint Petersburg, 1883), p. 67]; both Guards regiments were under the command of Chambers.

21 The infantry regiment of the Ingermanland governor Aleksandr Danilovich Menshikov. Raised in 1703 in Saint Petersburg from the "best and most handsome soldiers of various regiments". Commander – Lieutenant Colonel Fraser, Major Weide [Kurakin, p. 300]. Its numerical strength on 15 August 1,352 men. In February 1704, the regiment received five azure banners and the latest-model bayonets. [NIA SPbII RAN, F. 83, Op. 1, D. 101.]

22 James Gordon's (Iakov Petrovich Gordon's); also known as the Butyrsky Regiment. The regiment was raised in 1656/57 in Moscow as the Second *Vyborny* Regiment of Moscow. Its strength on 13 May was 969 men, on 15 September 862 men.

Lieutenant General Schönbeck[23]
Colonel Gulitz's regiment[24]
Colonel Deduit's regiment[25]
Field Marshal Ogilvy's regiment[26]
Colonel Pavel Berner's regiment[27]
Colonel Ivan Ridder's regiment[28]

---

23   Adam Schönbeck; a Brandenburg resident, he entered Russian service at the end of 1703. In 1704, a "general's" soldier regiment that carried his name was created; subsequently it received the designation Narvsky. On 16 May 1704 Schönbeck received an order to march from Schlisselburg to Kexholm with five infantry regiments, but already on 21 May he was sent to Narva. According to Adlerfeld, he directed the siege in the Tsar's absence until Ogilvy's arrival; although General-in Chief Repnin was senior in rank to him, it is possible to assume that Schönbeck at that time was the most experienced general in the Russian Army. He commanded a brigade of five regiments. On the day of the general assault on 9 August, he commanded an assault column during the capture of Narva's Victoria Bastion; according to B.I. Kurakin's version of events, it was instead the Gloria Bastion. Judging from the comments in B.P. Sheremetev's letters, Schönbeck did not get along well with the other generals and showed no concern for his soldiers when on the march – during the march from Narva to Pskov, his regiments' deceased and seriously ill soldiers were abandoned on the road [Zeziulinsky, N., *K rodosloviiu 34-kh pekhotnykh polkov Petra I*, pp 57–61].

24   Kashpar Andreevich Gulits's regiment. Formed from volunteers in Kazan in 1700. From 1708, known as the Rostovsky Regiment. Its strength on 13 May was 755 men, on 15 August 875 men, and on 15 September 784 men.

25   Aleksei Mikhailovich Dediut's infantry regiment; raised in 1700 in Kazan from conscripts as Nikolai Grigorievich von Werden's regiment. From 1708, known as the Lutsky or Velikolutsky Regiment [Zeziulinsky, p. 131]. On 12 July it became subordinate to P.M. Apraxin [Velikanov, V.S., "Initsiativy generala-feldmarshala G.B. Ogilvy when reforming the Russian Army in 1704-1705" *Voenno-istoricheskii zhurnal* (No. 5) 2015, p. 52]. Its strength on 13 May was 820 men, and on 15 September 794 men.

26   Field Marshal Iurii Iurievich Ogilvy's infantry regiment; prior to 2 July 1704, Matvei Matveevich Bordovik's regiment (who passed away at the start of the siege; see *Ofitserskie skazki*, Vol. 2, p. 1934). Raised in 1700 in Moscow from volunteers as Gustav Ivanovich Ivanitsky's regiment. From 1708, known as the Moskovsky Regiment [Zeziulinsky, p. 117]. Its strength on 15 August was 1,123 men.

27   Pavel Pavlovich Berner's infantry regiment. Raised in Kazan in 1700 from conscripts. From 1708, known as the Viatsky Regiment [Zeziulinsky, p. 134]. Its strength on 13 May was 681 men, on 15 August 919 men, and on 15 September 749 men. Colonel P.P. Berner was killed during the assault on 9 August, and in the roster of Repnin's regiments on 15 September, this regiment had already been re-named after Major General Scharf. This renaming is not reflected in the works of Zeziulinsky and Rabinovich, but Chernyshev confirms it – he indicates that "in May 1705 it was called the Viatsky Regiment, which had been under Major General Scharf's name" (Chernyshev, G.P. *Zapiski G.P. Chernysheva*, Vol. 5, No. 6 (1872), pp. 791–802). Maikinin also confirms that this regiment had been designated as "Major General Scharf's regiment, which today is known as the Viatsky Regiment with the same roster under Lieutenant Colonel Grigorii Chernyshev." [*Ofitserskie skazki*, Vol. 2, p. 1994]. A diagram of the Russian army's order of battle at the beginning of 1705 directly shows the regiment as "Scharf's, which had been Berner's" [OR BAN, F. 266, Vol. 3, p. 69]. This means that Alexander Scharf's regiment at the end of 1704 was the former regiment under Pavel Berner, the Viatsky Regiment, and was not Aleksandr Scharf's or Andrei Scharf's regiment, which later became the Olonetsky Regiment.

28   Ivan Ivanovich Ridder's regiment; raised in 1700 in Novgorod from volunteers and conscripts as Roman Vilimovich Bruce's regiment. From 1708, known as the Vologodsky Regiment [Zeziulinsky, p. 138]. Its strength on 13 May was 747 men, on 15 August 775, and on 15 September 745 men.

Major General Scharf[29]
Colonel Bovisch's regiment[30]
Colonel Busch's regiment[31]
Colonel Cooper's regiment[32]
Lieutenant General Schönbeck's regiment[33]
Major General Chambers' regiment[34]
General Prince Repnin's regiment[35]

---

29 Aleksandr Vilimovich Scharf, Major General, a British man; in 1692–1693 he served in the
    Semenovsky Regiment and took part in the Azov campaigns, then led a "settled" infantry
    regiment under his name in Kazan. In 1700 he was promoted to major general and commanded
    a brigade under Repnin. At the same time, in fact his younger brother Colonel Andrei
    Vilimovich Scharf commanded his brigade. In the winter of 1701 it defended the Pechersky
    monastery. In March 1702 at the head of an infantry brigade and regiment of dragoons
    Aleksandr Scharf was commanded by B.P. Sheremetev to raid from Pskov to Nöteborg and
    Nyen and had a successful engagement on the Retkin farmstead. In 1704 he commanded a
    brigade of six regiments, and on the day of the assault – the assault column that stormed the
    ravelin of the Gloria Bastion.

30 Benedikt Ottovich Bowisch (Povisch), until 2 July 1704 Major Jakov Kartashov's regiment;
    it was also known as the Schlisselburg First Regiment. It was formed in 1702 from conscripts
    and units from Tikhon Khristoforovich Gundertmark's regiment, which on its part had been
    formed in 1700 in Moscow from volunteers as Matvei Ivanovich Treiden's regiment. From
    1708, it was known as the Schlisselburgsky Regiment [Zeziulinsky and Rabinovich, No. 147].

31 Iurii Ivanovich Bush's regiment, formed in 1702 from units of Tikhon Khristoforovich
    Gundertmark's regiment, which in turn had been formed in 1700 in Moscow from volunteers
    as Matvei Ivanovich Treiden's regiment. From 1708 it was known as the Azovsky Regiment
    [Zeziulinsky and Rabinovich, Nos. 130, 208]. It strength on 15 August was 936 men.

32 Daniel Cooper's regiment, raised in 1703 in Ladoga by A.D. Menshikov as a select regiment
    from the men of three regiments, Treiden's, Bil's's and Inglis's [*Ofitserskie skazki*, Vol. 2, pp.
    2070, 2139, 2142, 2153, 2154, 2155, 2165 and 2168]). From 1708, known as the Riazansky
    Regiment [Zeziulinsky and Rabinovich, No. 194]. Its strength on 15 August was 930 men.

33 Adam Andreevich Schönbeck's infantry regiment. Raised in 1704 in Moscow from volunteers
    and conscripts. From 1708, known as the Narvsky Infantry Regiment [Zeziulinsky and
    Rabinovich, No. 194]. Its strength on 15 August was 964 men.

34 John Chambers' regiment, until 2 July 1704 Lieutenant Colonel Fedor Bulart's regiment; it was
    also known as Governor A.D. Menshikov's Second Infantry Regiment which was quartered
    in Saint Petersburg [Rabinovich, No. 173]. Formed in 1703 in Moscow, in 1706 Chambers'
    regiment was disbanded and merged into Aleksei Alekseevich Golovin's regiment. From 1708,
    known as the Koporsky Regiment [PiB, Vol. 4, p. 342; Tatarnikov, p. 219; Rabinovich, No.
    185]. Its strength on 15 August was 835 men.

35 General Prince Nikita Ivanovich Repnin's infantry regiment, prior to 2 July 1704 Major
    Weigner's regiment [Arkhiv SPbII RAN, F. 83, Op. Kart 2, D. 292, p. 2]. Formed in 1703. From
    1708, known as the Tobolsky Regiment [Zeziulinsky and Rabinovich, No. 175]. Mentioned as
    a "General's" among Repnin's regiments at the end of August 1704 [PiB, Vol. 3, pp. 140, 673].
    The diarist G.P. Chernyshev was a major of this regiment (from 27 July 1704) and took part in
    the storming of Narva. Its strength on 15 August was 1,170 men, on 15 September 819 men.

Major General Apraxin[36]
Colonel Bils' regiment[37]
Colonel Baishev's *streltsy* regiment[38]
Colonel Strekalov's *streltsy* regiment[39]
Colonel Titov's regiment[40]
Colonel Prince Shakhovsky's regiment[41]
Colonel Balabanov's regiment[42]
Colonel Inglis' regiment[43]

---

36 Petr Matveevich Apraxin (Apraksin). A major general, and the military governor of Ladoga. Until 1699, the military governor of Novgorod. With the start of the Northern War, he was responsible for the operations on the direction entrusted to him to the north of the Novgorod area. His "Swedish" campaign in 1702 was directed from Novgorod to Ingria, where he gained a number of victories over the Swedish General Kronhjort (for example at the Sarska and Dudorova estates and at the Izhora River. At the conclusion of the 1702 campaign he linked up with the Tsar's army and took part in the capture of Nöteborg. In 1703 he was at the siege of Nyen with the Novgorod noblemen cavalry and dragoons; later, on 15-16 September, he went on a reconnaissance raid towards Ivangorod and Narva. In 1704 he arrived from Jamburg at the mouth of the Narova River on 27 April and cut Narva's communications with the sea. According to Imperial edict from 7 March 1704 eight infantry regiments (Shakhovsky's, Bil's', Titov's, Balabanov's, Inglis', Dediut's regiments and Strekalov's and Baishev's *streltsy*) and two dragoon regiments (Souvas' and de Morel's) were assigned to Apraxin's "Jamburg Regiment" (corps) [Volynsky, Book 3, p. 25]. According to Kurakin, Apraxin had five regiments – Baishev's, Bil's', Shakhovsky's, Balabanov's and Titov's; according to the Specification there were six and they are listed here, while Dediut's and Inglis' regiments were included in other formations.

37 Ilia Iakovlevich Bils' infantry regiment. Raised in 1700 in Moscow from conscripts as T.Kh. Gundertmark's regiment. From 1708, known as the Smolensky Regiment [Zeziulinsky and Rabinovich, No. 119]. Its strength on 25 April was 496 men.

38 Colonel Miron Grigor'evich Baishev's and Lieutenant Colonel Fedor Mironovich Baishev's *streltsy* regiment in Novgorod. Raised in 1701 in Novgorod from Moscow and Novgorod streltsy [Rabinovich, No. 45].

39 Stepan Matveevich Strekalov's *streltsy* regiment. Raised in 1694 in Moscow. From 1708 – the Kargopolsky Infantry Regiment [Zeziulinsky, p. 177]. In August 1703 Strekalov's regiment was sent from Jamburg to Onezhitsy to build boats [Sheremetev's field campaign diary, p. 138; PiB, Vol. 2, p. 231.]

40 Grigorii Semenovich Titov's regiment. Raised in 1703 in Moscow from volunteers and townfolk [Rabinovich, No. 177]. Its strength on 25 April was 780 men. After the fall of Narva, it remained as its garrison [*Ofitserskie skazki*, Vol. 1, pp. 1119, 1207, 1252; Vol. 2, pp. 1656, 1977].

41 Prince Andrei Fedorovich Shakhovsky's infantry regiment. Raised in 1700 in Moscow from volunteers as Peter Matveevich Apraxin's regiment. In 1712 it merged with Galitsky's regiment (Rabinovich, No. 140); in the "Table" it was called Fedotov's regiment, obviously according to the patronymic name of the commander. Its strength on 25 April was 380 men.

42 Alexei Kuzmich Balabanov (Bolobonov's) regiment. Raised in Simbirsk in 1700 from select soldiers and soldiers' sons as Lieutenant Colonel Filipp Gavrilovich Kar's settled infantry regiment. From 1708, the Iaroslavsky Infantry Regiment [Zeziulinsky and Rabinovich, Nos. 116 and 144]. On 15 August 1703, "Aleksei Bolobonov was left in Jamburg garrison with a 1,000-man regiment" [PiB, Vol. 2, p. 231]. Its strength on 25 April 1704 – taken into the Narva campaign from the Jamburg garrison – was 300 men; the rest of the regiment was left in Jamburg.

43 Andrei Iurevich Inglis' regiment. Raised in 1700 in Novgorod from volunteers and conscripts as Ivan Kulom's regiment. From 1712, the Vyborgsky Regiment (Rabinovich, No. 139). It is known that Inglis' regiment was in P.M. Apraxin's unit before setting out on the campaign and on 4 April was considered "the worst of all" [PiB, Vol. 3, p. 610]; evidently, it joined the siege corps on 12 May. On 17 October it was assigned to the Ivangorod garrison [Arkhiv VIMAIViVS, F. 2, Op. 1, D. 1, l. 176 obr.]

Major General von Werden[44]
Colonel von Schweiden's regiment[45]
Colonel Aigustov's regiment[46]
Colonel von Delden's regiment[47]
Colonel Nikolai Balck's regiment[48]
Colonel Angler's regiment[49]
Colonel Shkot's regiment[50]

---

44   Nikolai Grigorievich von Werden, Major General, from Lübeck by birth. At the start of the war he was a colonel of an infantry regiment; however, subsequently he changed his branch of service. In 1702 in Sheremetev's army he commanded one dragoon regiment, but then a formation consisting of eight dragoon regiments, with which he carried out independent raids (for example, towards the towns of Smiltene, Rakvere and Wolmar [Valmiera in present-day Latvia] and was at Marienburg. Promoted to major general. In April 1703 with a separate corps that numbered 10,000 men in response to a Tsarist decree he was sent to the Jam fortress, which he forced to surrender on 14 May with a bombardment. On 3 May 1704, while commanding a formation of nine infantry and *streltsy* regiments, he gained a victory over the Swedish riverine flotilla not far from Dorpat on the Emajõgi River. Then as part of B.P. Sheremetev's force he participated in the siege of Dorpat, led an attack in the presence of the Tsar, and was wounded during the assault on 13 July. After capturing Dorpat, he set out with his infantry regiments "by water and by land" to Narva, where he arrived on 30 July and set up a separate camp upriver. The *Gistoriia Sveiskoi voiny* makes clear that von Werden's regiment, having arrived from Dorpat, in their sector "conducted blind *schanzen*;" in other words, launched a false attack. In a clarifying note to the map of the Narva siege found in the Book of Mars, it is recorded that the feigned attack was directed towards the Triumph and Fortune bastions. Prince B.I. Kurakin reports that von Werden commanded an assault column comprised of *streltsy*, Cossacks and soldiers that attacked the Triumph Bastion.
45   Willem von Schweiden's infantry regiment, also known as the Lefortovsky Regiment and as the First Moscow *Vyborny* Regiment. Raised in 1656 [Zeziulinsky and Rabinovich, No. 76]. Its numerical strength on 25 July was 30 officers and 791 men; on 15 August 765 men. Losses during the assault: 17 men killed and one officer and 32 men wounded.
46   Savva Vasilievich Aigustov's infantry regiment. Raised in 1696–1697 in Belgorod from soldiers of the Preobrazhensky, Semenovsky and other regiments as a select infantry regiment under Major General Regimon. Aigustov was virtually the sole, native-born Russian among the colonels of the field infantry regiments at that time. From 1708, it was known as the Belgorodsky Infantry Regiment [Zeziulinsky and Rabinovich, No. 80]. Its strength on 25 July was 30 officers and 694 men; on 15 August 759 men. Its casualties during the assault were 18 killed and 32 wounded.
47   Ivan Vilimovich von Deldin's infantry regiment. Raised in 1700 in Moscow from volunteers. From 1708, known as the Kazansky Regiment [Zeziulinsky and Rabinovich, No. 123]. Strength on 25 July was 22 officers and 625 men; on 15 August 752 men. Its casualties during the assault were 18 killed and 26 wounded.
48   Nikolai Nikolaevich Balck's regiment. Raised in 1700 in Moscow from conscripts. From 1708, known as the Novgorodsky Regiment [Zeziulinsky and Rabinovich, No. 126]. Its strength on 25 July was 28 officers and 676 men; on 15 August 810 men. Casualties during the assault: one officer and 10 men killed, one officer and 17 men wounded.
49   Ivan Ivanovich Angler's regiment. Raised in 1700 in Moscow from conscripts as Erik Grigorievich von Werden's regiment. From 1708, known as the Sibirsky Regiment [Zeziulinsky and Rabinovich, No. 122]. Its strength on 25 July was 26 officers and 652 men; on 15 August 784 men. Casualties during the assault: one man killed and two officers and 13 men wounded.
50   Iurii Iurievich Shkot's infantry regiment. Raised in 1700 in Moscow from volunteers as Willem von Schweiden's regiment. In 1705, Petr Petrovich Gasenius took command of the regiment, and in 1708 the regiment became known as the Chernigovsky Regiment [Zeziulinsky and Rabinovich, No. 125]. Shkot's command of this regiment is not noted in the works of Zeziulinsky and Rabinovich, but it is confirmed by the officers' stories [*Ofitserskie skazki*, Vol. 2, pp. 2326, 2332, 2340]. Its strength on 25 July was 30 officers and 654 men; on 15 August 704 men. Casualties during the assault: six killed and 25 wounded.

Colonel Mewes' Regiment[51]
Colonel Göring's regiment[52]
Colonel Kellin's regiment[53]
Colonel Denis Ridder's regiment[54]
Major Sheremetev's regiment[55]

Cavalry

Major General von Rönne[56]
Major General von Rönne's dragoon regiment[57]
Colonel Pflug's dragoon regiment[58]
Colonel Ostafiev's dragoon regiment[59]
Colonel Boltin's dragoon regiment[60]

51 Colonel John Mewes' infantry regiment. Raised in 1700 in Moscow from conscripts. From 1708 known as the Pskovsky Regiment [Zeziulinsky and Rabinovich, No. 118]. Its strength on 25 July was 29 officers and 845 men; on 15 August 801 men. Casualties during the assault: one officer and 10 men killed.

52 Nicklaus Göring's [Gerenk's] infantry regiment. Raised in 1700 in Moscow from conscripts as Willem von Delden's regiment. From 1708, known as the Kievsky Regiment [Zeziulinsky and Rabinovich, No. 124]. Its strength on 25 July was 30 officers and 793 men; on 15 August 732 men. Casualties during the assault: one officer and six men killed.

53 Aleksei Stepanovich Kellin's (Kelling's) infantry regiment. Raised in 1700 in Moscow from volunteers as Petr Andreevich Devson's regiment. From 1708 known as the Tverskoi Regiment [Zeziulinsky and Rabinovich, No. 114]. Its strength on 25 July was 29 officers and 715 men; on 15 August 723 men. Casualties during the assault: nine killed and one officer and 12 men wounded. Colonel A.S. Kellin was wounded during the assault.

54 Denis Ridder's infantry regiment. Raised in 1700 in Moscow from conscripts as Astafii Martynovich Polman's regiment. From 1708 known as the Nizhegorodsky Regiment [Rabinovich, No. 120]. Its strength on 25 July was 27 officers and 656 men; on 15 August 763. Casualties during the assault were 10 killed and 27 wounded.

55 Major Mikhail Borisovich Sheremetev's infantry regiment; in B.P. Sheremetev's campaign journal, it is called a battalion. Until 15 July 1704 the regiment was under the command of Lieutenant Colonel Petr Gasenius, who was wounded during the assault on Dorpat on 13 July. Raised in 1700 in Moscow from conscripts as Alexander Gordon's regiment. From 1708, known as the Astrakhansky Regiment [Zeziulinsky and Rabinovich, No. 128]. Its strength on 25 July was 31 officers and 755 men; on 15 August 708 men. Casualties during the assault: 14 killed and one officer and 12 men wounded.

56 Carl Ewald von Rönne (1663–1716). See the note about him under 29 June.

57 Colonel (from 29 June 1704 Major General) Carl Ewald von Rönne's dragoon regiment. Raised in 1700 in Preobrazhensky from palace courtiers as Colonel Efim Gulitz's Preobrazhensky Dragoon Regiment. From 1706, known as the Moskovsky Dragoon Regiment [Rabinovich, No. 542. Its strength on 15 September was 967 men.

58 Colonel Gebhardt Pflug's dragoon regiment. Raised in 1701 in Moscow as Aleksandr Aleksandrovich Malina's regiment. From 1706, known as the Sibirsky Dragoon Regiment [Rabinovich, No. 546]. Its strength on 15 September was 1,015 men.

59 Colonel Afanasii Denisovich Ostafiev's [Astafiev's] dragoon regiment. Raised in 1701 in Moscow as Daniil Romanovich Shenshin's regiment. From 1706 known as the Kazansky Dragoon Regiment [Rabinovich, No. 549; Volynsky, Book 4, p. 177; *Ofitserskie skazki*, Vol. 1, pp. 74, 956–957]. Its strength on 15 September was 954 men.

60 Colonel Morel de Carrier's dragoon regiment; from 6 August 1704 Lieutenant Colonel Ivan Vasilievich Boltin's regiment. Raised in 1702 in Novgorod from reiters, lancers, hussars and servicemen of the Novgorod regimental service as Ludwig Bodewy's regiment. From 1706

Colonel Gorbov's dragoon regiment[61]
Colonel Souvas' dragoon regiment[62]
Select noble company[63]

Artillery

Major General Bruce[64]

The roster of the "artillery servicemen" subordinate to James Bruce is known from documents of the Artillery Administration:

> Colonel Johann Goschka, Lieutenant Colonel Johann Gunter, Major Elias Kober, 5 captains, 1 adjutant, 13 lieutenants, 7 ensigns, 6 styck-junkers, 13 sergeants, 2 artisans, 1 doctor, 3 bombardier corporals, 21 cannoneer corporals, 66 bombardiers, 1 clerk, 158 cannoneers, 286 *handlangers* (matrosses), 13 drummers, 1 carpenter, 1 carver, 2 locksmiths, 3 tinsmiths, 3 "chandelier men" (whoever they were), 4 turners, 1 master joiner, 15 joiners, 1 master blacksmith, 19 blacksmiths and 2 coopers.[65]

Engineers

General-Engineer Lambert de Guerin[66]
Mark Heinson,[67] Andre de Brilli[68]
"Ensigns of the engineers" who were listed among the artillery officers who

known as the Novgorodsky Dragoon Regiment [Rabinovich, No. 553]. Its strength on 27 March was 35 officers and 924 men; on 15 September 836 men.

61   Colonel Ivan Stepanovich Gorbov's dragoon regiment. Raised in 1703 in Moscow from cavalry and lancers, city service-class men and their adolescents. From 1706, known as the Permsky Dragoon Regiment. Its strength on 15 September was 924 men.

62   Colonel Phillipe Souvas' dragoon regiment. Raised in 1702 from cavalry, lancers and servicemen of the regimental and landowning nobility of the Novgorod district as Dionisii Devgerin's regiment. From 1706, known as the Viatsky Dragoon Regiment (Rabinovich, No. 554). Its strength on 27 March was 33 officers and 808 men; on 15 September 746 men.

63   The select company of landowning nobility of the Novgorod district. Raised in November 1702.

64   Count James Bruce (in Russian Iakov Vilimovich Brius], Major General and military governor of Novgorod. He was in charge of the artillery during the sieges of Nöteborg, Nyenschantz and Narva. His work to prepare the artillery began in the autumn of 1701, and in 1704 became the factual leader of the Artillery, although the Chief General of the Artillery until his death in 1711 was General-Feldzeugmeister Alexander Archilovich, Prince Imeretinsky, who was being in Swedish captivity after the Battle of Narva in 1700.

65   Arkhiv VIMAIViVS, F. 2, Op. 1, D. 37, ll. 77–79, 484–489.

66   See the note about him in the text under 24 July.

67   Mark Heinson: "A colonel from Mecklenburg, sent by the King of Denmark" (*Specification* …). Engineer Heinson is also mentioned in von Huyssen's journal as a direct participant in the storming of Narva, sent on the attack together with the troops (von Huyssen, *Zhurnal Gosudaria Petra I s 1695 po 1709*, p. 455). In 1705, a lieutenant colonel (Arkhiv VIMAIViVS, F. 2, Op. 1, D. 10, ll. 2–7); in 1706 in the same rank he oversaw the construction of the Pechersk fortress in Kiev

68   Andre de Brilli or de Brili, "the Italian colonel" (*Specification* …). In Russian service in the rank of captain from 1701. "One plain Italian engineer, who made the approaches" (Kurakin, B.I., *Russko-shvedskaia voina*, p. 296). "Engineer Brilli" is mentioned in von Huyssen's

participated in the siege[69]: Carolus Antony Schkarbeck, Johann Lenzius, and Vences Ligoltsky.

Troops that did not take part in the siege of Narva

Colonel Bauer's Dragoon Corps[70]
Bauer's dragoon regiment[71]
Kropotov's dragoon regiment[72]
Ignatiev's dragoon regiment[73]
Volkonsky's dragoon regiment[74]
Meshchersky's dragoon regiment[75]
Inflant's dragoon regiment[76]
Grigorov's dragoon regiment[77]

journal as a direct participant in the storming of Narva, sent on the attack together with the troops (von Huyssen, *Zhurnal Gosudaria Petra I s 1695 po 1709*, p. 455).

69   Arkhiv VIMAIViVS, F. 2, Op. 1, D. 37, ll. 37–39.

70   Bauer, Adolph Felix (in Russian documents: Bour, Rodion Christianovich) (1667–1717). From Holstein, in 1700 in the rank of rittmeister he served in the Swedish garrison of Narva and went over to the side of Russians. From 1701 in Russian service in the rank of major. In 1704, now as a colonel, he commanded the dragoon regiments in Sheremetev's army and after the capture of Dorpat went on raids towards Pernau and Reval.

71   Colonel Rodion Christianovich Bauer's dragoon regiment. Raised in 1698 in Preobrazhenskoie from palace courtiers as the Preobrazhensky Dragoon Regiment; from 1699 known as A. A. Schnewentz's dragoon regiment. From 1706 known as the Kievsky Dragoon Regiment [Rabinovich, No. 541]. Strength on 9 June was 36 officers and 813 men, not including those without horses and left in their quarters.

72   Colonel Semen Ivanovich Kropotov's dragoon regiment. Raised in 1701 from cavalry, lancers and adolescents of towns along the Volga River. From 1706 known as the Troitsky Dragoon Regiment [Rabinovich, No. 543]. Its strength on 9 June was 30 officers and 912 men, not including those without horses and left in their quarters.

73   Colonel Ivan Artem'evich Ingat'ev's dragoon regiment. Raised in 1701 in Moscow as Colonel Prince Ivan Ivanovich Lvov's regiment. From 1706, known as the Astrakhansky Dragoon Regiment [Rabinovich, No. 550]. Its strength on 9 June was 33 officers and 949 men, not including those without horses and left in their quarters.

74   Colonel Prince Grigorii Semenovich Volkonsky's dragoon regiment. Raised in 1701 as Colonel Prince Nikita Fedorovich Meshchersky's regiment. From 1708 known as the Novgorodsky Dragoon Regiment [Rabinovich, No. 544]. Its strength on 9 June was 33 officers and 880 men, not including those without horses and left in their quarters.

75   Colonel Prince Petr Fedorovich Meshchersky's dragoon regiment. Raised in 1701 in Moscow as regiment of Colonel and courtier Mikhail Stepanovich Zhdanov. From 1706, known as the Vladimirsky Dragoon Regiment [Rabinovich, No. 551]. Its strength on 9 June was 34 officers and 940 men, not including those without horses and left in their quarters.

76   Colonel Nikolai Iustorovich Inflant's dragoon regiment. Raised in 1701 in Moscow as a regiment of Colonel and courtier Fedor Aristovich Novikov. From 1706 known as the Pskovsky Dragoon Regiment [Rabinovich, No. 548; Volynsky, Book 4, p. 189]. Its strength on 9 June was 34 officers and 789 men, not including those without horses and left in their quarters.

77   Colonel Vasilii Vasil'evich Grigorov's dragoon regiment. Raised in 1701 in Moscow as Colonel and courtier Nikita Ivanovich Poluektov's regiment. From 1706 – the Saint Petersburgsky dragoon regiment [Rabinovich, No. 547]. Strength on 9 June was 34 officers and 789 men, not including those without horses and left in their quarters.

Sheremetev's dragoon battalion[78]
Gagarin's dragoon regiment[79]
Select dragoon companies[80]
Kursk Kalmyks[81]

The garrison of Saint-Petersburg

Ober-commandant Colonel Roman Vilimovich Bruce[82]

Infantry

According to the records from 26 February 1704, the garrison had seven infantry regiments with a total strength of 6,184 men, including 757 absent due to illness.[83]
Colonel Gurik's regiment[84]
Colonel Treiden's regiment[85]
Colonel Bruce's regiment[86]
Colonel Tolbukhin's regiment[87]

---

78 Field Marshal Boris Petrovich Sheremetev's select dragoon battalion, commanded in 1704 by Lieutenant Colonel Iuda Vasilievich Boltin, and then by Colonel Shamordin. Raised in 1703 in Jamburg from select men of the dragoon regiments. From 1705 – a squadron; from 1708 known as the Arkhangelogorodsky Dragoon Regiment [Rabinovich, No. 564]. Being Sheremetev's personal escort, it arrived in Narva together with the Field Marshal after the capture of the town.

79 Lieutenant Colonel (and then Colonel) Prince Bogdan Ivanovich Gagarin's dragoon regiment. Raised in 1702 in Moscow from service men as Colonel Mikhail Iur'evich Frank's regiment. From 1706 known as the Smolensky Dragoon Regiment [Rabinovich, No. 558]. Its strength on 9 June was 33 officers and 505 men, not including those without horses and left in their quarters.

80 Select noble companies. Their strength on 9 June was 150 men [Sheremetev's field campaign diary, p. 150].

81 Their strength on 9 June was 55 men [Sheremetev's field campaign diary, p. 150].

82 Robert Bruce (in Russian Roman Vilimovich Brius) (1668–1720), Colonel and military governor of Saint Petersburg. Brother to James Bruce.

83 Ustrialov, Vol. 4, Part 2, p. 477.

84 Colonel Maksim Maksimovich Gurik's infantry regiment. Raised in 1700 in Simbirsk from soldiers of older ages from Shepelev's former command as Grigorii Andreevich Jankowsky's regiment. From 1724 known as the Kronstadt Infantry Regiment [Rabinovich, No. 142].

85 Colonel Timofei Ivanovich Treiden's infantry regiment. Raised in 1700 in Kazan from conscripts as Ivan Ivanovich Angler's regiment. From 1708 known as the Permsky Infantry Regiment [Rabinovich, No. 135].

86 Colonel Roman Vilimovich Bruce's infantry regiment. Raised in 1700 in Kazan from conscripts as Zachary Krog's regiment. In 1705 it was called the Saint Petersburg *Ober*-komendantsky Regiment, from 1708 the Arkhangelogorodsky Infantry Regiment [Rabinovich, No. 136]. Its strength on 30 April was 771 men [NIA SPbII RAN, F. 83, Op. 1, D. 217].

87 Tolbukhin in 1702-1703 commanded the regiment, which Colonel Andrei Vilimovich Scharf subsequently headed in 1704; raised in 1697–1698 from *streltsy* of the Kazan district as a settled infantry regiment in Tsaritsyn, from 1708 known as the Olonetsky Infantry Regiment [Rabinovich, No. 92]. This unit in May 1704 was sent from Pskov to Petersburg and served on Kotlin Island; however, it was called "Andrei Scharf's regiment from Kazan" [see *Ofitserskie skazki*, Vol. 1, p. 1032; Vol. 2, pp. 1906, 1916; and PiB, Vol. 3, pp. 50, 611]. Accordingly,

Colonel Neitert's regiment[88]
Lieutenant Colonel Hamilton's regiment[89]
Colonel Bordovik's regiment (in the summer of 1704 it was absent from Petersburg, because it had become part of the field army as Ogilvy's regiment)[90]
Colonel Andrei Scharf's regiment[91]

Irregular Cavalry

The total number of irregular cavalry in Saint-Petersburg's garrison was put at around 2,000 horsemen in Sheremetev's *Campaign Journal*.
Colonel Bakhmetev's irregular cavalry from the lower Volga[92]
Colonel Zazharsky's irregular cavalry from the lower Volga[93]
Colonel Temnik's Zaporozhian Cossacks[94]

Tolbukhin in the winter of 1704 was commanding a different regiment, from 1727 the Kronschlot garrison infantry regiment [Rabinovich, No. 94].

88   The settled infantry regiment of Lieutenant Colonel Nikolai Andreevich Neitert (Netert, Neidhart), it was at the same time called the settled Petersburg regiment, or military governor's regiment of Prince Aleksandr Danilovich Menshikov. Raised in Saint Petersburg from officers and rank and file of other regiments, "who had volunteered for garrison duty" [*Ofitserskie skazki*, Vol. 2, p. 2280]. In 1708, it became the Saint Petersburgsky Infantry Regiment [Zeziulinsky and Rabinovich, No. 174]. In 1704, the regiment was stationed in Saint Petersburg.

89   Lieutenant Colonel John Hamilton's (Ivan Gamilton's in Russian) infantry regiment. Raised in 1700 in Kazan from conscripts as Ivan Pavlovich Berner's regiment. From 1708, it was known as the Belozersky Infantry Regiment [Rabinovich, No. 133]. In May 1704 it escorted a load of artillery ammunition on small boats from Petersburg to Narva, then returned to Petersburg [*Ofitserskie skazki*, Vol. 2, p. 1987]. R.V. Bruce reported to A.D. Menshikov from Petersburg that "Hamilton had returned that same day [5 August] with all his men in good health aboard boats" [NIA SPBII RAN, F. 36, Op. 1, D. 693, l. 99 obr.]. In October 1704 he again went with provisions from Petersburg to Narva and on his return path was supposed to deliver cannons [PiB, Vol. 3, p. 178].

90   Matvei Matveevich Bordovik's infantry regiment, which was transferred from Petersburg into the acting army; Bordovik passed away at the start of the siege of Narva [see *Ofitserskie skazki*, Vol. 2, p. 1934]. From 2 July 1704, it was Field Marshal George Ogilvy's regiment. Raised in 1700 in Moscow from volunteers as Gustav Ivanitsky's regiment. From 1708, known as the Moskovskii Infantry Regiment [Zeziulinsky and Rabinovich, No. 117]. Its strength on 15 August was 1,123 men.

91   Major General Alexander Scharf's infantry regiment, though factually the commander from December 1702 was Andrei Scharf. From 1708, known as the Olonetsky Infantry Regiment [Zeziulinsky and Rabinovich, No. 92]. The "Andrei Scharf's regiment from Kazan" after the battle at Kaströ was sent by Sheremetev from Pskov to Petersburg on 9 May 1704 [PiB, Vol. 3, pp. 50, 611, 673]; it arrived in Petersburg in July and was dispatched to Kotlin Island [*Ofitserskie skazki*, Vol. 1, p. 1032; Vol. 2, p. 1906, 1916], from whence it was called back to Petersburg by R.V. Bruce on 5 August in connection with Maidel's second attack [NIA SPbII RAN, F. 36, Op. 1, D. 693, l. 59].

92   Dmitrii Efremovich Bakhmetev's regiment. In October 1704 it was sent from Petersburg into winter quarters at the Olonets shipyard.

93   Colonel Mikhail Zazharsky's settled mounted streltsy regiment in Astrakhan [Rabinovich, No. 32]

94   Matvei Temnik's regiment from Zaporozhie, numbering 113 mounted men [Bazarova, T.A., "Russkie voiska i mestnoe naselenie Ingermanlandii v 1702–1710 gg: problema vzaimootnoshenii" ["Russian troops and the local population of Ingermanland in 1702–1710: the problems of interactions" from *Severnaia voina, Sankt-Peterburg i Evropa v pervoi*

The general composition of Bakhmetev's and Zazharsky's irregular regiments apparently was described in two archival documents from Menshikov's Chancellery:[95]

1. "Which towns of the lower Volga, which ranks and how many men for service in the Swedish campaign … in the present 1704 has been sent" from 30 September 1704:
   Mounted: *streltsy* from Astrakhan – 300; Chernyi Iar – 70; Krasnyi Iar – 30; Tsaritsyn – 100; Samara – 100, Ufa streltsy and Cossacks – 200.
   Foot: From Astrakhan 500 *streltsy* and soldiers; Krasnyi Iar – 100; Chernyi Iar – 100; Tsaritsyn – 100; Dmitrov – 700 men.

2. An undated document from the book of copies of letters and reports to A.D. Menshikov for the year 1704:[96]
   "In the past 1703 on the 3rd day of December, an edict in the name of His Majesty has been sent from his Chancellery regarding service of mounted service men from the lower Volga towns in the Swedish campaign in the present year of 1704:
   From Astrakhan – 300 *streltsy*
   From Krasnyi Iar and Chernyi Iar: 100
   From Saratov, Samara, Tsaritsyn and Ufa – 100 men each, for a total of 400
   Iaik Cossacks – 500, Ufa Cossacks – 100, Greben Cossacks – 50; for a total of 650
   Ufa Bashkirs – 257
   Total mounted men: 1,707

His Majesty's pay for such service has been set at rate of 10 roubles for each man.

The Dorpat Garrison

Commandant Colonel Fedor Balck

According to the information from Sheremetev's Campaign Journal from 25 July, when Sheremetev's main forces left Dorpat, a garrison with a total strength of 2,664 men was left behind in the city.[97]
Colonel Balck's infantry[98]

---

chetverti XVIII v.: Materialy mezhdunarodnoi nauchnoi konferentsii [Northern war, Saint Petersburg and Europe in the first quarters of the 18th century: Materials of an international academic conference] (Saint Petersburg, 2007), p. 145].

95   NIA SPbII RAN, F. 83, Op. 2, D. 1, ll. 321–322.
96   NIA SPbII RAN, F. 36, Op. 1, D. 693, l. 61.
97   See Sheremetev's campaign journal, pp. 169–170.
98   Colonel Fedor Nikolaevich (Friedrich) Balck's infantry regiment. Raised in 1700 in Moscow. From 1708, the Voronezhsky Infantry Regiment [Rabinovich, No. 127]. Strength: "one lieutenant colonel, one major; in 10 companies: 10 captains, 10 lieutenants, 9 ensigns, for a

Colonel Polibin's *streltsy*[99]
Major Rukh's *streltsy*[100]
Nazimov's cavalry[101]
Murzenko's cavalry[102]

The personnel of the Russian artillery in the Narva and Ivangorod garrison

"On the 16th day of November 1704, the list of artillery officers in the town of Narva and in Ivangorod":[103]

Major Elias Kober
Captain Johann Friedrich Memmiger
Lieutenants: Otto Friedrich Ryttor, Gabriel Zart and Kliment Plimkö
Styck-junkers: Friedrich Schroeder and Karl Tamson
Sergeants: Danil Knop, Peter Dege, Jacob Bomhardt, Johann Schmidt
Bombardier Sergeant Grigorii Isaev
Bombardier Corporal Ivan Bykov
40 bombardiers
4 gunnery corporals
50 gunners, 95 *handlangers* (matrosses), 11 orderlies, 3 drummers and 1 blacksmith

Losses of the Russian Army

The 1704 campaign journal contains information on the casualties suffered "when on the assault", which is to say, on the day of the storming of Narva on 9 August 1704 (see Table 2):[104]

---

total of 32 [including the colonel]; and 926 non-commissioned officers and soldiers, including 120 wounded men, for a total of 958 officers, non-commissioned officers and men."

99   Colonel Polibin's *streltsy* regiment in Pskov; its strength on 26 April was 4 officers and 691 men; on 25 July 5 officers and 593 men.

100 Colonel Iurii Vestov's *streltsy* regiment in Pskov, which after 13 July 1704 was commanded by Major Rukh. Vestov was killed during the storming of Dorpat [Rabinovich, No. 53]. Its strength on 26 April was six officers and 625 men; on 25 July five officers and 402 men.

101 The regiment of cavalry under the command of the forward detachment (*ertaul*) leader and courtier Ivan Tikhonovich Nazimov. Raised in 1701 from Moscow nobles and service men from the Novgorod district [Rabinovich, No. 531]. Its strength on 2 June was 737 men and on 25 July 373 of the regiment's men had been left in Dorpat. According to Chambers, in Narva on 10 February 1705, "Nazimov had as few as less than 300 men and those men were irregular and without mounts" [NIA SPbII RAN, F. 83, Op. 2, D. 2, l. 215].

102 Colonel Moisei Murzenko's regiment of cavalry. Raised in 1700 from Smolensk gentry and cavalry; in 1701, it was staffed with Cossacks from the Novgorod district [Rabinovich, No. 515]. According to an edict in 1703 it was re-formed from Novgorod and Pskov nobility, cavalry, Cossacks and adolescents [Volynsky, Book 1, p. 223]. Its strength on 2 June was 993 men, and on around 20 July 700 men "of the Novgorod district and the cavalry of Murzenko's regiment" [PiB, Vol. 3, p. 110]; on 25 July, 370 men from the regiment had been left in Dorpat.

103 Arkhiv VIMAIViVS, F. 2, Op. 1, D. 1, l. 256.

104 *Pokhodnyi zhurnal 1704 goda*, pp. 114–115.

Table 2: Russian casualties suffered during the assault on 9 August 1704

	Killed	Wounded
Colonels	1	2
Lieutenant Colonels	–	2
Majors	1	4
Captains	3	15
Lieutenants	2	11
Ensigns	1	-
Non-commissioned officers	8	39
Quartermasters	4	23
Sergeants	1	2
Company clerks	1	2
Corporals	13	54
Privates	322	1,183
Drummers	1	3

This yields a total of 358 men killed and 1,340 wounded, for a total of 1,698 casualties from the assault.

The casualties prior to the assault are unknown. Judging from the nature of the combat operations and the intensity of the fighting, over the period of the siege the Russian forces might have lost no more than the number of casualties suffered during the assault.

Appendix II

The Swedish Forces

The garrison of Narva

According to Horn's letter to the Defence Commission in Stockholm, on 2 June 1704 there were 5,113 men in the garrison of Narva and Ivangorod (see Table 3):[1]

Table 3: Numerical strength of the Swedish garrison of Narva and Ivangorod

	Officers	Civil Officials	Non-commissioned officers and rank and file	Total
Artillery	7	5	326	338
Cavalry	38	4	627	669
Dragoons	12	–	264	276
Total:	57	9	1,217	1,283
Infantry				
Horn's regiment of 11 companies	36	10	1,551	1,597
Other regiments (20 captains and 60 subaltern officers)	94	18	2,121	2,233
Total:	130	28	3,672	3,830
Grand total:				5,113

Horn does not provide the name of any regiment other than his own; they can be identified from the testimony of Captain Staël and from other sources. A quick note is necessary to understand the classes of the Swedish regiments. The Swedish system of staffing and classification of units – the allotment (*indelta*), three-, four- and five-*männing* and *fördubbling* (doubling) regiments – is best described in specialised literature.[2] So now, a list of the

---

1   Rosen, p. 186. It is noteworthy that according to the information from captured Swedish prisoners, the garrison's strength in this period was significantly less. For example, Captain Stahl reported a total of 3,100 men.

2   Höglund, L.-E. and Sellnäs, A., *The Great Northern War 1700–1721, Vol. 1: Colours and Uniformes* (Karlstad: Acedia Press, 2000); Martinsson, Ö., *Svenska armén 1700–1721*, <www.tacitus.nu>. <http://www.tacitus.nu/karoliner/armeer/sverige/organisation.htm> (accessed

Swedish regiments and battalions:

Commandant Major General Henning Rudolf Horn
Major General Henning Rudolf Horn's Narva garrison regiment,[3] 1,100 men

Lieutenant Colonel Magnus Stjernstråle's Bjorneborgs doubling battalion,[4] 300 men

Colonel Jurgen Johann Lode's Tavasthus, Viborgs and Savolax three-*männing* regiment,[5] 300 men

Otto Rebinder's Estonian infantry regiment,[6] 600 men

Colonel Herman von Fersen's Estonian infantry regiment[7]

Colonel Carl Morath's Åbo county doubling cavalry regiment,[8] 300 men

Lieutenant Colonel Johann Kinnert's artillery

Narva's city militia, 300 men

Ivangorod Russian townsfolk, 200 men

Russian official documents give the following numerical strength of the Narva garrison at the start of the siege: 4,555 men, including 3,175 foot, 1,080 horse, and 300 artillerists, according to the Campaign Journal of 1704, and 4,375 men according to the engraved Relation.

Major General Schlippenbach's corps[9]
Major General Wollmar Anton Schlippenbach

Major General W.A. Schlippenbach Livonian dragoon regiment,[10] 600 men

Colonel F. Wachtmeister's Estonian nobility squadron,[11] 1,000 men

Colonel G.I. Burghausen's Karelian cavalry regiment,[12] 1,000 men.

Lieutenant Colonel A.I. von Schlippenbach's Livonian dragoon squadron,[13] 400 men

Lieutenant Colonel J. Kaulbars' Ösel dragoon squadron,[14] 400 men

on 4 August 2018); Wolke, L.E., *The Swedish army in the Great Northern War 1700–1721* (Warwick: Helion & Company, 2018).

3   Garnisonsregemente i Narva. H.R. Horn (Höglund, p. 107).

4   Bjorneborgs fördubblingsbataljon, M.S. Stefken, M. Stjernstråle (Höglund, p. 129).

5   Tavasthus, Viborgs och Savolax tremänningsregemente till foot, J.J. Lode (Höglund, p. 128).

6   Estländskt infanteriregemente, Jerwiska och Wieriska kretsen, O. Rebinder (Höglund, p. 109). It had on its unit roster one dragoon company.

7   Estländskt infanteriregemente, Wikiska kretsen, H. von Fersen (Höglund, p. 109).

8   Åbo läns fördubblingsregemente till häst, C. Pereswetoff-Morath (Höglund, p. 118). In the Narva garrison, the regiment consisted of cavalry and dragoons. A portion of the regiment was in Maidel's corps.

9   Information about the composition and strength of the garrisons of Narva, Reval and Schlippenbach's corps were reported by Captain Stahl, who was taken prisoner on 21 May 1704 (Volynsky, Book 3, pp. 15–18). The names of the regiments are given according to Höglund, L.-E. and Sellnäs, A., *The Great Northern War 1700–1721, Vol. 1: Colours and Uniformes* (Karlstad: Acedia Press, 2000).

10   Livländskt dragonsregemente, W.A. von Schlippenbach (Höglund, p. 86).

11   Adelsfanan i Estland och Ingermanland, F. Wachtmeister (Höglund, p. 82).

12   Karelska (Viborgs och Nyslotts län) kavalleriregementet, H.J. von Burghausen (Höglund, p. 54). In Stahl's testimony, this was "Colonel Baron Gusin's Vyborg regiment".

13   Livländskt dragonsqvadron, A.J. von Schlippenbach (Höglund, p. 86).

14   Öselska Lantdragonsqvadronen, J. Kaulbars (Höglund, p. 86).

The Reval garrison

Estonian General-Governor Count Axel Julius de la Gardie

Colonel K.A. de la Gardie's Estonian infantry regiment,[15] 1,024 men (of which 500 were assigned to von Schlippenbach's corps)

Colonel H.H. Liewen's Livonian infantry regiment,[16] 1,000 men (of which 500 were assigned to von Schlippenbach's corps)

Colonel B.I. Mellin's Estonian infantry regiment,[17] 800 men

Colonel B. von der Pahlen's Estonian infantry regiment,[18] 1,200 men (on the ships of De Prou's squadron)

Colonel O. Rebinder's Estonian infantry regiment, 600 men (on the ships of De Prou's squadron until 10 May, when it transferred into the Narva garrison).

Lieutenant General Maidel's corps

According to Maidel's report to the Defence Commission on 18 July, his corps in camp at Joutselkä (modern-day Simagino, Russia) had 4,145 men:[19]

Lieutenant General Georg Johann Maidel

Colonel J.G. von Tiesenhausen's Queen's Life-Regiment of the Horse, also known as the Estonian cavalry regiment,[20] 286 men

Colonel A.E. Ramsay's Nyland doubling cavalry regiment,[21] 500 men

Colonel A.G. Mühl's Karelian (Vyborg) doubling cavalry regiment,[22] 719 men

Lieutenant Colonel Dellwig's squadron of the Åbo three-männing cavalry regiment,[23] 129 men.

Colonel Morath's Åbo doubling cavalry regiment,[24] 134 men

General O. Wellingk's Ingrian dragoon regiment,[25] 202 men

Lieutenant Colonel C.F. Knorring's Estate Squadron/Finnish Stand Dragoon Squadron,[26] 134 men

General G.J. Maidel's Tavastahus infantry regiment,[27] 519 men

General O. Wellingk's Ingrian infantry regiment,[28] 283 men

A.F. von Krusenstierna's Åbo county doubling infantry battalion,[29] 475 men

15 Estländskt infanteriregemente, A.J. de la Gardie (Höglund, p. 107).
16 Livländskt infanteribataljon, H.H. Liewen (Höglund, p. 108).
17 Estländskt infanteriregemente, B.J. Mellin (Höglund, p. 109).
18 Estländskt infanteriregemente, Harriska kretsen, B. von der Pahlen (Höglund, p. 109).
19 Rosen, p. 198.
20 Drottningens Livregemente till häst (Estnika kavalleriregementet), J.H. von Tiesenhausen (Höglund, p. 83).
21 Nylands fördubblingsregemente till häst, A.E. Ramsay (Höglund, p. 118).
22 Karelska (Viborgs läns) fördubblingsregemente till häst, A.G. Mühl (Höglund, p. 118).
23 Åbo, Nylands och Viborgs läns tremänningsregemente till häst, S.M. Rebinder (Höglund, p. 116). Öfverste löjtn. Dellwigs Sqvadron.
24 Åbo läns fördubblingregemente till häst, C. Pereswetoff-Morath (Höglund, p. 118).
25 Ingermanlandska dragonregementet, General O. Wellingk (Höglund, p. 85).
26 Adelns, Presterkapets och Civile Betjenternas Dragoner/Finska Ståndsdragonsqvadron, S.F. Knorring (Höglund, p. 118)
27 Tavastahus regemente, General G.J. Maidel (Höglund, p. 72).
28 Ingermanländskt infanteriregemente, General O. Wellingk (Höglund, p. 108).
29 Åbo läns fördubblingbataljon, A.F. von Krusenstierna (Höglund, p. 129).

O.J. Maidel's Tavastehus doubling battalion,[30] 219 men
C. Boje's Nylands doubling battalion,[31] 131 men
C. von Hagen's Vyborg doubling infantry battalion,[32] 243 men
A. Pereswetoff-Morath's Nyslotts doubling infantry battalion,[33] 229 men

Vice Admiral Jacob De Prou's Naval Squadron
According to De Prou's letter to the King from Reval on 21 April, his squadron numbered 15 ships.[34] The ships' names are listed below with their number of guns:

Ship of the line: *Wachtmeister* (46)
Frigates: *Stralsundh* (36), *Revel* (32), *Falken* (30), *Snarswen* (20), *Ruschenfelt* (20)
Brigantines: *Castor* (14), *Kräftan* (14), *Scorpionen* (14), *Göija* (14), *Jungfrun* (14), *Wäduren* (14)
Bombardier ship: *Wulcanus* with two 60-pound mortars
Galleys: *Miöhunden* and *Stöfvaren*

According to a letter from De Prou to the King on 20 July, upon departing from Bjorke-Sund for Retusaari/Kotlin Island, the squadron included the warship *Wachtmeister*, four frigates, four brigantines and one bombardier ship.[35]

The losses of the Swedish garrison of Narva
The Campaign Journal of 1704 reports the following list of prisoners among the garrison:

Major General and Commandant Baron Horn
Colonels – 5
Lieutenant colonels – 4
Majors – 5
Rittmeisters – 3
Captains – 19
Lieutenants – 62
Adjutants – 1
Cornets – 4
Quartermasters – 4
Nobles – 4
Total: 111
Artillery servicemen – 125
Rank and file – 1,600

Kelch cites the names of the senior officers that were taken prisoner, but their total number does not match the figure given in the above-cited Russian

30   Tavastehus läns fördubblingbataljon, O.J. Maidel (Höglund, p. 130).
31   Nylands fördubblingbataljon, C. Boje (Höglund, p. 130).
32   Viborgs läns fördubblingbataljon, C. von Hagen (Höglund, p. 130).
33   Savolax (Nyslotts) fördubblingbataljon, A. Pereswetoff-Morath (Höglund, p. 130).
34   Rosen, p. 165.
35   Rosen, p. 200.

report:[36]

Colonels: Jurgen Johan von Lode, Otto Rebinder, Herman von Fersen, Johan Apolloff, Carl Morath;

Lieutenant Colonels: Moritz Lillie, Adam Johan von Treyden;

Majors: Adam Rheinhold Nieroth, Berend Rebinder, Ebert Grabbe, Jacob Gustav Rohr, Jobst Johan Barone;

As well as 4 rittmeisters, 21 captains, 5 lieutenant captains, 29 lieutenants, 6 cornets, 23 *fänrik* (ensigns) and more than 1,000 non-commissioned officers and rank and file.

The memoirist Kurakin indicates that they captured "7,500 lower officers and soldiers [this must be a mistaken figure, probably the correct number intended was 1,500], as well as 2,000 merchants and all sorts of estate owners, both male and female." He also gives the number of victims of the storming of Narva: "As for the killed people, 2,118 bodies have been carried out of the city."[37]

---

36   Kelch, p. 417.
37   Kurakin, B.I., *Russko-shvedskaia voina. Zapiski. 1700–1710*, p. 295.

Appendix III

"A letter about the fall of Narva, written in Reval on 5 September 1704"

News about the fall of Narva spread in pace with the arrival of refugees from the city on territory under Swedish control. For example, according to the terms of the accord, the author of the journal published by Adlerfeld – one of the members of the Ivangorod garrison – reached Revel overland under Russian escort.[1] Another portion of the garrison, apparently, was sent to Vyborg. Certain officers and citizens left Narva on 26 August (according to the Swedish calendar) aboard a ship, and after being delayed for several days by a head wind, and later because of windless conditions, arrived at Reval on 2 September (according to the Swedish calendar). Thus, news about what had happened arrived first in Reval, and possibly in Vyborg, from whence it began spreading wider. Personal letters of the citizens or notes from their stories were sent out in copies to Swedish bureaucrats and private individuals, and apparently, some of them became accessible to the compilers of news publications.

For example, a "letter from Reval from 15 September" (New style, that is 9 September in the Old style) was published in the Nuremburg *Mercurius* newspaper already in October 1704.[2] A different letter, from 13 October (according to the Swedish calendar, or 12 October per the Russian calendar), was published in a different German news publication in early 1705.[3] A number of similarities in Kelch's text allows one to assume that these

---

1   Adlefeld, Vol. 2, pp. 1–28.
2   *Mercurius:* "Welcher in sich enthält und vorstellig machet den gegenwärtigen Zustland von Europa, alles was in denen Europäischen Höfen sich ereignet, und vorfällt, das Interest der Printzen und Staaten, ihre Staats-Streiche, und überhaupt alles dasjenige, was da merkwürdig und curieux," Nuremburg, October 1704, pp. 1183 Acedia Press 1185.
3   "Der neubstellte Agent von Haus aus, mit allerand curieusen Missiven, Brieffen, Memoralen, Staffeten, Correspondencen und Commissionen, nach Erforderung der heutigen Staats- und gelehrten Welt." Freyburg, 1705, Vol. 6, pp. 492–496.

publications were among his sources. News from Danzig on 18 September about Narva's capture was published in a French gazette in October.[4]

A manuscript of a "letter" in the German language, which is published here, is preserved in General A.L. Lewenhaupt's collection of papers in the Linköping library in Sweden.[5] It was revealed and kindly offered by the scholar and archivist Bengt Nilsson. In Swedish historiography, the letter from the Narva burgher from 5 September was mentioned in Almquist's work;[6] however, it was never published in full and never used by historians either in Sweden or in Russia.

In the course of the work to decipher and translate this manuscript, we found out that the same information had already been published in a collection of documents in the French language in 1740.[7] The overwhelming degree of convergence between the two texts enabled a better understanding and a translation of the unclear portions of the German "letter". The existence of the two known copies of the text speaks to the fact that the letter had been copied. The majority of the information contained in the document is confirmed by other sources; some of the information, on the contrary, does not match the picture of events compiled on the basis of other sources. These contradictions, discussed in the accompanying commentary notes, can be explained by the author's poor information and the later date of the document's composition, as well as by our insufficient knowledge of the realities of 1704. With a high degree of confidence, it can be asserted that the manuscript does not appear to be a first-hand letter from any citizen, but it contains written or verbal evidence offered by an eyewitness (or eyewitnesses).

At the given point, one can offer two versions regarding the manuscript's origin:

1. The source of the German manuscript was the French text, published in 1740, but the author and translator added a number of new details to it;
2. Both the German manuscript and the French text are sketchy copies from an unknown original source in the German or some other language.

The proper names in the published text are given in accordance with the long-standing names in Russian historiography, but in the accompanying commentary notes, their names are cited in the language of the original. The dates in the text and the commentary notes are shown are in accordance with the Swedish calendar.

---

4   Gazette du 11 Octobre 1704// Recueil des Gazettes. Lyon, 1704, No. 42, p. 163.
5   Linköpings stifts- och landsbibliotek. LiSB H 79:4, no. 159.
6   Almquist H., *Ryska fångar i Sverige och svenska i Ryssland 1700-1709. II. Svenskarna i Ryssland* (Karolinska Förbundets Årsbok, 1943).
7   Lamberty, G., *Memoires Pour Servir a L'Histoire du XVIII Siecle: Contenant Les Negociations, Traitez, Resolutions, Et Autres Documens Autheniques Concernant Les Affaires D'Etat, Contenant Le Supplement A L'Anée MDCCIV* (Amsterdam, 1740), pp. 368–372.

Deciphering the handwritten manuscript, and translation from German to Russian: Oleg Sholin

Commentary: Boris Megorsky and Oleg Sholin

Reval, 5 September 1704

On Friday a schute[8] arrived from Narva, and on it a Russian drummer with letters from captured officers, as well as from residents to their [relatives]; on the same schute was the former commandant of Nöteborg Lieutenant Colonel von Schlippenbach, who had received freedom; Pastor Schwartz,[9] who had been freed by the Tsar at Schlippenbach's request; also, Pastor Habbe,[10] Henry Broun[11] and his spouse, the sons of the deceased Pastor Gnospelius;[12] and others who left Ivangorod according to the accord. Other than them, Heinrich Erik[13] arrived with a passport from Prince Aleksandr Menshikov,[14] the present governor general of Narva; several captains were left in Narva as a result of this as hostages. They are reporting that the city was attacked on 27 April, properly besieged on 23 May, subjected to bombardment from 31 July

---

8   *Schuit* (Dutch), *Schute* (German), *skuta* (Swedish) – during this period a North European flat-bottomed vessel with gaff rig, for coastal and riverine sailing (<http://www.debinnenvaart.nl/binnenvaarttaal/woord.php?woord=schr#schuit>). She departed from Narva at 5:00 p.m. on 26 August (Hansen H. J., *Geschichte der Stadt Narva* (Dorpat, 1858), S. 236).

9   Levin Andreas Schwartz (1699, Narva–1715/16, Sweden), the son of burgomaster Johan Christopher Schwartz, baptised in Narva on 30 December 1699. Educated in several universities (Bremen, Altdorf, Wittenberg, Leipzig, Dorpat); defended his doctorate in Leipzig on 25 April 1693; ordained in Narva in 1697; vicar in Gubanitsy (from 1697); vice pastor in Kosemkina until 1704; in Sweden from 1704 [Akiande M., *Bidrag till kännedom om Evangelisk-lutherska församlingarne i Ingermanlands stift* (Helsingfors, 1865), p. 74; YrjöKotivuori, Ylioppilasmastrikkeli 1640–1852: Levin Andreas Schwartz (Verkkojulkaisu, 2005) – <http://www.helsinki.fi/ylioppilasmatrikkeli/henkilo.php?id=U446> (accessed 24 May 2015).

10 Johannes Habbe (16??? Reval–14 October 1710, parish of St. John, Harjumaa). Preacher in landmilitia regiment in Narva (March 1703); deacon in von Pahlen's regiment (10 May 1705); preacher in St. John parish (29 December 1706); died of plague (Paucker H. R. Ehstlands Geistlichkeit in geordneter Zeit- und Reihenfolge. Revel, 1849. S. 130).

11 In the French version of the text, given as Henry Bruin. Possibly, Henry Broun or Brown, a merchant and citizen of Narva (14 December 1682); city councilman (21 November 1698) [EAA.1646.1.599; 1666–1832].

12 Jacob Gnospelius (born May 1646, Mittenwald [Brandenburg]–died on 15 October 1703, Reval). Studied in Frankfurt-am-Main. Conrector in Pritzwalk (from 1667); rector in Havelberg (from 1675); professor of poetry of the Reval gymnasium (from 1678); deacon of the German community in Narva (1682–1685); compastor (from 1685); pastor in Vaivara (1691–1700) [Akiander M., Bidrag ... p. 70].

13 In the French version of the text, given as Henri Erich. Possibly, Heinrich Erich, a merchant and citizen of Narva (6 October 1682); he is mentioned among townsfolk deported to Vologda in 1708 [EAA.1646.1.599; 1666-1832; Hansen H.J. Geschichte... S. 254.

14 From 1702 Menshikov was a count and received his title of "prince" only later, in 1706. Possibly, the use of the title of "prince" in the 1704 source reflects his high position as one of the Tsar's favourites in the eyes of himself and those around him, but did not correspond to his formal status.

on, and on 10 August[15] – at a half past 1:00 subjected to a 45-minute assault, as a result of which it was unfortunately taken, to a great extent because of the splendid bastion named Honour, which was built according to all the rules, to everyone's surprise began to collapse on Sunday 7 August at 5:00 p.m.[16] The masonry began to slide down into the ditch, and in addition even the rampart was collapsing. On Monday the Tsar through a letter to the commandant demanded a surrender of the city; by the way announcing in it the impossibility of relief; on Tuesday everything was quiet, but once Commandant Horn replied that he had no intention to capitulate, the general assault began on the above-indicated day; the enemy stepped off for the most part towards the Honour bastion, towards which 100 men abreast began marching towards the ravelin and breach,[17] where they could place 12 men in a row; here, Major Funk,[18] Captains Hochmuth, Menschgeber[19] and Gyllenspang and his brother – a lieutenant were all killed, and along side them, 12 grenadiers; the citizens and soldiers fought off several enemy

---

15   The dates in the text are given according to the Swedish calendar. The storming indeed occurred on 9/10 August, and the bombardment began on 30/31 July. However, the other dates, which were more distant for the author of the text, are not fully correct: P.M. Apraxin began to besiege the fortress on 27/28 April, but the formal siege did not begin until June, once the main siege army reached the city in the last days of May.

16   The collapse of the face of the Honour Bastion occurred in the morning between 9:00 and 10:00 a.m., according to the chronology published by Adlerfeld and the citizen's diary [Adlerfeld, Vol. 2, p. 18; Archiv., p. 273].

17   The author has in mind the breach in the Victoria Bastion.

18   According to Adlerfeld (p. 21), the defence was being directed by Lieutenant Colonel von Treyden, Major Funk, Captains Aminoff and Gyllenspang, two lieutenants and two ensigns; other than von Treyden and Aminoff, they were all cut down in the fighting together with their soldiers. Captain Hochmuth was a participant in the sorties and fighting on 28 May and 30 June.
     Funk [Carl Philip von Funcken], killed on 10 August 1704 at Narva – a participant of the campaigns in Hungary (1685) and Brabant (1696); captain of the Narva garrison regiment (14 July 1683), made major of the same regiment on 29 March 1700 [Lewenhaupt, A., *Karl XII:s officerare. Del. 1* (A.K. Stockholm, 1920), p. 218.
     Hochmuth, most likely, is Casimir Ertman Wisocki-Hochmuth, killed on 10 August 1704 at Narva – a sergeant of the Vyborg infantry regiment; *fändrik* of the same regiment (9 April 1700); lieutenant of Welling's dragoon regiment (24 September 1700); captain of the same regiment (27 April 1701) [Gustav Elgenstierna, *Den introducerade svenska adelnsättar tavlor. 1925–1936.* Wisocki-Hochmuth nr. 829 <http://www.adelsvapen.com/genealogi/Wisocki-Hochmuth_nr_829> (accessed 27 May 2015)].
     Rheinhold Gyllenspång, born in Kexholm and killed on 10 August 1704 at Narva. Clerk (*mönsterskrivare*) of Horn's regiment in Kexholm (1679), a musketeer in the Foot Guards (in 1685), a pikeman until 14 August 1686; sergeant of the Åbo infantry regiment (1686), sergeant of Pistolekors' regiment in Kexholm between 1686 and 16 December 1693); in the Narva garrison regiment: *fänrik* (17 September 1695), lieutenant (16 March 1698), regimental quartermaster (May 1703), captain (May 1704).
     Albrekt Johan Gyllenspang, born in 1650 in Kexholm and killed on 10 August 1704 in Narva. Brother to Captain Reinhold; gunner in artillery (1670), *styck-junkor* in Reval, *fänrik* in artillery in (18 May 1689), lieutenant in artillery in Narva (10 May 1704). (Gustaf Elgenstierna, *Den introducerade svenska adelnsattar tavlor. 1925–36.* Gyllenspång nr 1018 <http://www. adeslvapen.com/genealogi/Gyllenspång_nr_1018> (accessed 27 May 2015).

19   Probably, Henrik Johan Mentscher, killed on 10 August 1704 at Narva. In the Narva garrison: a volunteer (1679); a *furir*; a *förare*; sergeant; *fändrik* (July 1683); lieutenant (October 1684); regimental quartermaster (16 March 1698); captain (19 March 1701) [Lewenhaupt A., *Karl XII:s officerare.* Del. 2, p. 454]

attacks and detonated a mine next to the King's Gates,[20] where the enemy lost 400 killed and even a greater number of wounded; however, just at this time a portion of the troops had been dismissed in order to get some rest from their great fatigue, while another portion was occupied with preparing provisions[21], and the enemy with all its forces ferociously attacked the city. It proved impossible to resist, so therefore some of the garrison quickly escaped to Ivangorod, while the rest were compelled to lay down their arms and beg for mercy; even so, initially many were killed because of the fury, namely burgomiester Ekholm[22] at his own doorway, *Ratsherr* Porten[23] on the bridge, as well as Neandr Strahlenborn,[24] lawyer Herbers[25] and a large number of craftsmen, their employees, household servants and others. Even more blood would have been spilled, if the Tsar himself had not stopped the soldiers; he first rushed to the cellar of Lieutenant Colonel Marquard's home, where his wife was hiding, and posted a guard there; he then headed to Commandant von Schlippenbach's home and escorted him away from there. Then he headed to burgomeister Dittmar[26], counsellor Baumhardt [*sic*],[27] and the home of the

---

20 According to all of the other documents, a mine exploded only at the Victoria bastion.

21 In the French version, the text of this phrase has a completely different meaning: "<…> qu'une autre partie étoit occupée à faire sortir les provisions dudit bastion (<…> another portion was engaged in covering this bastion [the Honour bastion]". In other words, Kelch's report and the Reval letter in the German language that state at the moment of the assault many defenders were busy with preparing provisions are dubious. Provisions in the besieged fortress had long ago been inventoried and stockpiled, so there was no need to begin to prepare them.

22 Alexander Georgii Ekholm (born in Sweden in 1662, killed at Narva on 10 August 1704), a secretary in Stockholm; in Narva a town councilman (rattsher), adviser (Rathsverwandter), justice-burgomaster (Justizbügermeister), 26 February 1704 ["Narva's Belagerung und Einnahme von den Russen" in Archiv für die Geschichte Liv- Est- und Curlands. Band VI (Reval, 1851), p. 237]

23 Matthias Poorten (born 1656 in Narva and killed on 10 August 1704 in Narva), the son of the merchant Caspar Poorten; Matthias studied in Leipzig and Jena (1678); became a secretary in Narva on 12 January 1688 and town councilman (from 1694); chairman of the city supreme court [OberGerichsVogt] on 21 October 1699. [Yrjö Kotivuori, Ylioppilasmatrikkeli 1640-1852: Matthias Poorten. Verkkojulkaisu 2005 <http://www.helsinki.fi/ylioppilasmatrikkeli/henkilo.php?id=U381> (accessed 24 May 2015)].

24 Here the author confuses together two different men. According to Kelch, two merchants were killed: Jürgen Strahlenborn and Christian Neandr [Kelch, Ch., *Lieflnädische Historia*, Vol. 2 (Dorpat, 1875), p. 416].

25 Gustav Herbers (born in 1674 in Narva, killed on 10 August 1704 in Narva) – son of burgomaster Ulrich Herbers; baptised on 25 March 1676; studied in Åbo and Vyborg; legal practice in Narva [Yrjö Kotivuori, Ylioppilasmatrikkeli 1640–1852: GustavHerbers. Verkkojulkaisu 2005 <http://www/helsinki.fi/ylioppilasmatrikkeli/henkilo.php?id=3778> (accessed 25 May 2015)].

26 Hermann Dittmar [Ditmer, Ditmar, Dittmer] (born in Narva). He became a town councilman on 2 May 1687, police burgomaster [Polizeibürgermeister] on 31 October 1699; chairman of the city construction collegium, which was striving to follow the models of Swedish monumental architecture (for example, the building of the city exchange, 1695–1704). After the fall of Narva, he was suspected of colluding with the Russians; exiled to Vologda (1713) [Anger G., *Svensk adelns Ättar-taflor*, Vol. 1 (Stockholm, 1858), p. 583; Dittmer, slätt in Svengst biografiskt lexicon (art av Bengt Hildebrand), <http://sok.riksarkivet.se/sbl/artikel/17552> (accessed 24 May 2015)].

27 Johann Boomgard had become, according to Hansen, a member of the town council only on 13 September 1704, after the city's capture [Hansen, H.J., *Geschichte* … p. 242].

deceased burgomeister Schwartz;[28] the Prince meanwhile took up quarters in Baumhardt's home. Town Commandant Horn was captured by one Russian officer near the Cattle Drive (Karri Pforte) Gates and led back to his own home, where he was subjected to insults and outrage; however, if you think about it, he could count upon even worse treatment by the Tsar after the above-mentioned impertinent reply [to the Tsar's call to surrender]; however, he was arrested and placed in the same jail in which *he had* been holding Tsarist prisoners, and was forced to spend 12 days there, after which he was transferred to a guard house and held there. His four daughters were staying in an apartment owned by Lieutenant General Chambers, and the Tsar order not to harm them. Immediately after the capture, looting began, which lasted for 24 hours, and the majority of homes, with the exception of Lieutenant Colonel von Schlippenbach's, and as some say, burgomeister Dittmar's home, were plundered; such misfortune did not exceed the fact that many lost everything when their homes and basements were broken into by Russians with unsheathed swords. They killed the old man Gerckens,[29] who refused to yield his goods and residence; the teacher Böttscher[30] together with his wife and children; and others. Seven thousand bombs were discharged [on the city][31], which killed many people and destroyed many buildings; 40-, 80-, 120- and 360-pound bombs. In the commandant's home they found 83,000 riksdaler, in addition to the 14,000 riksdalers that personally belonged to him; the Tsar distributed the money among his men.

It seems if not for the collapse of the Honour Bastion, the town might have held out for a longer time, since it had provisions for two months. In Ivangorod, the commandant Lieutenant Colonel Stjernstråle had 400 or 500 men, and when those arrived from Narva, the number of soldiers reached 900 men, and 3,000 souls altogether.

The enemy did not fire a single shot at the given fortress, but only blockaded it, until an agreement was concluded on 17 August; at the same time only 14 days of provisions remained.

The capitulation accord contained nine articles, of which to the present moment only two have been observed.[32] Personal weapons were taken from

---

28 Johann Christoph Schwarz (born in Reval in 1627, died in Narva on 16 September 1699) – a Narva justice burgomaster (1664–1699), county judge (haradshöfing) of Ingria [Hansen, H.J., *Geschichte* …. p. 346; Recke, J.F. and Napiersky, K.E., *Allgemeines Schriftsteller- und Gelehrten-Lexicon der Provinzen Livland, Esthland und Kurland*, Vol. 4 (S.Z. Mittau, 1832), p. 159].

29 Dietrich Gerckens, killed on 10 August 1704 – a merchant and citizen of Narva since March 1666 [EAA.1646.1.599; 1666-1832; Kelch, *Lieflnädische Historia*, Vol. 2 (Dorpat, 1874), p. 416].

30 Matthias Böttscher (born in Osnabrück, killed on 10 August 1704 in Narva), studied in Königsberg (defended his thesis in 1684); became a teacher of a German school in Narva (1688–1704) [Geerkens, S.D., *Narva literata* … p. 172].

31 According to the information contained in Narva diaries, between 31 July and 8 August 4,567 bombs were hurled at the city; according to the Artillery Administration, during the siege of Narva 5,714 bombs were expended, ranging from one to nine poods in calibre.

32 The draft of the accord about the surrender of Ivangorod, offered by Stjernstråle, included eight articles. Ogilvy approved most of them: 1) exiting with personal weapons; 2) release of the family members of the Swedish garrison; 3) free exiting of the local inhabitants; 4) transport to Reval for the garrison and their wounded; 5) liberation of the family members of

the garrison, and in return they were given completely useless weapons, so many of our soldiers tossed them aside.[33]

Yesterday those very same 300 or 400 men arrived by land and stopped in the suburbs.

Fifty men were transported from Ivangorod to Finland, and others remaining in the town are also in need of transportation like the sick and ill.

The gentlemen colonels: Colonel Morath, Colonel Lode, Colonel Rebinder, Colonel von Fersen and Lieutenant Colonel von Treyden are being held in Narva, while other officers are being held in a camp for prisoners and are to be sent to Moscow.

Georgii Oginsky spent time in Narva and received in the form of assistance from the Tsar 13,000 infantry for Lithuania; the Bishop of Kulm [Chelmno] and certain other Polish gentlemen were also here, as well as emissaries: the Danish Heinz, King August's Arnstedt, the King of Prussia's Kaiserling, who followed the Tsar to Dorpat.

The garrison of Narva today consists of 5,000 men under the command of governor general Aleksandr Menshikov. The Tsar has sent 8,000 dragoons to Pernau; the remaining are in camp near Narva.

All of the forces that he deployed against Narva numbered up to 15,000 men of infantry and 16,000 horse, a significant portion of which, taking up quarters at Pühajõgi and in its surroundings, were not dispersing across the country, so a large herd was supposed to be near Narva.[34] This now should be around 40,000 men, which seems almost unbelievable. In the next few days Dorpat and Russian peasants[35] and 500 stone masons are expected for participating in the city works.

In the city they are supporting cleanliness, and in order to prevent a possible contagion, it was ordered to throw the dead, the half-dead and sick into the river.

---

the Ivangorod garrison captured in Narva; 6) provisions for one month. Ogilvy rejected the article about coming out with flags, music and cannons; the prisoners being held by the Swedes in Ivangorod were supposed to be released. Ogilvy was unable to carryout Stjernstråle's seventh request to gather their belongings in Narva, since the city was being plundered at that time; the eighth article about a possible future return of the fortress back to the Swedes was left "to the will of the Almighty God" [*The full collection of laws of the Russian Empire* (PSZRI), Vol. 4, pp. 264–265].

33 The interpretation of the articles of the accord in favour of the victor was the common practice. If the accord foresaw the release of the garrison with their weapons, then the soldiers in place of their flintlock muskets were given broken or aged matchlock muskets. That is what happened during the surrender of Koporie, Dorpat and Mitau [Jelgava].

34 In the French manuscript this excerpt carries a different sense: *On compte que toutes les Troupes qu il a eues devant cette Ville montent à 15000 hommes d infanterie & 1600 de Cavalrie, outre le renfort qui leur est venu de Dorpat dont la plus part ont été postez près de Pihagaggi & environs d'ou ils ont chassé tout le bétail des champs, & il y en doit avoir un gros troupeau près de Narva* (the approximate total numerical strength of the forces activated during the siege of the city amounts to 15,000 infantry and 16,000 cavalry, in addition to those that arrived from Dorpat and concentrated for the most part near Pühajõgi; all of the grazing cattle had been taken to here, so a sizable herd was to be near Narva).

35 In the French version of the text there is also mention of Finnish peasants, and the total number of labourers is put at more than 1,000 people.

Doctor Döhnel[36] entered Tsarist service, burgomeister Dittmar was appointed as burgrave, ratsherr Boomgard – as burgomeister, and merchant Christian Götte[37] – as commissar.

Unmarried women were given away in marriage, and among them ought to have been the deceased councillor Portehn's widow, who kept refusing, therefore the Tsar ordered the Russian mayor[38] take her away only to Russia, where she was supposed to give her consent.

Sir Pastor Helvig[39] asked to retire, in order to be sent back to Rostock, but the Tsar replied that it was not befitting to abandon his flock, and gave him a passport to Moscow, where Lutherans also lived.

The garrison of Narva consisted of 1,000 men (Rebinder – 400, von Fersen – 300, Lode – 300 men), half of which were sick and many died. There remained 300 cavalrymen, but they were not fit for combat, since the enemy had taken away the horses not only from the cityfolk but from the troopers and had also taken away 300 pairs of boots [from the latter].

The Tsar ordered to raise the 10 Pomeranian ships that had arrived in Narva that spring and had been sunk at Commandant Horn's orders, and 8 of them were still seaworthy.[40]

The pilings, driven into the mouth of the Narova at an order from the Tsar were also lifted.[41]

Twenty-eight sailors and boatmen also arrived here from Narva.

During the siege, a ton of rye cost 6 riksdalers, a pound of meat – 4, 5 or 6 riksdalers, a pound of pork – eight riksdalers, a *shtof* [1.23 litre] jug of beer – three or four *vitten*,[42] and by the end, it was nearly impossible to acquire something.

36   Johann Justin Döhnel (born in 1661 in Gotha, died in 1711 in Poznan), the great grandson of the first pharmacist in Gotha; pharmaceutical practice in Nyen and Narva; Doctor of Medicine in Leiden (dissertation: De Paralysi. Lugd. Bat. 1695); *Stadt*-physician of Narva and Ingermanland, member of the medical board in Stockholm. Peter the Great's personal physician (from 1704) [*Bol'shaia biograficheskaia entsiklopediia. Donel', Iogann-Iustin* {Polovtsov} <http://gufo.me/content_bigbioenc/donel-iogann-justin-193703.html#ixzz3bMjTyiC> (accessed 27 May 2015)].

37   Christian Götte became, according to Hansen, a member of the town council on 13 September 1704 [Hansen, H.J., *Geschichte* … p. 242].

38   In those places where the German manuscript speaks about Russian officers, the French text has them as German.

39   Johann Andreas Helvig (born in Berlin on 26 January 1668, died on 7 February 1720 in Reval). Studied in Rostock Griefenwalde and Wittenberg, where he received a master's degree in 1692 and became an adjunct in the philosophy department in 1693. He visited Stockholm and Uppsala; ordained in a cathedral in Reval on 19 June 1695; compastor (1696–1699) and senior pastor (1699–1708) of the German community in Narva. He served as a preacher among the prisoners in Vologda exile (1708–1713); pastor of the Church of St. Olaf in Reval (1714); and superintendent of the Reval consistory (1715) [Akiander, M., *Bidrag* … pp. 69–70].

40   The list of the ships taken by the Russian fleet in Narva is known: the *Juffroun Maria, Santa Maria, Sant Pieter, Mosus, Provat Daniel,* and the *Aleksander* [RGA VMF, F. 223, Op. 1, D. 8, l. 17a, obr.] (The information was kindly offered by Alexei Melnov).

41   Other sources are silent about the piling driven into the river bottom at the mouth of the Narova in 1704. The bridge, built here in May, was a pontoon bridge. Possibly, the author has in mind the sealing of the mouth of the river with an *estacade* – a French term for a palisade that crosses a river to prevent the passage of boats. In the French text, this sentence is absent.

42   In other words, Swedish *öre*. In the given period, 1/72 of a riksdollar. See: Robert Petre, "Dagbok under Kriget ifran ar 1702 till Slaget vid Pultava" in *Karolinska krigares dagböcker*

Several Russian and other officers from Smolensk came to see the Tsar.

Money was generously distributed to the men, as if it was a salary.

All of the troops were dressed in German uniforms, but the officers' uniforms were trimmed in lace.[43]

Certain regiments wore uniforms in the Swedish style.

Wigs were fairly common among the officers.

The Tsar and prince do not wear any other than a German uniform with the Order of St. Andrew, the cross of which is made from gold and is worn on the chest and with which his Tsarist Majesty bestows to important sirs.[44]

The Foot Guards consist of 2 regiments with a strength of 6,000 men, one uniformed in green coats, red waistcoats, red cuffs and brass buttons. The second regiment – in blue and red with the same buttons.[45]

The Horse Guards, which are called Yellow Dragoons, are dressed in green velvet waistcoats and cuffs with green velvet sword belts and shoulder belts;[46] their karpus caps have been fabricated from yellow cloth and green velvet; the horses are light grey and the regiment numbers 1,000 men.

There are entire regiments, the horses of which are completely similar; in each regiment there is one company of grenadiers wearing tall bearskin caps,[47] dressed in green and red, blue and red, totally light red, white and red, or yellow uniforms. There are also entire regiments of such grenadiers.[48]

Mail between Moscow and Narva runs constantly.

---

jämte andra samtida skrifter, Vol. 1 (Lund, 1901), p. 17; Rassmuson, L.N., "Inte en vitten": in *Ur ett myntnamms historia* (Fornvännen, 1947(2)), p. 70; Edvinsson, R., "The multiple currencies of Sweden-Finland 1534–1803", DEH Stockholm University, 2009, p. 41.

43 In the German text: "die Offieceren Cammeriert gekleidet"; in the French text: "les habits des Officiers ont été richement galonez".

44 In the document's text, the expression "Tsar and his prince" might be interpreted as an indication of his successor. However, Tsarevich Aleksei Petrovich received the Order of St. Andrew later, in 1711. Therefore, apparently, the author has in mind the cavalier of St. Andrew and untitled Prince A.D. Menshikov, at that moment a count.

45 It is not hard to guess that the Foot Guards meant the Preobrazhensky and Semenovsky Regiments with their traditional uniform colours. The mention of the copper buttons is valuable; up to now it was known that when manufacturing the first German coats for the Guards in 1702, buttons covered in cloth were used [PiB, Vol. 2, p. 446].

46 In the French version of the text, the phrase contains the same information about the yellow coats of the dragoons, which makes the indicated name of the regiment logical. There was no Horse Guards in the Petrine army in 1704. By all appearances, the author has in mind an elite dragoon unit – Boris Sheremetev's select dragoon battalion, which could have been in Narva after its fall as the personal escort of the field marshal. The information about the battalion's uniform is unknown in Russian historical sources for the year 1704; however, there is evidence about the yellow and green uniforms of Sheremetev's dragoons later [Letin, S. A, Leonov, S.G., *Russkii voennyi kostium [Russian military dress]*, Vol. 1 (Moscow, 2008), pp. 56, 57 and 135]. The description of the headgear is the earliest mention of karpus caps in the Russian army; to this point the first known mention relates to 1706 [PiB, Vol. 4, pp. 317, 986]; the karpus entered wide circulation after 1708.

47 "*aufgestützeten Bähren Mützen*".

48 In the French text, the phrase about the grenadier elements begins with a new sentence, which means the description of the uniforms relates not so much to the dragoon as to the entire army. The reference to "entire regiments of grenadiers" is doubtful, since in 1704 the grenadiers comprised separate companies in the infantry regiments; consolidated grenadier regiments appeared in the Russian army in 1709, while the earliest evidence of the existence of consolidated grenadier battalions relates to 1706 [Adamovich, B.V., *Sbornik voenno-istoricheskikh materialov Leib-Gvardii Keksgol'mskogo polka [Anthology of the military-*

On 14 August they had a celebratory holiday for the capture of Narva to the accompaniment of the thunder of guns. The Muscovites are taking Swedish churches into their own hands; German churches are still closed.

During the celebration for the capture of Dorpat, which was marked in the Russian camp at Narva, they [the Russians] put the flags taken in Dorpat on display on their batteries.

The Tsarist soldiers and cavalry no longer carry their sabres, but use Solingen swords with brass hilts, while the officers have swords of Swedish, Saxon and other work.

There is news: The Tsar with all of his forces and those quartered in Narva intends move out from Dorpat into Lithuania.

During the assault, the enemy lost approximately 1,000 men in addition to those killed when the mine exploded.

Those also arriving from Narva report that the Tsar has promised to free the community for any exactions for 7 years, and also to distribute 60,000 roubles, which in the course of the next 7 years might provide restitution for all the assets through the development of all main trades and production facilities. Here, however, no one wants to believe this.

P.S. Today it has become known to us that during the storming of Narva somewhere around 2,000 Muscovites were killed, while the entire siege cost the Tsar 5,000 men.

In the course of the siege the Tsar twice sent out drummers with a proposal to allow women and children to come out freely, but the commandant did not want to enter negotiations.

---

historical materials of the Life-Guards Kexholm Regiment], Vol. 1 (Saint Petersburg, 1910)], p. 103.

Colour Plate Commentaries

1 The battle between Petr Matveevich Apraxin's battery and the Swedish ships in the Narova estuary on 28 April 1704. Andrei Anatol'evich Tron'; Saint Petersburg, 2016.

2 The defeat of the Swedish flotilla by von Werden's regiments in the mouth of the Emajõgi River, 3 May 1704. Andrei Anatol'evich Tron'; Saint Petersburg, 2016.

3 The capture of Lieutenant Colonel Marquard. Valentin Vadimovich Taratorin; Smolensk, 2015.

4 Battle of Narva 19 November 1700 Alexander von Kotzebue (1815-1889), Russia, 1846 Artillery Museum (VIMAIViVS), Saint-Petersburg.

The onrushing victorious Swedes are being kept separate from the bridge, across which Russian troops are fleeing, only by the tenacious resistance of Peter's Guardsmen. The appearance of the opponents doesn't reflect the realities of 1700 but corresponds to the level of knowledge about it in the 1840s; the Russians back then still weren't wearing tricorn hats and were still dressed in the East European fashion. The Swedish grenadiers in the foreground are shown in a captured Swedish grenadier's cap that had been preserved in Russia and with a company flag of Colonel Horn's Narva garrison regiment that also remained among the trophies kept in Saint-Petersburg.

5 The defense of the moat and covered way of the Narva fortress. Valentin Vadimovich Taratorin, Smolensk, 2015.

6 The Battle of Narva 19 November 1700. Nikolai Valentinovich Zubkov, Saint Petersburg, 2014-2016.

This is the moment of the breakthrough of the Russian fortified line by the Swedes. The Swedish column of Major-General Maidel consisted of two groups. The left group is what we see on the foreground. At the head of it marched a platoon of grenadiers of Dal Regiment. Then followed 2nd battalion of Dal Regement, and converged battalions from Finnish (Viborgs, Bjorneborgs) regiments. The commanding General, Maidel, with his staff on horses is seen between the two groups. The right group consisted of Narke-Warmlands Regiment, Vastmanlands and Savolax Regiments. Farther away towards horizon the Swedish right flank column of General Vellingk is barely seen. The Swedish flags and uniforms are depicted according to available sources. The grenadiers brought fascines to fill the ditch; the battalions in four rank formation supposedly had their pikemen in the center around the flags.

During the siege of Narva the Russians built a fortified line of countervallation that faced the besieged town, and the line of circumvallation with bastions that faced the field. The earthen parapet had 'Spanish horse' placed on the top; the ditch separated the parapet from the field.

The defenders of this part of the Russian circumvallation line, according to the plan of engineer General Hallart, was Infantry Regiment of Colonel Biels (Smolensky Infantry since 1708). Note that the costume is oriental yet – the Tsar introduced West European costume couple years later, but in 1700 his men fought in what was called 'Hungarian' uniforms. The color of uniforms of this particular regiment is unknown, but generally the Russian army in 1700 wore coats of dark green, green, blue, red and brown colors. The green became traditional color for the Russian infantry since then. What was color of the flags is unknown, too.

A curious detail is that in 2015 in Narva an amateur archeologist with the metal detector managed to find two Russian flag finials roughly on a place where Biels' Regiment stood; the flags must had been captured and travelled to Stockholm but their finials remained in the ground for 315 years since 1700.

Although the Russian army amounted to between 35 and 40 thousand, it had to occupy the lengthy line; the chief Engineer of the Tsarist army, General Hallart wrote that the line needed 70,000 men to defend it properly. So, in order to cover all the front, the troops were distributed in one line without reserves; and the regiments instead if six ranks, as was prescribed by the Russian 1699 regulation, formed only three or even two ranks deep, which made rather weak defense.

According to the anonymous Russian manuscript of 1700 – a unique eyewitness account of the battle from the Russian side, the Swedish soldiers filled the ditch with fascines, climbed over the parapet and threw down the 'Spanish horse' to open way to the infantry and cavalry. They fired their fusils and stabbed with their pikes. The Russians that stood behind the parapet, offered little resistance and fled.

7 The Russian trench works at Narva. Andrei Karashchuk, Moscow, 2015

8 The fighting in the dark for the Dorpat palisade. Maksim Vladimirovich Borisov, Moscow, 2015.

9 The breaching battery on the Ivangorod bank of the Narova River. Maksim Vladimirovich Borisov, Moscow, 2016.

10 The Swedish artillery Colonel Johann Kinnert at the Honor Bastion a moment before Russian bullet will hit his head. Sergei Igorevich Shamenkov; Odessa, 2015.

11 The storming of the Honor Bastion. Oleg Konstantinovich Parkhaev; Moscow, 2015.

12 The victory – troops mounting Viktoria Bastion. Nikolai Valentinovich Zubkov; Saint-Petersburg, 2016.

13 Mounting bastion Victoria. By Oleg Vladimirovich Fedorov, Moscow 2015.

14 Peter I pacifies his enraged troops after taking Narva in 1704. Nikolai Aleksandrovich Zauerveid (1836-1866); Russia, 1858, The State Tret'iakov Gallery.

15 The Swedish garrison's departure from Ivangorod. Oleg Konstantinovich Parkhaev; Moscow, 2015.

Sources and Literature

Archival materials

Archive of the Military-historical Museum of the Artillery, Engineers and Signal Troops (VIMAIViVS), F. 2: The Artillery Administration (Prikaz Artillerii).

Archive of Saint Petersburg Institute of History of the Russian Academy of Sciences (NIA SPbII RAN), F. 83: A.D. Menshikov's chancellery; F. 36: Vorontsov's chancellery; F. 270: Commission regarding the publication of Peter the Great's letters and papers.

Library of the Russian Academy of Sciences (BAN). Manuscripts; PiB: Library of Peter I; Department of Cartography.

Linköpings Stifts- och Landsbibliotek. LiSB H 79:4.

Riksarkivet. Krigsarkivets kartor och ritningar. Russian State Archive of the Navy (RGA VMF), F. 177: Administration of the Naval Fleet; F. 233: Manuscripts of Peter the Great;

Russian State Military-historical Archive (RGVIA), F. 2584: Life-Guards Semenovsky Regiment. Regiment headquarters.

The University of Nottingham. Manuscripts and Special Collections. Letters and Papers of Robert Harley, 1st Earl of Oxford.

Published documents

Adlerfeld, Gustavas, *The military history of King Charles XII, King of Sweden, written by the express order of his Majesty*, Vol. 2 (London, 1740).

Defoe, D., *British Officer in the Service of the Czar. An impartial history of the life and actions of Peter Alexowitz, the present Czar of Muscovy* (London, 1723).

Gordon, A., *The History of Peter the Great, Emperor of Russia: To which is Prefixed a Short General History of the Country from the Rise of that Monarchy and an Account of the Author's Life,* Vol. 1 (Aberdeen, 1755).

Kelch, C., *Lieflandisch Historia oder Kriegs- und Friedens-Geschichte. Continuation* (1690–1706). Dorpat, 1875. [*Livonian History, or the History of war and peace. Continuation*].

Lohenstein J.H. von, *Des Moscowitischen grossen Czaars Petri Alexiewiz Leben und Thaten* [Life and deeds of Moscow's Tsar Petr Alekseevich], Vol. 2 (Frankfurt and Leipzig, 1710).

Nordberg, J.A., *Histoire de Charles XII, Roi de Suede* [*History of Charles XII, King of Sweden*], Vol. 1 (Haye, 1748).

PETER THE GREAT'S REVENGE

In the Russian language

Adamovich, B.V., *Sbornik voenno-istoricheskikh materialov Leib-Gvardii Keksgolmskogo polka* [*Collection of the military-historical materials of the Life-Guard Keksgolmsky Regiment*], Vol. 1 (Saint Petersburg, 1910).

Gistoriia Sveiskoi voiny (Podennaia zapiska Petra Velikogo) [*History of the Swedish war (Chronological notes of Peter the Great)*]. In two volumes (Moscow, 2004).

Huyssen, H. von, "Zhurnal Gosudaria Peta I s 1695 po 1709" in *Sobranie raznykh zapisok i sochinenii, sluzhashchikh k dostavleniiu polnago svedeniia o zhizni i deianiiakh Gosudaria Imperatora Petra Velikogo. Izdannoe trudami i izhdiveniem Feodora Tumanskogo* ["Journal of His Majesty Peter I, from 1695 to 1709" in *Anthology of various letters and essays, used for delivery of full information about the life and works of His Majesty Emperor Peter the Great. Published by the efforts and means of Feodor Tumansky*, Vol. 3 (Saint Petersburg, 1787).

Kniga Marsova, ili voinskikh del ot voisk ego tsarskogo velichestva rossiiskikh vo vziatii preslavnykh fortifikatsii, i na raznykh mestakh khrabykh batalii uchinennykh nad voiski ego korolevskogo velichestva sveiskogo. S pervogo sanktpeterburgskogo 1713 goda izdaniia vtorym tisneniem napechatannaia [*Book of Mars*, or the military exploits of the troops of the Russians' Tsarist Majesty when taking very famous fortifications, or the brave battles in various places over the troops of the Royal Swedish Majesty. From the second printing of the first Saint Petersburg 1713 edition. (Saint Petersburg, 1766).

Pisma i bumagi Petra Velikogo (1704–1705) [*Letters and papers of Peter the Great (1704–705)*], Vol. 3 (Saint Petersburg: Gos. tipografija, 1893).

Pokhodnyi zhurnal 1704 goda [*Campaign Journal of 1704*] (Saint Petersburg, 1854).

Severnaia voina 1700–1721 gg. K 300-letiiu Poltavskoi pobedy. Sbornik dokumentov [*Northern War of 1700–1721. On the 300th anniversary of the Poltava victory. Collection of documents*], Vol. 1 (Moscow, 2009).

Shafirov, P.P., *Rassuzhdenie, kakie zakonnye prichiny Petr Pervyi k nachatiiu voiny protiv korolia Karla XII v 1700 godu imel* [*Consideration of what legal justifications Peter the First had for starting the war against King Charles XII in 1700*]

Sheremetev, B.P., "Voenno-pokhodnyi zhurnal (s 3 iunia 1701-go po 12 sentiabria 1705-go goda) general-fel'dmarshala Borisa Petrovicha Sheremeteva" in *Materialy voenno-uchenogo arkhiva glavnogo shtaba* [Military campaign journal of General Field Marshal Boris Petrovich Sheremetev from 3 June 1701 to 12 September 1705] (Saint Petersburg, 1871), Vol. 1.

Ustrialov, N.G., *Istoriia tsarstvovaniia Petra Velikogo* [*History of the reign of Peter the Great*] Vol. 4, Part 2. Appendices (Saint Petersburg, 1863).

Vedomosti. Moscow, 1704 [News]

Volynsky, N.P., *Postepennoe razvitie russkoi reguliarnoi konnitsy v epokhu Velikogo Petra s samym podrobnym opisaniiam ee uchastiia v Velikoi Severnoi voine. Istoricheskoe issledovanie po pervoistochnikam* [*Gradual development of the Russian regular cavalry in the era of Peter the Great with the most detailed description of its participation in the Great Northern War. Historical research according to original sources*] (Saint Petersburg, 1912), Books 3 and 4.

Zhurnal ili Podennaia zapiska, blazhennyia i vechndostoinaia pamiati gosudaria imperatora Petra Velikogo [*Journal or chronological notes, the blessed and eternally worthy recollections of His Majesty Emperor Peter the Great*] Part 1 (Saint Petersburg, 1770).

Memoirs

Hallart, L.N., *Tagebuch des Generals von Hallart uber die Belagerung und Schlacht von Narva, 1700* [*Diary of General Hallart about the siege and battle of Narva, 1700*] (Reval: F. Kluge, 1894).

Hallart, L. N., "Podrobnoe opisanie osady goroda Narvy i srazheniia pod sim gorodom v 1700 gody" ["Detailed description of the siege of the town of Narva and the battle for the same town in 1700"] in *Severnyi arkhiv*, 1822, Part 1, No. 1, pp. 3–28; No. 2, pp. 117–143.

Hermann Poorten, "Aufzeichnungen uber die Belagerung und Ennahme der Stadt Narva durch den Russen im Jahre 1704" in *Archiv für die Geschichte Liv-, Esth-, und Curlands, Band II* (Reval 1861), pp. 191–197.

"Narva's Belagerung und Einahme von den Russen, nach Aufzeichnungen dasiger Einwohner in Jahre 1704" in *Archiv für die Geschichte Liv-, Esth-, und Curlands, Band VI, Heft 3* (Reval, 1851), pp. 225–287.

Kurakin, B.I., "Voennaia khitrost' tsaria Petra Alekseevicha pod Narvoiu 8-go iunia 1704 g.: Rasskaz ochevidtsa kniazia B.I. Kurakin" [Military ruse of Tsar Peter Alekseevich at Narva on 8 June 1704: Tale of the eyewitness Prince B.I. Kurakin" in *Arkhiv kn. F.A. Kurakin* [*Prince F.A. Kurakin's archive*], Book 3 (Saint Petersburg, 1892).

Kurakin, B.I., "Russko-shvedskaia voina. Zapiski. 1700–1710" ["Russian–Swedish war. Notes. 1700–1710"] in *Arkhiv kn. F.A. Kurakin* [*Prince F.A. Kurakin's archive*] (Saint Petersburg, 1890).

"Letopisets 1700 goda" ["Chronicler of 1700"] in *Letopis' zaniatii Arkheograficheskii Komissi, 1865–1866* [*Chronicle of the lessons of the Archeological Commission, 1865-1866* (Saint Petersburg, 1868), 4th Ed., pp. 131–157.

Chernyshev, G.P., "Zapiski G.P. Chernysheva" ["Notes of G.P. Chernysheva"] in *Russkaia Starina*, 1872: Vol. 5, no. 6, pp. 791–802.

Juel, J., *Zapiski datskogo poslannika v Rossii pri Petre Velikom* [*Notes of a Danish envoy to Russia under Peter the Great*] (Moscow: Lavry Poltavy, 2001).

Military treatises

Bland, H.A., *A Treatise of Military Discipline; in which is laid down and explained the duty of the officer and soldier thro' the several branches of service* (London, 1727).

Feuquières, A., *Memoirs historical and military: containing a distinct view of all the considerable states of Europe. With an accurate account of the wars … from the year 1672, to the year 1710.* (London, 1735–1736).

Kane, R., *A system of camp-discipline, military honours, garrison-duty, and other regulations for the land forces* (London, 1757).

Mallet, A.M., *Les Travaux de Mars ou L'art de la Guerre*, Vol. 1–3 (Paris, 1685–1691).

Muller, J.A., *A treatise of artillery* (London, 1768).

Saxe, M., *Reveries, or, memoirs concerning the art of war* (Edinburgh, 1776).

The Art of War, In four parts. Written in French by Four Able Officers of Long Service and Experience, and Translated into English by an English Officers (London, 1707).

In the Russian language:

Borgsdorf, Ernst, *Poverennye voinskie pravila kako nepriiatselskie kreposti siloiu brati* [*Trusted military rules how to take enemy fortresses by force*] (Moscow, 1709).

Braun, Ernest, *Noveishee opisanie i praktika artillerii Ernest Broun kapitana artillerii vo Gdanske 1682* [*Latest description and practice of the artillery of Ernest Broun, Captain of Artillery in Gdansk 1682* (Moscow, 1710).

Montecúccoli, R., *Zapiski Montecúccoli, generalissimusa imperatorskikh voisk, ili Obshchie printsipy voennogo iskusstva* [*Notes of Montecúccoli, Generalissimo of Imperial forces, or the General principles of military art*. In three volumes [Translated by Ia. S. Semchenkov] (Montreal, 2012).

Saint-Remy, S., *Memorii, ili Zapiski artilleriskie* [*Records, or Artillery notes*] (Saint Petersburg, 1733).

Vauban, S., *Kniga o atake i oborone krepostei.* [*Book about the attack and defence of fortresses*] (Saint Petersburg, 1744).

Voinskii Ustav, sostavlennyi i posviashchennyi Petru Pervomu Generalom Veide v 1698 [*Military Regulations, compiled and dedicated to Peter the first by General Wade in 1698* (Saint Petersburg, 1841).

Monographs and articles

Anderson, R.C., *Naval wars in the Baltic during the sailing-ship epoch, 1522–1850* (London: Francis Edwards, 1910)

Hansen, H.J., *Geschichte der Stadt Narva* (Dorpat, 1858).

Kaljundi, E.A. and Kiprichnikov, A.N., "Kreposti Ingermanlandii i Karelii v 1681. Po doneseniiu Erika Dalberga pravitelstvu Shvetsii" ["Fortresses of Ingermanland and Karelia in 1681. According to Erik Dahlberg's report to the government of Sweden"] in *Skandinavskii sbornik*, 20th Edition (Tallinn, 1975), pp. 68–81.

Koroliuk, V.D., "Vstuplenie Rechi Pospolitoi v Severnuiu voiny" ["Entry of the Reczpospolita in the Northern War"] in *Uchenye zapiski Instituta slavianovedeniia* [*Academic notes of the Institute of Slavic Studies*] Vol. 10 (1954), pp. 239–347.

Laidre, M., *Severnaia voina i Estoniia: Tartu v godinu ispytanii (1700–1708)* [*Northern war and Estonia: Tartu in the years of trials (1700–1708)*] (Tallinn, 2010).

Nikitiuk, A.N., "Arkheologicheskie issledovaniia bastionov Narvskoi kreposti v 2008–2009 gg." ["Archeological research of the bastions of the Narva fortress in 2008–2009"] in *Pamiatniki fortifikatsii: istoriia, restavratsiia, ispol'zovanie. Sbornik statei i materialov Pervoi mezhdunarodnoi nauchno-prakticheskoi konferentsii, 18–19 sentiabria 2009* [*Monuments of fortifications: History, restoration and use. Anthology of articles and materials of the 1st International Academic-practical Conference, 18–19 September 2009* (Arkhangelsk), 1st ed., pp. 244–257.

Palli, H.E., *Mezhdu dvumia boiami za Narvu: Estonia v pervye gody Severnoi voiny 1701–1704* [*Between two battles for Narva: Estonia in the first years of the Northern War 1701–1704*] (Tallinn, 1966).

Petrov, A., "Narvskaia operatsiia" ["Narva operation"] in *Voennyi sbornik*, No. 7 (1872), pp. 5–38.

Petrov, A., *Gorod Narva, ego proshloe i dostoprimechatel'nosti* [*City Narva, its past and places of interest*] (Saint Petersburg, 1901).

Pototsky, P., *Gvardiia russkogo tsaria pod Narvoiu v 1700 i 1704* [*Guards of the Russian Tsar at Narva in 1700 and 1704*] (Saint Petersburg, 1890).

Slavnitsky, N. R. "Osada i vziatie Narvy russkimi voiskami v 1700 i 1704" ["Siege and capture of Narva by Russian forces in 1700 and 1704"] in *Mir i Novoe vremia* [*World and the Modern Era*] (Saint Petersburg, 2005), pp. 111–117.

Smolokurov, A., "Narodonaselenie Narvy: Demograficheskii obzor istorii goroda" ["Population of Narva: Demographic review of the city's history"] in *Sbornik Narvskogo muzeia* [*Anthology of the Narva Museum*] (Narva, 2000), pp. 15–66.